Drugs and Rights

DOUGLAS N. HUSAK
RUTGERS UNIVERSITY

CAMBRIDGE
UNIVERSITY PRESS

Published by the Press Syndicate of the University of Cambridge
The Pitt Building, Trumpington Street, Cambridge CB2 1RP
40 West 20th Street, New York, NY 10011-4211, USA
10 Stamford Road, Oakleigh, Victoria 3166, Australia

© Cambridge University Press 1992

First published 1992

Printed in the United States of America

Library of Congress Cataloging-in-Publication Data
Husak, Douglas N., 1948–
Drugs and rights / Douglas N. Husak.
p.   cm. – (Cambridge studies in philosophy and public policy)
Includes bibliographical references and index.
ISBN 0-521-41739-2 (hardback). – ISBN 0-521-42727-4 (pbk.)
1. Drug abuse–Government policy.   2. Drug legalization.
3. Narcotic laws–Philosophy.   I. Title.   II. Series.
HV5801.H84   1992   92-4407
364.1'77–dc20   CIP

A catalog record for this book is available from the British Library.

ISBN 0-521-41739-2   hardback
ISBN 0-521-42727-4   paperback

Contents

Contents

Acknowledgments

People who have assisted me with all or part of this manuscript include Jim Jacobs, David Maiullo, Donna Mancuso, Harold Rubenstein, Jonathan Shonsheck, and Andrew von Hirsch. I owe a special debt to Phyllis Schultze, who taught me the value of a good librarian.

Introduction

This book does not propose yet another solution to our nation's intractable drug problem. As H. L. Mencken is reputed to have said about the alcohol problem during the era of prohibition, "No intelligent man believes the thing is soluble at all." Whether or not the drug problem can be solved, many commentators have addressed the issue from the perspective of social policy. I have little new to add to their discussions.

I approach drug use from an individual rather than a social perspective. My central concern is to identify the *moral rights* of adult users of recreational drugs. I discuss social policy only insofar as it has a bearing on these rights. Moral rights have been all but ignored both by the state in its war on drugs and by theorists who have written, oftentimes critically, about this war. It is easy to see why rights are neglected by a state at war. What is more difficult to understand is why commentators have been so passive in calling attention to this neglect. Those scholars who have dissented in the war on drugs are seldom motivated by a desire to protect the rights of drug users. More frequently they have protested that the war cannot be won, or that it is too costly, or that it exacerbates the very problems it is designed to solve.

When individual rights are mentioned at all, they are usually the rights of innocent persons jeopardized by overzealous law enforcement. Criminal procedure provides the legal battleground for these debates. The war on drugs has expanded the police power of the state in a variety of ways. However, the nonusing public did not become alarmed until

1

they were directly affected by this expansion. A modest out-
cry was expressed about such practices as random roadblocks
of drivers, mandatory drug testing of employees, early cur-
fews for juveniles, and police searches of garbage. These
tactics threaten the innocent and the guilty alike.

But what about the substantive rights of many of the very
persons against whom the war is waged, that is, adults who
use drugs recreationally? The war, after all, cannot really be
a war on drugs, since drugs cannot be arrested, prosecuted,
or punished. The war is against persons who use drugs. As
such, the war is a civil war, fought against the 28 million
Americans who use illegal drugs annually. And unlike previous battles in this apparently endless war, current cam-
paigns target casual users as well as drug abusers.

Millions of Americans have been punished – oftentimes
severely – for breaking criminal laws against the recreational
use of drugs. A majority of these persons have been punished
simply for drug possession and use. If existing statutes turn
out to violate their moral rights, the cumulative injustice is
among the greatest in American history. Yet neither the public nor the intellectual community has expressed much sympathy for the plight of drug users who are prosecuted and
convicted. I believe that such sympathy is long overdue. No
laws enforced by such harsh punishments rest on a more
flimsy rationale than those prohibiting the use of recreational
drugs.

The very suggestion that adults may have a moral right to
use drugs for recreational purposes is bound to strike many
readers as ludicrous. I offer three quick responses to persons
who share this initial reaction. First, proposals to countenance new and unfamiliar rights are typically greeted with
disdain and ridicule. The moral rights of women and blacks
were recognized reluctantly. Second, the right to use drugs
recreationally is not really new. Less than a century ago, few
commentators thought that the state had the authority to
prohibit the use of recreational drugs. Finally, the issue of
whether a moral right should be recognized depends on phil-

osophical argument, not consensus. If belief in this right is outrageous, its existence should be easy to refute.

I pursue two closely related projects in this book's four chapters. The first is an exercise in moral and legal theory, involving an attempt to clarify the limits of the criminal law. I seek to answer the following questions. Does the state have the legitimate authority to punish adults who use drugs recreationally? If so, for what reason(s)? May the state punish persons for using any drug recreationally? What properties must a hypothetical drug possess before the state has the authority to prohibit it?

My second project applies the theoretical conclusions I reach. I attempt to identify the existing recreational drugs that satisfy or fail to satisfy the criteria for criminalization I have described. Thus I seek to determine whether laws against the use of actual recreational drugs violate moral rights. This project is more tenuous, and my conclusions are more qualified. Some of the criteria for criminalization are vague, imprecise, and hard to apply to particular cases. Moreover, the empirical data about drugs and drug use on which I rely are inconclusive and subject to constant challenge and revision. No factual claim I make about a particular drug is beyond controversy. Although important progress has been made, we still have much to learn about drugs and drug users. Still, I hazard any number of observations about the justifiability of criminalizing the use of existing recreational drugs. Much of my attention is focused on heroin and cocaine (crack and powder), since many drug prohibitionists believe them to be our greatest problems. If adults have a moral right to use heroin and cocaine, they probably have a moral right to use most or all other existing recreational drugs.

I attempt to describe what a drug would have to be like before adults would have a moral right to use it for recreational purposes and what a drug would have to be like before adults would not have a moral right to use it for recreational purposes. On the basis of the evidence I will cite, I conclude that a strong case can be made that the use of most or perhaps all existing recreational drugs should be permitted. This does not imply that adults would have a moral right to use any conceivable drug recreationally; the prohibition of drug use is not inevitably beyond legitimate state authority. Someday a recreational drug might be created that the state would have compelling reasons to prohibit. However, I am skeptical that such a recreational drug exists today.

Few philosophers have addressed either the theoretical or the practical questions I raise here. Despite the growing attention contemporary philosophers purport to pay to current moral and legal issues, almost all of their focus has been directed to a very few matters, usually involving life and death. Discussions of abortion, euthanasia, capital punishment, and animal rights tend to dominate the philosophical landscape. The scant literature on the moral status of recreational drug use is greatly oversimplified. Much of it defends one or another extreme position. Commentators believe either that the prohibition of drugs is not the business of government or, more often, that drugs are a scourge that no responsible state would tolerate. I reject both of these extremes in favor of a more moderate position.

In the first three chapters, I assess the justifiability of prohibiting the recreational use of drugs altogether. Other than caffeine, alcohol, and tobacco, the recreational use of drugs is almost totally proscribed throughout America today. I critically examine what can be said for and against these general laws. In Chapter 4 I investigate what restrictions may be placed on recreational drug use if a total ban is indefensible.

My approach to these issues makes frequent reference to other recreational activities that I compare and contrast with drug use. One reason persons are confused about this issue is that drug use is treated as sui generis. But drug use is similar to, and yet dissimilar from, any number of other recreational activities about which most Americans have strong feelings. Clear thinking about the rights of drug users is facilitated by exploring these similarities and differences.

I will proceed as far as possible without immediately distinguishing between the several different kinds of drugs. An alternative to my approach would begin by sorting drugs into different categories, depending upon their pharmacological properties, and discussing each drug separately. This organizational device might seem more likely to yield valuable insights. The arguments for and against the legalization of caffeine and heroin may appear to differ so radically that little progress can be made by assimilating them. Nonetheless, a surprising number of the arguments for and against prohibitions of recreational drug use can be evaluated without attending to the differences between various drugs. Of course, I will note these differences at the several places they become important.

My arguments make use of pharmacological data about the effects of drugs and, to a greater extent, of sociological evidence about drug users. There are good reasons to pay more attention to sociology than to pharmacology. The effects of drugs on users and nonusers is a function of a complex set of variables, of which pharmacology is only one. Evidence about how recreational drugs are actually used by human beings in the real world – and not, for example, by rats in laboratories – provides the most reliable perspective. Conclusions drawn from this data are surprising. Even well-informed Americans tend to have a distorted stereotype of drugs and drug users. As a result, bad arguments in favor of criminal legislation prohibiting recreational drug use appear better than they are, whereas more respectable arguments appear virtually unassailable.

I am concerned to understand the best principled reasons for denying that adults have a moral right to use any or all recreational drugs. No doubt I will omit a discussion of several such reasons. Some of these reasons are foolish: It is hard to resist the temptation to respond to them, if only to indicate how nonsensical some of the rhetoric of drug prohibitionists has been. For example, I do not take seriously the suggestion that laws against recreational drug use are needed to stop the growth of satanic cults. Other reasons I will neglect are not so foolish. For example, I will not respond to the objection that persons have no moral rights at all, or that they have only those moral rights that the state chooses to give them. Moral argument must begin somewhere, and mine begins with the assumption that persons have moral rights against the state.

I do not attempt to derive the moral rights of drug users from a single, simple principle. Nor do I begin with a theory about the limited role of state authority and conclude that the prohibition of drug use lies beyond its scope. In fact, I will have almost nothing to say about the foundations of the moral rights I presuppose. This neglect may disappoint philosophers who are unpersuaded by anything less than a comprehensive moral theory in which rights are ultimately justified. I fear that presenting such a theory would detract more than it would add. Anyone who is antagonistic toward my philosophical foundation would be likely to resist the edifice I build upon it. I hope that the assumptions I make, and the inferences I draw from them, are congenial to philosophers who may disagree radically about the deeper foundational issues I try to avoid. My arguments should appeal both to libertarians and to those who share the ideal of an activist government with the authority to cope with a wide range of social problems. The foundations of political authority need not be challenged to appreciate the weakness of the case in favor of criminal laws against the recreational use of drugs.

I will not discuss the very real possibility that the prohibition of drug use should not be understood in rational terms. Some commentators have suggested that the war on drugs is largely symbolic, serving to express the anxiety that authorities with political power feel toward persons who are deviant and unconventional. I am not especially interested in the psychology of drug prohibitionists. To suppose that drug laws cannot withstand rational scrutiny concedes what I believe must be demonstrated. I trust that no one is prepared to argue that the symbolism of the drug war serves to justify it.

Introduction

For two reasons, I approach this project with modest expectations about my ability to change the minds of those who are firmly opposed to any suggestion that adults may have a moral right to use drugs recreationally. First, since my arguments depend on a balancing of several factors, reasonable minds can and will differ about how these factors should be weighed. Moral and legal argument is difficult because it often requires a balancing of incommensurables. Second, for reasons that are deep and mysterious, this topic is among a small handful of issues that seem almost immune to rational debate. One might as well attempt to shake the confidence of a fundamentalist about the existence of God.

Nor do I anticipate sparking an interest in legislative reform. The current political climate is unfavorable to the decriminalization of any recreational drugs. Although political climates have been known to change rapidly, a real debate on the issue of drug decriminalization would be likely to polarize the country even more divisively than the abortion controversy. In the meantime, I appeal to those whose capacity to remain open-minded is not constrained by their need to be reelected.

In defending a moderate position about whether adults have a moral right to use drugs recreationally, my arguments necessarily become somewhat complex. I draw lines in new and unfamiliar places. This complexity creates three concerns. First, it might discourage and frustrate persons who are initially interested in the topic but who hope for simple solutions. If the problem were easy, reasonable minds would not differ about it. Second, clear and easily applied answers to the questions I raise are not forthcoming. At no time do I pretend to have said the last word about a particular argument for or against drug prohibitions. Finally, the tone of my discussion is academic and serious. I am reminded of a comment made by a student who evaluated a course entitled "Philosophy and Sex." The professor treated this topic with the serious care it deserves, but the course disappointed many of the students who enrolled in it. One complained:

Introduction

"I never knew sex could be so dull." I hope that my attempt to provide a serious assessment of the moral rights of recreational drug users does not give rise to a similar reaction. I know of no better way to make a topic exciting than to treat it with philosophical sophistication.

Chapter 1

Drugs, drug use, and criminalization

THE WAR ON DRUGS

For a period of sixteen months from 1989–1990, a majority of Americans identified drugs as our nation's greatest concern, surpassing crime, the environment, taxes, the homeless, education, and the deficit.[1] War in the Middle East temporarily focused attention elsewhere. But President George Bush promised to restore the problem to its "number one" status "when the international situation has calmed down."[2] According to William Bennett, America's first "drug czar," "drugs remain . . . our gravest domestic problem."[3]

So great is the problem perceived to be that the public has enthusiastically responded to the latest call for a "war on drugs." This declaration of war is not new. The military metaphor has dominated thought about drug policy ever since Richard Nixon became the first president to declare war on drugs.

The war metaphor is, of course, an exaggeration; the resources mobilized against drugs are not comparable to efforts during wartime. The costs of enforcing criminal laws against the recreational use of drugs (henceforth shortened to "laws against drugs," or LAD) are modest by comparison to our military budget, even when we are officially at peace. Still, by any measure, a massive effort is under way to attempt to eliminate illegal drug use in our society. This effort is built on a broad, if not an especially deep, social consensus. Most of the opposition to the level of current expenditures for the

9

war on drugs has come from congressional Democrats who argue that the commitment from Republicans is too meager. Americans perceive that drug use is out of control and that an extreme response is needed to curb it.

Is this perception accurate? No one can be sure. Three factors contribute to this uncertainty, and they cannot be overcome simply by collecting more reliable data. First, there is no agreement about what constitutes a drug. Definitions of "drugs" are not especially helpful, as I will show later in this chapter. Second, there is no basis to compare and contrast the extent of drug use in the same country at different times, or in different countries at the same time. If Americans consume more of one drug but less of another than at some previous time, no common denominator is available to show whether we are using greater or lesser quantities of drugs. Third, there is no obvious starting point from which to measure trends. Drug use seems to have remained relatively constant over the last century, but it has increased dramatically throughout the most recent two-and-a-half decades, only to decline again in the past few years. These statistics can be manipulated to be used as evidence of whatever trend one wants to find.

Not surprisingly, the exact extent of illegal drug use in America today is subject to dispute, although the quality of the data keeps improving.[4] Estimates are based primarily on three annual studies: the High School Senior Survey, conducted by the Institute for Social Research at the University of Michigan; the Drug Abuse Warning Network (DAWN), which collects data from 535 hospital emergency rooms and county medical examiners in twenty-one cities; and the National Household Survey on Drug Abuse, conducted by the National Institute on Drug Abuse. Additional data are available from a growing number of sources, such as companies that screen applicants and employees and police departments that administer drug tests on arrestees. Each survey is imperfect. However, they combine to provide reasonably accurate sociological information about drug use.

According to the National Household Survey on Drug

Abuse, more than 28 million Americans violated LAD in
1990. Violations occurred "on literally billions of occasions."[5]
Illegal drug use in America remains at significant levels. But
because of or despite the war on drugs, illegal use in virtually
all categories has declined significantly throughout the last
several years. Over 60% of high school seniors reported having tried marijuana during the peak year of 1979; that figure
dropped to 44% in 1990.[6] Daily use has declined from a high
of 10.7% in 1978 to only 2.9% in 1990. Cocaine use has peaked
in high schools as well. During the peak year of 1985, 17.3%
of high school seniors reported having tried cocaine; that
figure dropped to 10.3% in 1990.[7] The use of psychedelics
and amphetamines has followed a similar trend. Heroin use,
never a significant problem in schools, has remained relatively stable throughout American society. And a 20% drop
in cocaine-related medical emergencies in the fourth quarter
of 1989 provides hope that the so-called crack epidemic may
have peaked as well.[8]

Accurate or not, the perception that drug use is out of
control has triggered an enormous state response. Illegal
drugs have become the single most important concern of our
criminal justice system. Although estimates are imprecise,
tens of billions of dollars are probably spent to enforce LAD
every year,[9] and the less direct costs of the war on drugs are
several times greater. Ronald Hamowy describes this war as
"the most expensive intrusion into the private lives of Americans ever undertaken in the nation's history."[10]

About 750,000 of the 28 million illegal drug users are arrested every year. Between one-quarter and one-third of all
felony charges involve drug offenses.[11] The severity of a sentence has almost no limits for, as the Supreme Court has
recently held, a term of life imprisonment without parole for
the offense of possession of 677 grams of cocaine is not cruel
and unusual punishment.[12] As a result, courts have become
clogged, and prison overcrowding is legendary. The U.S.
Sentencing Commission has estimated that within fifteen
years the Anti-Drug Abuse Act passed by Congress in 1986
will cause the proportion of inmates incarcerated for drug

violations to rise from one-third to one-half of all defendants sentenced to federal prison. The costs of punishment threaten to drain the treasury, as each prisoner requires expenditures of between $10,000 and $40,000 per year. Since the average punishment for a drug conviction has risen to seventy-seven months in prison, each new inmate will cost taxpayers approximately $109,000 for the duration of the sentence.[13]

Law enforcement officials continue to exercise broad discretion in arresting and prosecuting drug offenders. More than three-quarters of those arrested are eventually charged with possession, typically of marijuana.[14] Many crimes of possession involve amounts that include a presumption of intent to distribute. Sometimes the quantity of drugs that creates this presumption is small. Moreover, the means used to measure the quantity of given drugs can be peculiar. Since statutes typically refer to a "mixture or substance containing a detectable amount" of a drug, the weight of the entire mixture or substance is included when calculating the quantity of a drug. If a tiny dose of LSD has been placed on a tab of paper or a cube of sugar, the weight of the tab or cube is included in the determination of the amount of the drug. The Supreme Court has recently held this practice to be constitutional.[15]

The true extent of the war on drugs cannot be measured in quantities of dollars spent or numbers of defendants punished. The enforcement of drug laws has diminished precious civil liberties, eroding gains for which Americans have made major sacrifices for over two centuries. Increasingly common are evictions, raids, random searches, confiscations of driver's licenses, withdrawals of federal benefits such as education subsidies, and summary forfeitures of property. Atlanta has sought to reduce drug use and drug-related violence by imposing an 11:00 P.M. weekday curfew on youths under age seventeen. If successful, this experiment could be followed in other cities.

And matters may get worse before they get better. Since existing efforts are widely perceived to be ineffective, more severe measures have been advocated. Red Auerbach, general manager of the Boston Celtics, captures the public mood by suggesting that the drug problem has become so overwhelming that "you have to put this altruistic civil rights stuff down the toilet."[16] Governor Douglas Wilder of Virginia proposes mandatory testing of college students for drug use. Chester Mitchell describes some of the more draconian ideas as follows:

> In recent years members of Congress have proposed bills that would, if passed, permit the military to assist in drug law enforcement, create a northern Arctic "gulag" for drug offenders, restrict bail for drug suspects, permit disclosure of IRS data, eliminate the exclusionary rule, punish foreign drug producers, and repeal the prohibition against use of herbicides abroad.[17]

This list could be expanded. Texas state legislator Al Edwards proposes cutting off a finger for each drug conviction. Delaware state senator Thomas Sharp suggests flogging drug felons.[18] Bennett has responded that "I don't have any problem" with a proposal to "behead the damn drug dealers."[19] President Ronald Reagan reserved judgment when asked whether "drug dealers" should be executed, but he was quick to add, "I know they deserve it."[20] The fact that many of our politicians take these measures seriously indicates that, in the words of Charles Rangel, chair of the House Select Committee on Narcotics Abuse and Control, "We have yet to begin the fight. We have not even fired the first shot."[21] Perhaps no politician has ever lost a vote by promising to take a harder stance on drugs than an opponent. A 1989 Gallup poll revealed that 77 percent of all respondents favored "tougher laws for drug users."

These facts, figures, and attitudes are staggering, but they cannot begin to tell the entire story of the war on drugs. Several important dimensions of this war cannot be reduced to raw numbers. At least three additional (and frequently overlooked) matters must be discussed if this war is to be understood and evaluated.

First, why do so many Americans use recreational drugs? Or, more specifically, why do so many Americans use the kinds of recreational drugs of which the majority disapproves? The power of drugs per se can only be part of the explanation. Illegal drug use is less prevalent in many countries where drugs are plentiful, inexpensive, and higher in quality than those available in America. A more viable strategy to combat drugs might attempt to identify and change the conditions peculiar to America that have led to widespread use. For present purposes, I am less concerned to attempt to identify these conditions than to ask why this issue has received so little attention from drug prohibitionists. It is hard to see how a long-term solution to the drug problem can be found without knowing why so many Americans are motivated to break the law in the first place.

This "root cause" argument is usually greeted with disdain. Bennett has dismissed it with the following analogy:

> If we want to eliminate the drug problem, these people say, we must first eliminate the "root cause" of drugs. . . . Twenty-five years ago, no one would have suggested that we must first address the root causes of racism before fighting segregation. We fought it, quite correctly, by passing laws against unacceptable conduct. The causes of racism was an interesting question, but the moral imperative was to end it as soon as possible and by all reasonable means: education, prevention, the media, and not least of all, the law. So too with drugs.[22]

Bennett purports to explain why "the drug problem" can and should be "eliminated" without paying much attention to the "root causes" of drug use. Is his analogy between drug use and racial segregation sound?

Perhaps efforts to combat segregation continue to prove difficult precisely because the root causes of racism have not been addressed. But I will not press this response here. Suppose it is true that the state should fight segregation without addressing the root causes of racism. Why might this be so? Segregation is a public manifestation of racism, and it may

14

be possible to alter the structure of racist institutions without undermining racism itself. If the state sought to criminalize all manifestations of racism, law enforcement alone could not have much effect without addressing root causes. However, not all expressions of racism are subject to criminal penalties. In our private lives, we Americans remain free to act according to whatever racist beliefs we happen to hold. No laws prevent private displays of racism. One need not invite a member of a particular race to his private parties, but he is obliged to serve him in his public restaurants. Racism itself is not the target of desegregation efforts.

But the war on drugs is different. LAD criminalizes both private and public acts. The state does not recognize a personal sphere in which individuals remain free to behave according to their preferences; it enacts a general prohibition of recreational drug use. For this reason, law enforcement in this area has a much more ambitious task than is assigned to those who fight against public segregation. It is less likely that the war on drugs can succeed without attending to the root causes of drug use.

A second issue is typically neglected in understanding and evaluating the war on drugs: Why has war been declared on illegal drugs? The simplistic answer is that drugs pose a threat to American society comparable to that of an invading enemy. Self-protection requires the mobilization of resources equivalent to those employed in time of war. For reasons that will become clear, I do not believe that this answer can begin to explain the extraordinary efforts of the state in combating drugs. Few wars – and certainly not the war on drugs – can be understood as a purely rational response to a grave social crisis.

No one doubts that the drug problem calls for state action, but why has a militaristic response been thought appropriate? The metaphors used to describe a phenomenon constrain what will appear to be an acceptable solution to it. If we really are at war against drugs, the alternative of decriminalization can be characterized only as a shameful retreat. William von Rabb, commissioner of the U.S. Customs Ser-

otests that legalization would be "an unconscionable
ler in a war [in which] there can be no substitute for
ctory."[23] But what is "total victory," and why is it
ry? A policy that does not work can always be
changed, but a war that is not won can only be lost. With
hindsight, it appears that Americans may have been hasty
in rallying to the call for a war on drugs. Perhaps we should
not be talking about a drug *war* at all, but rather about a drug
policy. A rational policy might well include massive efforts
by our criminal justice system, but other components of a
sensible policy – treatment, education, and the option of
simply leaving people alone – are not easily expressed within
a war mentality.

What needs to be explained is why some problems are
singled out for attention, whereas others are relatively ignored.[24] The abuse of legal drugs such as alcohol and tobacco
is not the only hazard likely to be overlooked by the war on
illegal drugs. Another such problem is lead. Federal authorities estimate that one out of every six children under the
age of six suffers from irreversible lead poisoning.[25] Children
with elevated lead levels have impaired auditory and language functioning, decreased attention spans, liver and kidney damage, altered electroencephalogram readings, and a
median IQ deficit of six points compared to their low-lead
classmates.[26] Despite these alarming data, no one has called
for a declaration of war on lead. Why not? There is no need
to suppose that the state is conspiring to deliberately manufacture a crisis in order to support an Orwellian expansion
of Big Brother. An alternative account explains why the public has been so receptive to a militaristic response to drug
use.

The public fears that America is a nation in decline. Crime,
poverty, poor education, corporate mismanagement, and an
unproductive and unmotivated work force are cited as evidence of this deterioration. Who, or what, should be blamed?
The political climate limits the range of acceptable answers.
Conservatives will not allow liberals to blame institutional
structures for our problems. The difficulty cannot be that

government has failed to create the right social programs to help people. Nor will liberals allow conservatives to blame individuals for our problems. The difficulty cannot be that people are lazy, stupid, or egocentric. What alternative explanations remain?

Illegal drugs provide the ideal scapegoat. Drugs are alleged to be so powerful that persons cannot be blamed very much for succumbing to them, as they could be blamed for not studying or working. And drugs are so plentiful and easy to conceal that government cannot be blamed very much for failing to eliminate them. Even better, most drugs are smuggled from abroad, so Americans can attribute our decline to the influence of foreigners. In blaming drugs, politicians need not fear that they will antagonize a powerful lobby that will challenge their allegations and mobilize voters against them. Almost no organized bodies defend the interests of drug users. Illegal drugs represent a "no-lose" issue, the safest of all political crusades.

A scapegoat would be imperfect unless there were at least some plausibility in the accusations of drug prohibitionists. Perhaps illegal drug use *has* increased crime, contributed to poverty, exacerbated the decline in education, and decreased the productivity of workers. Sometimes it may have done so in dramatic ways. The stories of the most decrepit victims of drug abuse lend themselves to biographies and television docudramas that make a deep and lasting impression on viewers. Everyone has seen vivid images of persons who were driven by drugs to commit brutal crimes, abandon their children, steal from their friends, drop out of school, stop going to work, and perhaps even die. In light of these consequences, who can condone illegal drug use?

I will attempt to show that a more accurate profile of the typical adult user of illegal drugs is less negative. This picture should emerge as a result of two factors that help to keep the drug problem in perspective. First, any number of other problems that receive almost no media attention and have not been made the target of a war contribute enormously to the problems America would like to solve. Second, the terrible problems associated with drug use occur in only a very small minority of cases. A persistent theme of this book is that drug policy has too often been framed by unwarranted generalizations from worst-case scenarios that seldom conform to the reality of typical drug use.

I will not further explore these two issues I believe to be significant in understanding and evaluating the war on drugs. A more detailed treatment, however important, would only reinforce the social perspective on drugs that I am anxious to replace. I am not primarily interested in showing that the disutility of drug use has been exaggerated. Instead, my position is that moral and legal questions about drug use have been approached from too narrow a perspective. In a society that boasts of its concern for moral rights, debates about drugs have tended to lose sight of individuals. Decriminalization theorists have done as much to encourage this misperception as apologists for the status quo. Both sides frame the central question in similar terms: Do drugs cause more harm than drug laws? If the answer is no, LAD should be opposed; if the answer is yes, war should be waged. But this utilitarian approach, however insightful, is not the only perspective worth adopting. I will argue that utilitarian thinking is inappropriate to apply to the act of recreational drug use unless prohibition does not infringe the moral rights of drug users. It is by the standard of moral rights that the justifiability of the war on drugs should be assessed, and it is by the standard of moral rights that the justifiability of the war on drugs is most vulnerable.

A third and final issue about the war on drugs raises a matter that I will explore in greater depth: If there is to be a war on drugs, against which drugs should it be waged? Usually this question is answered by naming acceptable and unacceptable recreational drugs: Heroin and crack are terrible; cocaine is only slightly better, but poses a comparable threat because it is more widely used; marijuana is not quite so worrisome, but still is bad enough to prohibit; alcohol and tobacco are not good, but should be tolerated. This kind of response, however, simply identifies a number of conclusions without indicating the reasoning that supports them. It does not articulate a set of principles to test the accuracy or coherence of these judgments. Particular drugs obtain their evaluations because they are believed to possess certain characteristics; conceivably, some of these drugs could lack those characteristics. Criteria are required to show why some recreational drugs should be prohibited, and others should be allowed.

I believe that progress in thinking about drugs can be achieved by shifting the focus of debate from real to hypothetical cases. What properties would a recreational drug have to possess so that adults would have a moral right to use it? What properties would a recreational drug have to possess so that adults would lack a moral right to use it? Only if these questions are answered is it possible to identify those existing drugs, if any, that satisfy these criteria. Without answers to these questions, no one should be too confident that a war on a given recreational drug is justified. Even if these questions do not seem urgent today, they are certain to become more pressing in the future. As Bennett warns: "New illegal products will no doubt continue to appear. . . . Whichever happens to be the drug of the day, our job is to persist in making it difficult to buy, sell, or use it."[27] But why? Simply because it is a drug? What is it about drugs that makes their prohibition seem so urgent? Is it impossible even to imagine a new recreational drug that society should condone and perhaps welcome?

MEDICAL AND LEGAL DEFINITIONS OF DRUGS

Labeling a substance a "drug" has extraordinary significance in the eyes of the public. The belief that a recreational activity involves a drug automatically evokes wholly different attitudes and reactions than are thought to be appropriate for a recreational activity that does not involve a drug. War has been declared on *drugs*. If war is to be declared on something, one would hope that two conditions would be satisfied. First, the enemy should be clearly identified. Second, the special significance of the enemy should be demonstrated. Unfortunately, neither condition is satisfied by the war on drugs.

Rarely do makers of policy bother to propose a definition of drugs. According to Franklin Zimring and Gordon Hawkins, this failure reflects "a long-standing tradition generally respected throughout the available literature on drug abuse and most clearly evident in previous reports on the subject published by federal departments and agencies."[28] Why has this failure been tolerated? Zimring and Hawkins offer no explanation. Lyndon Johnson's declaration of "war on poverty" gave rise to endless controversies about how poverty should be defined. But the declaration of war on drugs has stimulated little dispute about what drugs are. The problems I will raise in this section are not due to sloppiness in defining terms. They cannot be overcome simply by exercising greater care and ingenuity in the crafting of definitions. Instead, they indicate that the very concept of a drug is vague and imprecise.

How is "drug" defined by those who make the effort to define it at all? The answer depends on the discipline where an answer is sought. Perhaps the most frequently cited medical definition is "any substance other than food which by its chemical nature affects the structure or function of the living organism."[29] Undoubtedly this definition is too broad. Nonetheless, I tentatively propose to adopt it until a better alternative becomes available.

Notice that this definition refers only to the pharmacological effect of a substance and not to its legal status. For two reasons, "drugs" must not be defined as synonymous with "illegal drugs." First, it would be absurd to suppose that a non-drug could become a drug, or that a drug could become a non-drug, simply by a stroke of the pen. A legislature can change the legal classification of a substance, but not the nature of that substance; it has no more power to decide that a substance is a drug than to decide that a substance is a food. Second, a philosophical study designed to evaluate the moral rights of drug users can hardly afford to rely uncriti-

20

ARGUMENT IS WHY CERTAIN DRUGS A THE CLASSIFIED
AS BEING ILLEGAL ?

cally on the existing legal status of substances, since the legitimacy of these determinations is part of what is under investigation. To suppose that "drugs" means "illegal drugs" begs important questions and concedes much of what I will challenge. In what follows, I will use the word "drug" to refer to both legal and illegal substances that satisfy the medical definition I cited.

No doubt this usage will create confusion. Despite the desirability of distinguishing "drugs" from "illegal drugs," there is ample evidence that the public tends to equate them. Surveys indicate, for example, that whereas 95 percent of adults recognize heroin as a drug, only 39 percent categorize alcohol as a drug, and a mere 27 percent identify tobacco as a drug.[30] This tendency is pernicious. The widespread premise that only illegal substances are drugs lulls persons into accepting unsound arguments such as the following: Drugs are illegal; whatever is illegal is bad; we drink alcohol; what we do isn't bad; therefore, alcohol is not a drug. Clear thinking about this issue is impossible unless one realizes that whether a substance is a drug is a different question from whether that substance is or should be illegal.

How did the "semantic fiction"[31] equating "drugs" with "illegal drugs" arise? The story of nicotine may be instructive. The inability of the public to recognize nicotine as a drug is due less to the pharmacological effects of the substance than to the powerful political influence of the tobacco industry throughout American history. The regulation of tobacco is not under the authority of the Food and Drug Administration (FDA). Tobacco appeared in the 1890 edition of the *U.S. Pharmacopeia,* an official listing of drugs published by the government. But the drug was deleted from the 1905 edition, which automatically withdrew it from FDA supervision. The removal of tobacco from the *Pharmacopeia* was the price that had to be paid to induce legislators from tobacco-growing states to support the Food and Drug Act of 1906. The FDA had another opportunity to gain authority over nicotine when the Hazardous Substances Labeling Act of 1960 empowered it to control the sale of dangerous substances with

21

ty to produce illness through inhalation. But the
f the Department of Health, Education, and Wel-
V), the parent organization of the FDA, argued
t should not be construed to create FDA authority
to regulate cigarettes until Congress amended the act to make
this interpretation more explicit. Congress subsequently rejected such an amendment.[32] The familiar health warnings
on cigarette packages were eventually required by the Federal
Trade Commission (FTC) as part of its authority to regulate
unfair and deceptive trade practices. The status of nicotine
as a "drug" is irrelevant to the basis of the FTC's authority. The moral of this story is that the categorization of a
substance as a drug is a function of politics and not just of
pharmacology.

The unfortunate equation of "drugs" with "illegal drugs"
runs throughout the policy statements of the National Drug
Control Strategy. Bennett alleges that "the majority of American city residents . . . do not take drugs," but he also cites
statistics to show that alcohol is "the most widely abused
substance in America."[33] These two statements suggest that
Bennett believes that alcohol is not a drug. What, then, *is* a
drug? Bennett does not say.

Legal definitions of "drugs" are somewhat more compli-
cated than the earlier medical definition. The federal Controlled Substances Act incorporates the following definition
of "drugs" from the Food, Drug, and Cosmetic Act:

"Drugs" means (a) substances recognized in the official United
States Pharmacopeia, official Homeopathic Pharmacopeia of
the United States, or official National Formulary, or any subsequent to any of them; and (b) substances intended for use
in the diagnosis, cure, mitigation, treatment, or prevention of
disease in man or other animals; and (c) substances (other
than food) intended to affect the structure or any function of
the body of man or other animals; and (d) substances intended
for use as a component of any article specified in subsections
(a), (b) and (c) of this section; but does not include devices or
their components, parts or accessories.[34]

22

I will offer two critical observations about this elaborate definition.

First, the conjunction "and" that separates the four criteria, (a)–(d), in this definition cannot be taken literally. Would anyone seriously maintain that a substance fails to satisfy this statutory definition because it is not used in the diagnosis or treatment of a disease, even though it is listed in the *Pharmacopeia* and affects the structure or function of the body? On the other hand, no one would argue that a substance qualifies as a drug simply by satisfying any of these four criteria. Is a stethoscope a drug because it is a substance used in the diagnosis of disease?

Second, criteria (b), (c), and (d) make a peculiar reference to *intentions*. A substance satisfies criterion (b) if it is intended to be used for the diagnosis of a disease and criterion (c) if it is intended to affect the structure or function of the body. The statute does not explicitly identify the person(s) to whose intentions it refers. One would think that the intentions of the person who makes the diagnosis are relevant in (b), whereas the intentions of the person who dispenses or uses the substance are relevant in (c). This reference to intentions produces some very curious results. Users may be mistaken about whether a particular substance has an effect. Suppose that someone believes that the consumption of a placebo will affect his bodily structure or function. If so, the placebo qualifies as a drug according to this definition. One can only speculate about why the drafters of this statute thought it advisable to define drugs not according to their true properties or effects, but according to the properties or effects that an unspecified person intends them to have.

Only criterion (a) does not make reference to intentions. It provides what might be called an operational definition; it describes a simple test to determine whether a substance is or is not a drug: A substance is a drug if and only if it is contained in the *Pharmacopeia*. This process is like defining a word as whatever configuration of letters appears in an authoritative dictionary. Ultimately, however, operational definitions resolve nothing; they merely shift the burden to experts who prepare the authoritative sources. How do the experts decide what drugs are? As I have already suggested in the case of tobacco, the exclusion of a substance from the *Pharmacopeia* need not be a function of its pharmacological properties. If the manufacturers of tobacco products had lacked political clout around the turn of the century, or if tobacco had been discovered later in history, tobacco would certainly have appeared in the *Pharmacopeia*, thereby satisfying criterion (a) of the legal definition of "drug."

For these two reasons, this legal definition is deficient. Do these defects contaminate any legal results that invoke this definition? Since so much depends on whether the public regards a substance as a drug, one might naturally anticipate that the same would be true of the law. Many difficult questions arise in the course of interpreting this definition. Consider two examples. Since a given substance becomes a drug when it is intended for use in the treatment of "disease," it becomes crucial to know what a disease is. Philosophers of medicine have debated the nature of disease since Plato. And because "foods" are contrasted with drugs, it becomes crucial to know what a food is. Statutory definitions are unhelpful.[35] In light of the propensity of lawyers to stir up litigation, enormous controversy should have surrounded attempts to define "disease" and "food."

Surprisingly, these legal controversies have rarely taken place, and it is important to understand why. The simple explanation is that modern statutes do not rely on the term "drug" very much. Nothing of legal significance depends on whether or not a substance satisfies the preceding definition and qualifies as a drug. The terms of the Controlled Substances Act create the authority to regulate "drugs or controlled substances," not "drugs" per se. As I will describe in more detail in the following section, regulation under this act is achieved by placing a drug on one of five schedules. The statute defines "controlled substance" to mean "a drug, or other substance, or immediate precursor, included in Schedule I, II, III, IV, or V."[36] Thus a "controlled substance" can refer to either a "drug" *or* an "other substance," as long as it is placed on a schedule. The act does not define "substance," and it provides no guidance about how the distinction between substances and non-substances should be drawn. Remarkably, the concept of a drug has no special significance in this statutory scheme.

In other words, legislators can admit that a substance is *not* a drug without surrendering any of their authority to regulate it under the Controlled Substances Act. Nothing prevents this statute from being used to prohibit the manufacture, sale, distribution, possession, or consumption of non-drugs, as long as what is regulated qualifies as a substance. As one might expect, this broad, almost unlimited authority to control substances rather than drugs produces some very peculiar results. However, the authority created by the act is not boundless. Some materials – "distilled spirits, wine, malt beverages, or tobacco" – are explicitly excluded from the definition of a "controlled substance."[37] Alcohol and tobacco are not controlled substances for the simple reason that the statute says they are not. With this stroke of the legislative pen, two of the most dangerous drugs are placed beyond the scope of regulation under the Controlled Substances Act.

The circularity in this definition of a "controlled substance" is evident. A controlled substance is any substance that appears on any of the five statutory schedules. In other words, a controlled substance is any substance that is controlled. From all that has been said so far, water and chocolate could qualify as controlled substances. The definition of drugs explicitly distinguishes drugs from foods, but since foods would seem to be substances, this statute could be used to prohibit the consumption of foods after all. Beyond the explicit exceptions for alcohol and tobacco, the only limitations on what substances can be controlled are found in the criteria for appearance on each of the five statutory schedules. In effect, these criteria substitute for a definition of "drugs." Even more importantly, they specify what it is about substances that makes them eligible for regulation.

Although almost anything would seem to be a substance

25

and thus eligible for regulation under the Controlled Substances Act, I do not suppose for a moment that courts would actually allow air, water, or other fanciful examples to be prohibited under this statute. Obviously, this act was not intended to create the authority to proscribe the sale of handguns. But nothing in this statute requires that a "drug or other substance" be consumed; surely a bullet in the brain can "affect the structure or function of the body," partly as a result of its chemical properties. It would be fascinating to examine the reasoning of a court about why such fanciful examples are ineligible for regulation under the act.

Despite the fact that legal regulations effectively abandon the concept of a drug in favor of the amorphous concept of a substance, I will continue to follow popular usage and discuss the moral and legal issues involved in recreational *drug* use. In most of what follows, I will pretend that the act does not create the authority to regulate substances that are not drugs. Yet I do so with reluctance and not simply because "drug" is hard to define. Shifting the inquiry from drugs to substances would help to overcome the tendency to believe that the drug problem is sui generis. The fact that a substance is or is not a drug does not seem especially important to the case for or against its legal regulation. Suppose that a new food were discovered that was no more or less dangerous or subject to abuse than cocaine and had exactly the same side effects. The fact that this new substance is a food rather than a drug is not, I think, relevant to the decision about whether it should be prohibited.

In fact, I see no reason why the same criteria of justification that pertain to the regulation of substances, drugs or otherwise, should not pertain to the regulation of all recreational activities. Suppose, for example, that a new activity were invented that was no more or less dangerous or subject to abuse than cocaine and had exactly the same side effects. The fact that this new recreational activity does not involve the consumption of a drug is not, I think, relevant to the decision about whether it should be prohibited.

In other words, the fact that something affects the function or structure of the organism by its chemical properties does not seem to be especially significant. The personal and social effects of an activity are important to the case for prohibiting it, not the means by which they result. I will test the hypothesis that "drugs are not different" throughout this book. This hypothesis will not lead me to abandon the use of the word "drug," but it will allow me to draw frequent analogies between the use of drugs, the consumption of unhealthy foods, and the performance of dangerous activities. If these analogies fail, it will not be because drugs and non-drugs should be evaluated by different criteria. Or so I will tentatively suppose.

Those who regard these analogies as inapt must make a case that drugs *are* different. But no support for the belief that drugs are different can be drawn from the legal definition of "drug" found in the statutory scheme that controls drug use. This belief, which tends to be taken for granted by the public, seems to have been repudiated by those who drafted the Controlled Substances Act, and who did not attach any special significance to drugs per se.

LEGAL REGULATION OF DRUGS

Mark Moore writes:

> One of the most frustrating aspects of the current debate about legalization is that the debaters often seem ignorant about the current legal regime. The system of laws regulating drug use is often painted as moralistic and paternalistic rather than as a rational scheme for regulating the uses of psychoactive drugs.[38]

Moore is correct that both friends and foes of LAD are often unaware of how recreational drug use is regulated by law. In this section, I propose to remedy this deficiency. However, my examination does little to support Moore's judgment that LAD comprises a "rational scheme."

The Comprehensive Drug Abuse Prevention and Control

Act, popularly known as the Controlled Substances Act of 1970, provides the basis for understanding the legal regulation of drugs. This act supplanted previous statutory schemes for prohibiting the use of drugs and serves as a model for a uniform state law. Forty-five states have adopted the Uniform Controlled Substances Act in some form or another; only Alaska, Colorado, Maine, New Hampshire, Vermont, and the District of Columbia have failed to do so. This act divides "drugs or other substances" into five schedules. The placement of a drug in one schedule or another affects manufacturing quotas, import restrictions, dispensing limits, and criminal penalties for unlawful trafficking. The schedule where a drug is placed has no affect on the punishment for unlawful possession.

This act does not criminalize drug use per se. This fact is not especially significant. The comparable statutes in twelve states create "use provisions," which punish "using" or "being under the influence" of a controlled substance. Most states follow the federal act and do not criminalize use itself. The difference is unimportant, since it is virtually impossible to use a drug without possessing it. As I will argue in Chapter 3, possessory offenses are anticipatory; they provide a means to prevent the consummate harms associated with drug use before they occur. If drugs were not used, no one would worry about their possession. In case there is any doubt, Bennett writes that "the drug problem in its essence" is "use itself";[39] drug use is "the chief and seminal wrong."[40] No one thinks that possession is the "seminal wrong" or the "essence" of the drug problem. For these reasons, I will continue to refer to the crime of drug use, although I am fully aware that the Controlled Substances Act does not explicitly create such an offense. This fact does not affect any of my arguments for or against LAD.

Although there is some variation among states about the particular schedule where a given drug is placed, the federal act categorizes drugs roughly as follows: Schedule I includes heroin, LSD, and marijuana; Schedule II, cocaine and amphetamine-type stimulants; Schedule III, nonamphetamine-

28

type stimulants and barbiturates; Schedule IV, barbiturate and nonbarbiturate depressants; and Schedule V, compounds with low amounts of narcotics, stimulants, and depressants. Three states (Arkansas, Tennessee, and North Carolina) have created a special "Schedule VI" solely for marijuana.[41]

The criteria governing the schedule where a drug is placed are controversial, important, and resistant to a quick summary, so I will reproduce them in full:

(1) SCHEDULE I:
(A) The drug or other substance has a high potential for abuse.
(B) The drug or other substance has no currently accepted medical use in treatment in the United States.
(C) There is a lack of accepted safety for use of the drug or other substance under medical supervision.
(2) SCHEDULE II:
(A) The drug or other substance has a high potential for abuse.
(B) The drug or other substance has a currently accepted medical use in treatment in the United States or a currently accepted medical use with severe restrictions.
(C) Abuse of the drug or other substance may lead to severe psychological or physical dependence.
(3) SCHEDULE III:
(A) The drug or other substance has a potential for abuse less than the drugs or other substances in schedules I and II.
(B) The drug or other substance has a currently accepted medical use in treatment in the United States.
(C) Abuse of the drug or other substance may lead to moderate or low physical dependence or high psychological dependence.
(4) SCHEDULE IV:
(A) The drug or other substance has a low potential for abuse relative to the drugs or other substances in schedule III.
(B) The drug or other substance has a currently accepted medical use in treatment in the United States.
(C) Abuse of the drug or other substance may lead to limited physical dependence or psychological dependence relative to the drugs or other substances in schedule III.
(5) SCHEDULE V:

(A) The drug or other substance has a low potential for abuse relative to the drugs or other substances in schedule IV.
(B) The drug or other substance has a currently accepted medical use in treatment in the United States.
(C) Abuse of the drug or other substance may lead to limited physical dependence or psychological dependence relative to the drugs or other substances in schedule IV.[42]

These criteria are used to decide whether and under what circumstances a drug will be regulated. In addition, they identify what it is about a drug in virtue of which prohibition is thought to be justifiable.

An examination of these criteria is central to my theoretical project to describe a recreational drug that adults would have or would lack a right to use. Apparently, the state concedes that persons have a legal right to use those recreational drugs that fail to satisfy the criteria for inclusion on any of the five statutory schedules. Hence these criteria contain the state's answer to the question of what properties a recreational drug would have to possess before adults would have or would lack a right to use it. Interpretations of this act should make it possible to describe a hypothetical drug that is not controlled and that adults have a right to use recreationally.

Applications of this complex statutory scheme require a number of very difficult determinations. I will discuss some of the more controversial issues that arise in deciding where (or whether) to schedule a given drug.

First, the drafters of the act neglect to specify the relationship among the several criteria used to schedule a given "drug or other substance." As with the definition of "drug" I described earlier, no "and" or "or" clearly separates the end of one criterion from the beginning of the next. Perhaps the more natural reading of the act is that the criteria should be conjoined. In other words, a "drug or other substance" should not be placed on Schedule I unless it satisfies criterion (A) *and* (B) *and* (C). If so, the number of existing schedules is grossly inadequate to classify all drugs. For example, a "drug or other substance" with "no accepted medical use" but with less than a "high potential for abuse" cannot be placed on any of the five schedules.

In order to avoid this difficulty, one might expect that courts would construe the criteria disjunctively. According to this interpretation, a "drug or other substance" may be placed on Schedule I if it satisfies criterion (A) *or* (B) *or* (C). But this interpretation is absurd. No one would think that possession of a "drug or other substance" without a medical use should give rise to criminal penalties. A lump of coal may lack a medical use, but surely its possession could not be made criminal under the act. But why not? Much of the difficulty is due to the failure of the drafters to restrict the application of the act to "drugs" rather than to "drugs or other substances."

Judicial interpretations of the terms of the act have not resolved the confusion over the relationship among the several criteria used to schedule a given drug. Courts have held that "the three statutory criteria for Schedule I classification ... should not be read as being either cumulative or exclusive."[43] These criteria "are guides in determining the schedule to which a drug belongs, but they are not dispositive."[44] Apparently, the relationship among the criteria should not always be construed either conjunctively or disjunctively.

This holding is unhelpful in providing any guidance about how the statutory criteria *should* be interpreted. This failure is serious. As a result, the criteria for placing a substance on one schedule rather than another can be, and often are, indeterminate. Thus the Controlled Substances Act offers no definitive answer to the question: What properties must a drug possess before its use can be prohibited? Of course, the use of a recreational drug that satisfies none of the criteria of the act will be permitted. For this reason, it should still be possible to describe the properties of a hypothetical drug that falls beyond the reach of the act.

Several criteria in the act must be interpreted before such a recreational drug can be described. Criterion (B) in Schedules I–V is especially difficult to understand. Applications of the Controlled Substances Act require a determination of

31

whether a "drug or other substance" has a "currently accepted medical use." Drugs without a currently accepted medical use are placed in Schedule I; otherwise, they are placed in subsequent schedules. How does one decide whether a given drug has an accepted medical use?

According to one possible answer, a drug has an accepted medical use only when the FDA approves an application to market it. But this answer cannot be correct. The FDA might reject an application to market a drug for seven distinct reasons, including the failure of the application to contain relevant patent information.[45] The absence of medical use cannot be inferred simply from the lack of FDA marketing approval.

A second possible answer is that a drug has an accepted medical use when sufficient numbers of the medical community believe that it has such a use.[46] But this interpretation opens a Pandora's box. If medical practitioners agree that the best treatment for drug addicts includes administration of an addictive drug under medical supervision, then no addictive drug will satisfy this criterion for placement on Schedule I. According to this interpretation, any addictive drug could have a medical use. But this result cannot be what the drafters of the act had in mind by an "accepted medical use."[47] They clearly had no intent to duplicate the so-called British System and to allow medical practitioners to prescribe Schedule I narcotics to addicts.

A closely related problem is to determine how a drug can acquire an "accepted medical use" once it has been placed on Schedule I. According to some commentators:

> The true test of [the statutory scheme] will be in loosening restraints when justified. A scheme that is directed only towards tighter and tighter controls will, in time, lose its most important attributes, flexibility, and the capacity to adjust to changing social circumstances.[48]

But flexibility is hard to achieve under the act. A drug that is illegal for doctors to prescribe cannot possibly have a medical use that *is* accepted. Nearly half of the cancer specialists responding to a questionnaire answered that they would prescribe marijuana if it were removed from Schedule I.[49] But it is not clear that this poll shows that marijuana *has* an accepted medical use. Thus the debate about how a drug gains or loses an "accepted medical use" remains unresolved.

Deciding whether a drug has or lacks a medical use has turned out to be a quagmire. But applications of criterion (A) in Schedules I–V are even more troublesome. This criterion, which requires a determination of a drug's potential for abuse, is perhaps the most important basis for deciding where a given drug should be scheduled. A drug with a "high potential for abuse" will be placed on Schedule I or II (depending on whether it has a medical use), and drugs with a "low potential for abuse" relative to those on Schedules I or II will be placed on successively higher schedules. How is the relative potential for abuse of a drug to be ascertained? The act does not define "abuse" or "high potential for abuse," although attempts to challenge the constitutionality of the act for this reason have proven unsuccessful.[50]

The legislative history of the Controlled Substances Act reveals the following four guidelines to identify the extent of a drug's potential for abuse:

(1) There is evidence that individuals are taking the drug . . . in amounts sufficient to create a hazard to their health or to the safety of other individuals or of the community; or
(2) There is significant diversion of the drug . . . from legitimate drug channels; or
(3) Individuals are taking the drug . . . on their own initiative rather than on the basis of medical advice from a practitioner licensed by law to administer such drugs in the course of his professional practice; or
(4) The drug or drugs . . . are new drugs so related in their action to a drug or drugs already listed for having a potential for abuse to make it likely that the drug will have the same potentiality for abuse.[51]

Although these guidelines are helpful, many problems remain.

First, notice that these guidelines only address whether a drug has *some* potential for abuse but do not speak to the more difficult question of how to measure the *extent* of this potential. Unless the degree of the potential for abuse can be quantified, no drug can be assigned to a particular schedule. Only guideline (4) provides a basis of comparison. Pursuant to (4), a new drug should be placed on a schedule by estimating its potential for abuse relative to drugs that are already scheduled. Of course, this approach is sound only if the drugs in the comparison class have been scheduled properly. Without understanding how the relative potential for abuse is to be measured, it is impossible to know if the drugs already scheduled have been placed correctly or incorrectly. In short, the entire scheduling process lacks an anchor.

Moreover, practically any "drug or other substance" will be abused by some persons to some degree at some time or another. Very curious results can be produced by temporarily suspending the pretense that the act controls drugs rather than substances. From all that has been said so far, nothing would preclude placing chocolate on Schedule I.

But problems remain even if applications of the act are restricted to drugs. These guidelines fail to specify whether a potential for abuse becomes high because a great percentage of users abuse the drug a little, or because a small percentage abuse the drug a lot. Judicial interpretations of the act indicate that the latter circumstance suffices to allow a drug to be placed on Schedule I or II. Evidence that a few users have required treatment in hospital emergency rooms has helped to persuade courts that a drug belongs on Schedule I, even though those who require emergency care may represent a tiny fraction of the total number of users. As a result, the act has the effect of sacrificing the interests of the (perhaps overwhelming) majority of persons who use a drug without undue hardship to promote the interests of the (perhaps small) minority of persons who use a drug abusively.

34

Perhaps this sacrifice of the many for the sake of the few can be justified – I will return to this issue later – but it cannot be taken for granted.

In addition, guideline (3) seemingly identifies *any* nonmedical use of a drug as abuse. The very act of taking a drug for a nonmedical reason constitutes abuse and allows the drug to be regulated under the act. Some commentators appear to go so far as to *define* drug abuse in terms of recreational use.[52] From this perspective, the suggestion that drugs have a nonmedical use is incoherent, and not merely false. Understanding how a drug might properly be used recreationally is no easier than understanding how a square could be round.

A final difficulty in interpreting (A) in Schedules I–V is that the placement of a drug depends on its *potential* for abuse. The scheduling of a drug need not wait "until a number of lives have been destroyed or substantial problems have already arisen."[53] But how is the potential for abuse of a given drug to be determined in the absence of evidence of actual abuse? Some commentators have argued that the "strong euphoria" produced by a given drug "suggests a high abuse potential."[54] In other words, a drug is subject to great abuse simply because it is a lot of fun to use. The finding that a drug produces pleasure is all that is required to subject it to the most stringent controls under the act.

In any event, difficulties in scheduling a particular drug turn out to be irrelevant for purposes of answering my central question. Adults have no legal right to use a drug recreationally, regardless of where it is scheduled. Even more significantly, the extent of punishment for illegal possession, and thus for use, does not change with the scheduling of a drug. "Simple unlawful possession" of any controlled substance is punishable by "a term of imprisonment of not more than one year, a fine of not more than $5,000, or both."[55] Under federal law, unlawful possession of heroin is punished no more severely than is possession of a Schedule V substance without a prescription.

Perhaps the difficulties in interpreting and applying these

statutory criteria should come as no surprise. Political factors having nothing to do with the harm or likelihood of abuse of a drug have clouded the act since it was drafted. According to David Musto, "The history of drug laws in the United States shows that the degree to which a drug has been outlawed or curbed has no direct relation to its inherent danger."[56] The very creation of Schedule I was partly due to the efforts of manufacturers and distributors of "legitimate" substances to ensure that their products were not classified along with illicit drugs.[57]

I hope to have cast doubt on the accuracy of Moore's description of LAD as "rational." Nonetheless, my central concern has not been to expose the deficiencies of the Controlled Substances Act. I have explored the terms of this act primarily because the criteria for inclusion on the statutory schedules provide the state's answer to the question: What properties must a drug possess before adults have or lack a right to use it recreationally? The answer to this question is now apparent. Except for the ad hoc statutory exemptions for tobacco and alcohol, the recreational use of drugs is totally proscribed. This result follows from two related strains of thought. First, since recreational use is nonmedical, a drug is subject to prohibition on this ground alone. Even if a given drug has a medical use, its consumption for recreational purposes constitutes abuse. Second, since the effects of a drug must be enjoyable before anyone would want to take it recreationally, the use of a drug to produce pleasure is tantamount to abuse, again making that drug eligible for prohibition. Therefore, it is impossible to imagine a drug that anyone would want to use recreationally that would be permitted for such a purpose under the Controlled Substances Act.

These extraordinary results can hardly be described as "rational" inasmuch as they express an unreasonable prejudice against recreational drug use per se. It is unthinkable that any other activity would become eligible for harsh punishment solely because it is euphoric. Ordinarily, the discovery that an activity produces pleasure would be an occasion for celebration – unless that activity involves drug use. Why should the fact that a drug is pleasurable but lacks a medical use be a sufficient reason to prohibit it for recreational purposes?

Understanding the terms of the Controlled Substances Act has proved to be difficult. Moreover, problems go beyond statutory interpretation. My final observation about this act is perhaps the most important, as it raises constitutional questions about legal prohibitions of recreational drug use.

Challenges that a particular drug should not be controlled at all, or that it should be placed on a different schedule, are typically adjudicated according to the "rational basis test." According to this test, "those challenging the legislative judgment must convince the court that the legislative facts on which the classification is apparently based could not reasonably be conceived to be true by the governmental decisionmaker."[58] The judge must determine "whether there exists any set of facts which can be shown or which could reasonably be assumed to provide support for the classification selected by Congress."[59] The application of this test results in near-absolute deference to legislative judgments; rarely have plaintiffs prevailed in showing that a rational basis for a legislative determination is lacking. Judges have almost never upheld challenges to the legal classification of a drug, despite enormous dispute about its dangerousness and considerable vagueness in the statutory scheme.

Courts seldom subject legislative regulation of drugs to heightened levels of scrutiny. They have declined to apply the demanding "compelling state interest" test to assess challenges that a given drug should be placed on a different schedule or should not be controlled at all. According to this test, a law is unconstitutional unless it is "necessary, and not merely rationally related, to the accomplishment of a permissible state policy."[60] If this test were applied, courts would be forced to decide whether a less restrictive alternative might better achieve whatever objectives are sought by LAD. To make this determination, the objectives of LAD would have to be identified. These issues need not be confronted as long as the rational basis test is applied.

Applications of the rational basis test make hard cases seem easy. Consider the all-too-familiar conflicts about smoking cigarettes in public places. One might think that these conflicts pit the "right to smoke" against the "right to breath clean air." If so, the conflict cannot be resolved without some procedure to decide which right is entitled to a greater degree of protection. According to Robert Goodin, the rights of nonsmokers take precedence. Goodin does not categorically reject the existence of a right to put a substance into one's body. Yet he maintains that "there is no larger social interest of free speech or any other to be served by allowing [smoking]."[61] The rationale for curbing smokers is no different from the basis for regulating "smelly factories."[62] The fact that smokers may enjoy smoking does not count for very much. Although I have little quarrel with his conclusion, I suspect that Goodin reaches it too easily. The right to put a substance into one's body should not be weighted so lightly.

Occasionally courts have invoked standards of review that are intermediate between the rational basis and compelling state interest tests. In *Ravin v. State*, the most noteworthy case to invoke an intermediate test, the Alaska Supreme Court held that "the right to privacy would encompass the possession and ingestion of substances such as marijuana in a purely personal, non-commercial context in the home."[63] This conclusion was reached by applying a test of constitutionality that required courts to decide "whether the means chosen suitably furthered an appropriate governmental interest."[64] As a result of applying this intermediate test, the private use of an illegal recreational drug was held to be protected by a constitutional right in the state of Alaska. Because this decision was so controversial, voters have recently sought to overturn it through the process of initiative and referendum.[65]

Constitutional law requires that statutory classifications

with a disproportionate impact on race must be subjected to strict scrutiny. Until recently, this rationale for applying a heightened level of judicial review seemed to have little application to LAD. However, many states have begun to treat possession of crack as a more serious offense than possession of identical amounts of powdered cocaine. Since blacks are more likely to use crack than powdered cocaine, they tend to be punished more severely than whites. This disparity led a judge in Minnesota to subject that state's crack statute to strict scrutiny. As a result, she overturned·this law until scientific rather than merely anecdotal evidence establishes that crack is a different and more dangerous drug than powdered cocaine. Her ruling was upheld by the Minnesota Supreme Court, which said it found little hard evidence to support a distinction between the two substances.[66]

But these examples represent the exception rather than the rule. Why have heightened degrees of scrutiny been applied so infrequently? The Supreme Court has never provided a coherent explanation of the characteristics that trigger higher levels of judicial review.[67] Infringement of "important" or "fundamental" rights or interests usually gives rise to stricter scrutiny.[68] The unwillingness to assess questions about recreational drug use according to more exacting tests indicates that personal decisions about recreational drug use are not thought to be protected by an important or fundamental right.

Why are whatever rights may be involved in recreational drug use regarded as so insignificant? Sometimes a policy or practice is so familiar and widespread that it becomes all but impossible to return to a state of innocence and to imagine how strange and peculiar it would appear from the perspective of an outsider. Suppose that a person who did not have a particular issue in mind were asked to prepare a list of general rights that are most important or fundamental in a free society. General rights that could easily be interpreted to protect recreational drug use would be prominent on this list. One such right is the right to determine what happens in and to one's body. Another such right is the right to regulate the ways in which the mind processes the sensory data it receives from the world. According to Laurence Tribe, it would seem "preposterous" that courts would allow the state to regulate these rights without applying heightened standards of review. Yet, he adds, "Courts that affirm the power of government to ban the use of such psychoactive substances as marijuana appear to be saying something very much like that."[69]

Almost no one seems to have cared. As Ethan Nadelmann points out, "Even the civil-liberties groups shy away from this issue."[70] It is easy to interest the American Civil Liberties Union (ACLU) in the question of whether adults should be tested for drug use. But ACLU has little interest in the question of whether and under what circumstances adults should be allowed to use recreational drugs in the first place. These priorities are misplaced. Surely the best reason to oppose drug tests is because adults have a moral right to engage in the very activity the tests are designed to detect.

Suppose that the state were to interfere with various applications of whatever rights are implicated by LAD. Imagine that the state attempted to regulate dress by forbidding anyone to wear high heels. Or that it attempted to regulate appearance by prohibiting anyone to grow long hair. Compound the difficulty by supposing that these interferences purported to reach private citizens, not just public employees. Even worse, imagine that these regulations applied in the home. In other words, suppose that high heels or long hair were proscribed, even if offenders did not appear in public. It seems clear that the state would need excellent reasons to enact such general legislation and that courts should be encouraged to scrutinize these reasons very carefully. These interferences affect rights that should be placed high on a list of protections in a free society. Why is recreational drug use any different? In Chapter 2, I will explore whether a theory of personal autonomy can be defended that would entitle recreational drug use to a lesser degree of protection than the activities on this list.

For better or worse, the constitutionality of hypothetical

statutes that interfere with decisions regarding dress or appearance, in public or in private, will remain unsettled as long as states do not intrude in these matters. Little constitutional law has developed here precisely because these regulations are so outlandish. Most of the few existing precedents involve attempts to interfere with the dress and appearance of schoolchildren. My examples, however, involve regulations of private citizens that apply even in their own homes. Sometimes, but not always, the fact that laws regulate behavior in the privacy of one's home is constitutionally significant. In numerous cases, courts have held that persons have a right to do in private what they are not permitted to do in public. Surely dress and appearance are entitled to a greater degree of protection in private than in public, and one might naturally expect the same to be true of recreational drug use.

I do not mean to prejudge how such cases ultimately should be decided. To propose that a given test of constitutionality is appropriate for deciding a case is not tantamount to actually deciding it. My more modest point is that the constitutionality of these laws would and should depend on the stringency of the standard of review by which they are adjudicated. Suppose that the rational basis test, which is presently applied to regulation of drug use, were applied to the hypothetical laws just discussed. It is easy to see why a state might have a rational basis for regulation of dress or appearance. According to Tribe, "History abounds with examples of governments asserting virtually boundless authority over the details of personal appearance and manners."[71] On the streets of our cities, persons are sometimes killed for their sneakers or leather jackets. Suppose that the state responded by prohibiting persons from wearing these clothes. These laws might be constitutional if plaintiffs were required to show that "the legislative facts on which the classification is apparently based could not reasonably be conceived to be true by the governmental decisionmaker." Surely "there exists [a] set of facts which can be shown or which could reasonably be assumed to provide support for the classification." But interferences with dress or appearance should not be accepted uncritically in a free society.

I do not conclude that an interference with recreational drug use is as objectionable as an interference with dress or appearance. However, I maintain that the larger rights that are implicated by each of these interferences seem to be of comparable importance, so that the same test should be applied to decide their constitutionality. Dress and appearance are and ought to be subject to regulation. The state routinely controls these matters when students, military personnel, police, and fire fighters are involved. Such regulation, however, should be made to satisfy very stringent criteria. The same stringent criteria should be applied to assess the justifiability of interferences with recreational drug use.

It is unclear whether the objectives sought by LAD could satisfy the more stringent criteria of constitutionality involved in heightened levels of scrutiny. This issue has not been resolved, because the state has been allowed to interfere with the right of adults to use the recreational drug of their choice according to a more lenient standard. What *is* clear is that plaintiffs would have much greater prospects for success in challenging classifications under the Controlled Substances Act if their allegations were assessed according to a more demanding test.

Despite the fact that these questions about the Controlled Substances Act raise important constitutional difficulties, I will not further pursue the constitutional dimensions of LAD. Although I am centrally concerned to evaluate arguments for and against the claim that adults have a moral right to use drugs recreationally, I will not attempt to elevate these arguments to the plane of constitutional law. Moral rights should be protected by legal rights, so the existence of a moral right to use recreational drugs would provide an excellent reason to oppose LAD. Still, I will make no serious attempt to argue that any such legal right can be "found" in the Constitution. I am not especially concerned about whether a moral right to use drugs recreationally should be vindicated ultimately by the legislature or the Court.

I have several reasons for not undertaking a more detailed examination of these constitutional issues. First, David Richards has already made a powerful case that many aspects of LAD are unconstitutional.[72] Although I am suitably impressed by Richards's arguments, the weaknesses of his position are apparent as well.[73] The Constitution makes no explicit reference to drug use. If recreational drug use is entitled to constitutional protection, some existing right must be interpreted to protect it. The right to privacy is the most likely candidate for this constitutional right. Thus two conditions must be satisfied before recreational drug use is entitled to constitutional protection. First, the Constitution must create a right to privacy. Second, this right to privacy must apply to and protect the right to use some or all recreational drugs.

Neither proposition is beyond controversy. Largely because of the abortion dispute, the very existence of a right to privacy continues to be debated by scholars of constitutional law. The application of any such right to the decision to use recreational drugs is equally unclear. Many different conceptions of the right to privacy have been defended, and only some of them would protect recreational drug use. The Supreme Court seems currently disposed to reject the right to privacy altogether or, more likely, to confine its scope to decisions pertaining to marriage, procreation, and the family.[74] An extended critical discussion of these issues would take us too far afield. I hope that the arguments I will make in favor of a moral right to use recreational drugs can be expressed in constitutional terms, but I will make no serious effort to do so here.

Still, I cannot refrain from adding one brief twist to the constitutional arguments involving recreational drug use. Many of the social conservatives who are least sympathetic to the decriminalization movement favor a "jurisprudence of original intent." According to this principle of interpretation, the Constitution is to be construed according to the intentions of its drafters. A jurisprudence of original intent is favored largely because it tends to generate results that are congenial

to the agenda of social conservatives. For example, the founding fathers tended to be less liberal about most matters of
criminal procedure. However, this jurisprudence may produce unacceptable results for drug prohibitionists. Thomas
Jefferson was not alone among the founding fathers in opposing state authority to prohibit the use of drugs, medical
or otherwise. "Was the government to prescribe to us our
medicine and diet," he observed, "our bodies would be in
such keeping as our souls are now [under the state
church]."[75] Federal control over drug use was widely regarded as unconstitutional as late as 1900.[76] Even in 1937,
the Treasury Department prohibited marijuana separately
from narcotics because it feared an attack on the constitutionality of the Harrison Act.[77] An effort to apply the original
intent of the founding fathers might create surprising difficulties for LAD.

RECREATIONAL DRUG USE

No one pretends that drugs are good or bad per se. Trying
to decide whether drugs are good or bad is like trying to
decide whether fires are good or bad: It depends on the
purpose(s) for which they are used. As the examination of
the Controlled Substances Act demonstrates, war has not
really been declared on *drugs*. War has been declared on
persons who make a certain *use* of drugs. I will describe this
use as *recreational*.

By "recreational use," I mean consumption that is intended
to promote the pleasure, happiness, or euphoria of the user.[78]
The more specific purposes that are encompassed under this
broad umbrella include sociability, relaxation, alleviation of
boredom, conviviality, feelings of harmony, enhancement of
sexuality, and the like. Although borderline cases are numerous, paradigm examples of recreational drug use are
plentiful. Interviews with users indicate that they are most
likely to consume drugs on two general occasions. First, they
use drugs to attempt to improve what they anticipate will be
a good time. Hence drug use is frequent during parties, con-

certs, and sex. Second, they use drugs to attempt to make mindless and routine chores less boring. Hence drug use is frequent during house cleaning and cooking. I regard these as paradigm examples of recreational use.

The distinction between recreational and nonrecreational drug use does *not* purport to sort drugs into categories based on their pharmacological properties. Instead, this distinction sorts drug *use* into categories. The claim that a given drug is "recreational" can only mean that it is typically used for a recreational purpose. More precisely, "recreational drug" is elliptical for "drug that is used recreationally." Any drug can be, and probably has been, used for almost any purpose.

The concept of recreational use can be clarified by contrasting it with other purposes for using drugs. The most familiar nonrecreational reason to use drugs is medical. Although most drug use is either recreational or medical, these categories do not begin to exhaust the purposes for which drugs are consumed. Some persons take drugs for the explicit purpose of committing suicide. Others take drugs ceremonially, in the course of religious rituals. Still others take drugs in order to enhance their performance in competitive sports. Undoubtedly this list could be expanded, but I will make no attempt to provide a comprehensive account of the many reasons for using drugs.

I have two general reasons for focusing on recreational drug use in inquiring whether and under what circumstances adults have or lack a moral right to use drugs. I have already mentioned the first reason. Different justificatory issues arise depending on the purpose for which drugs are consumed. Personal attitudes toward drugs are incomprehensible without attempting to distinguish between legitimate and illegitimate uses. I will evaluate arguments for and against the moral right to use drugs recreationally; I will have little to say about the possible justifications for nonrecreational drug use.

Second, I hope to avoid commitment on dubious empirical claims that have been made about the benefits of drug use. Anecdotal evidence from members of the "drug culture" suggests that nonmedical drug use may contribute to a variety of purposes that any reasonable person would concede to be valuable. Drugs have been alleged to foster creativity, increase self-awareness, promote artistic inspiration, and the like. Andrew Weil is among the earliest defenders of this point of view. Tired of hearing "users rambling on about the purely hedonistic aspects of drug experience," Weil sought to set the record straight by describing how "altered states of consciousness have great potential for strongly positive psychic development."[79] He proceeded to elaborate upon these alleged benefits in great detail.

Some critics of LAD believe that the pendulum may have swung too far in the other direction. Bruce Alexander claims that "the rhetoric of the resisters [in the war on drugs] celebrates, and typically overstates the virtues of drugs in personal development and growth."[80] Many an insight one had judged profound while intoxicated turns out to be less impressive when evaluated while sober. Perhaps the claims made by Weil are true, or perhaps they are false. In either event, my arguments in favor of the moral rights of adult drug users will not depend on them. The arguments I will evaluate allege no greater benefits of drugs than that many users regard them as enjoyable. This benefit, I think, is virtually immune from empirical falsification. If users sincerely believe that drugs are pleasurable, no empirical evidence is likely to prove otherwise.

For reasons that are deep and mysterious, many persons become apologetic and defensive about arguing in favor of a right to engage in an activity simply because it is pleasurable. Apparently the pursuit of fun is perceived to be so shallow and trivial that many persons feel obliged to find some other basis to defend their choice. Suppose that someone challenged whether the state should permit adults to engage in a given dangerous activity, such as skiing. According to the line of thought I reject, skiing should not be defended because it is exhilarating but because of some tangible benefit it produces. For example, a defense might appeal to the cardiovascular advantages of skiing. However, this strategy divorces the justification of the activity from the reason why most person perform it. Persons would continue to ski, and would oppose state interference, even if skiing did not increase their fitness. Many skiers would resort to cardiovascular benefits as a pretext to publicly criticize what they would privately resist for wholly different reasons.

Nowhere is this peculiar tendency to attach nonrecreational defenses to recreational pursuits more evident than among drug users. Many express guilt about their indulgence, insist that they use drugs only for "serious" purposes, and show disdain for those who want to get "high" and experience only the sensual effects of drugs.[81] But the production of euphoria should not be regarded as an insignificant benefit. Even if illegal drug use does nothing more than induce immediate gratification, good reasons would be needed to prohibit it. If drug use happens to produce more profound advantages, the case against LAD is that much stronger.

Only rarely do authorities acknowledge that the euphoria of recreational drug use might be valuable. A federal district court judge, Robert Sweet, shocked his colleagues by calling for the decriminalization of all illicit drugs. After reciting some of the cost-benefit advantages of decriminalization, he continued: "Cocaine gives a sense of exhilaration, heroin a glow, a warmth, and marijuana a sense of relaxation and ease. What then is wrong?"[82]

Nonetheless, my attempt to confine the context of discussion to the recreational use of drugs is not entirely unproblematic. Weil has challenged the viability of distinctions between the several purposes for which drugs apparently are consumed. He claims that "the desire to alter consciousness periodically is an innate, normal drive analogous to hunger or the sexual drive."[83] The "omnipresence of the phenomenon" of drug use in various societies throughout human history has led him to conclude that "we are dealing ... with a biological characteristic of the species."[84] Behavior that satisfies a biological need cannot be understood as a purely recreational form of activity, comparable to scuba diving or mountain climbing.

More recently, a variation of this basic theme has been developed by Ronald Siegel. Studies of animal behavior persuade him that "we must expand the definition of self-medication to include drug use for purposes of intoxication."[85] Siegel believes that even the most dangerous of intoxicants really function as medicines.[86] He contends that the distinction between medical and nonmedical drug use should be dissolved in favor of conceptualizing drugs as "adaptogens," defined as "substance[s] that help people to adjust to changes in their physical or physiological environments."[87] Thus Siegel denies a principled distinction between the use of "esterene, to alleviate the pain and depression of arthritis," and the use of "heroin, to fight the gloom and despair of consciousness."[88]

The majority of Americans who do not question the legitimacy of the war on drugs will surely dismiss these remarks out of hand. Yet these attacks on the traditional distinction between medical and nonmedical drug use are stubbornly resistant to a quick refutation. A plausible criterion of medical use is easy to state: The use of a drug is medical if it is intended to treat a disease, illness, injury, or other interference with normal functioning. But this criterion is less easy to apply. Difficulties in determining whether a given incidence of drug use is medical result from uncertainty about whether the condition for which a drug is taken qualifies as a disease, illness, injury, or other interference with normal functioning. An attempt to identify drug use as medical by reference to the standard practice of doctors is obviously inadequate to meet Siegel's challenge. Siegel would demand a deeper explanation of how doctors make their decisions. Drug use does not become medical because of what doctors do; rather, doctors do what they do because of some characteristic(s) in virtue of which their use of drugs qualifies as medical.

Millions of Americans consume caffeine in order to combat

drowsiness and lethargy, or drink alcohol in order to relax and relieve stress. As a housewife lamented: "I have four children and a house to clean. I couldn't get through the day without Dexedrin."[89] Can any of the conditions that lead these Americans to consume drugs be construed as a disease, illness, injury, or other interference with normal functioning, so that their drug use can be labeled as medical rather than as recreational? The answers to these questions may seem simple. Neither doctors nor the public would classify moderate lethargy or stress as medical conditions. But it is precisely these judgments that need to be reevaluated. In the absence of a theory about disease, illness, injury, or abnormality, there is no firm basis to decide whether the use of a substance is medical. A narrow conception of "normal functioning" will expand the range of medical drug use and shrink the range of recreational drug use proportionately. As James Bakalar and Lester Grinspoon argue:

> When we talk about the dangers to health caused by drugs, we tend to use the broadest possible definition of health to justify the strongest restrictions. When we establish legitimate purposes for using drugs, of which health is obviously one, we try to define health narrowly so that again we can justify severe restrictions. Health as positive liberty – total well-being – is a legitimate reason for banning drugs but not for using them.[90]

If the perspectives taken by either Weil or Siegel are correct, a critical examination of the moral right to use recreational drugs becomes both too difficult and too easy. On the one hand, it seems clear that the war on drugs must be completely rethought if all drug use is medical and responsive to a biological drive. The state should not be in the business of frustrating the satisfaction of innate needs. On the other hand, these positions are of no help in evaluating the reason why many people at least claim to use drugs. It is one thing to consume drugs to combat the alleged "gloom and despair of consciousness," but what is to be said about the drug use of adults who do not regard life as so dismal? Those who support their drug use because it is euphoric are unlikely to be thankful for a defense that construes their behavior as responsive to an underlying pathology. Thus I will continue to discuss the moral and legal questions that arise in recreational drug use. I propose to evaluate the justifiability of laws prohibiting adults from using drugs for the express purpose of increasing their pleasure or happiness.

Undoubtedly my focus on recreational drug use will give rise to the criticism that my approach is academic, middle class, and unresponsive to the realities of drug use in impoverished neighborhoods. Drug use in ghettos, it will be said, is not recreational. The less fortunate members of our society do not use drugs to facilitate their enjoyment at concerts but to escape from the harsh realities of their daily lives. Here, at least, gloom and despair play a central role in explaining the high incidence of drug use.

In fact, the black community has expressed little enthusiasm either for the war on drugs or for drug decriminalization.[91] But theorists who favor one approach or the other divide, sometimes bitterly, over the implications of decriminalization for the lower classes. According to Nadelmann, "The minority communities in the ghetto" would be "the greatest beneficiaries of repealing the drug laws."[92] Other theorists reach the opposite conclusion. Since drug use is a "mode of adaptation" to the "disadvantages of ghetto life," James Inciardi and Duane McBribe contend that drug legalization "would be a nightmare" for the underclass.[93] They express their verdict in the strongest possible terms: "The legalization of drugs would be an elitist and racist policy supporting the neocolonialist views of underclass population control."[94]

Several replies to this criticism should help to defend my focus on recreational drug use. First, I explore decriminalization as a means to protect moral rights, not as a policy to improve conditions in ghettos. The utilitarian tone in which this debate is usually cast ignores the perspective of the individual. Members of lower classes have rights too. If they choose to use drugs to help make their desperate situation more bearable, members of privileged groups should be uncomfortable about telling them that they may not. No one proposes to ban alcohol because members of lower classes tend to drown their sorrows rather than to sharpen their palates. Moreover, a strategy of decriminalization should not be advocated as a substitute for redressing the genuine grievances of minorities.

Finally, the empirical facts are ambiguous in proving that illegal drug use is a special problem for the black community.[95] Only 20 percent of all illegal drug users are black.[96] Whites are more likely than blacks to have tried illegal drugs, and cocaine in particular, at some time in their lives.[97] The more drug prohibitionists succeed in portraying drug use as a ghetto phenomenon, born of frustration and despair, the easier it is to lose sight of the repudiation of liberal values that LAD entails. As I will emphasize time and time again, too much of our policy about illegal drug use is based on generalizations from worst-case scenarios that do not conform to the reality of typical drug use. I hope to undermine the inaccurate stereotypes of drug use and drug users reinforced by this objection. LAD prohibits drug use by members of all races and classes; a legal policy applicable to all should not be based on the perceived problems of a few.

THE DECRIMINALIZATION MOVEMENT

Intelligent opposition to the war on drugs is increasingly heard. Academics, insulated from political pressure by the tenure system, have been more vocal in questioning the drug war than public officials, who remain accountable to voters. Nonetheless, a few politicians, including Kurt Schmoke, mayor of Baltimore, and George Schultz, former secretary of state, have joined Nobel economist Milton Friedman and conservative pundit William Buckley in advocating the decriminalization of some or all illegal drugs.

The decriminalization movement brings together strange allies who are far apart in their political ideologies. Despite

fundamental differences, almost all decriminalization theorists begin from the same premise: America is losing the war
on drugs. Our approach to the drug problem is ineffective
and counterproductive. It has not and will not succeed, and
it actually compounds many of the problems it is designed
to solve. Since I hope to shift the focus away from utilitarian
arguments to issues of principle, I will only summarize the
allegations of decriminalization theorists here. In subsequent
chapters, I will return to several of their criticisms insofar as
they have a bearing on the questions of whether and under
what circumstances adults have a moral right to use drugs
recreationally.

The first of two related themes that run through the decriminalization literature is that the war on drugs is and always will be futile. Many theorists who defend this
conclusion begin (and sometimes end) by stressing economic
considerations. They argue that most of the tens of billions
of dollars spent by the criminal justice system to enforce LAD
has been wasted. Despite the numbers of drug traffickers
arrested and the volumes of contraband seized, the supply
of drugs available to consumers, as reflected by street price,
remains relatively unchanged. Nadelmann's conclusion is
especially pessimistic: "Criminal justice efforts to stop drug
trafficking . . . have little effect on the price, availability, and
consumption of illicit drugs."[98] Besides saving billions of dollars currently squandered in law enforcement, the decriminalization of illegal drugs would bring additional economic
rewards. Depending on the price of legalized drugs, their
sale could allow the state to collect vast tax revenues.

Attempts to curtail the supply of illegal drugs are bound
to fail. Efforts to eradicate production are doomed because
of what has been called the "push down, pop up" effect: As
drug supplies are destroyed here, they reappear there. The
prospects for marked improvement in the interdiction of imported drugs are remote and unrealistic. Because of the
"needle-in-a-haystack" phenomenon, commentators estimate that only about 10 percent of imported marijuana and
cocaine is seized.[99] Since much of what is interdicted is re-

placed, administration officials admit that imports of cocaine have not been reduced by more than 5 percent.[100] No one thinks that our overmatched customs agents can do much better. In any event, improvements would probably accomplish little. Even dramatic increases in source control and interdiction would have a limited impact on the price and purity of drugs.[101]

Somewhat more success has been achieved by curbing demand. Despite reports of unprecedented availability of cocaine, the percentage of high school seniors who used cocaine in 1990 tumbled to its lowest level since 1976.[102] The public appetite for drugs has steadily declined throughout the last decade, although there is room for disagreement about the extent to which law enforcement has contributed to this trend. The use of legal drugs, most notably tobacco, has decreased noticeably with little input from the criminal justice system.

The second theme that runs through the writings of the decriminalization theorists is that the war on drugs has been counterproductive. Many commentators claim that the evils of criminalization are greater than the evils of drug use itself, so that the "cure" of law enforcement is worse than the "disease" of drug use. I will briefly describe fifteen of their more specific allegations; I will not quibble about whether this list should be lengthened or shortened.

1. The drug trade has created enormous opportunities for organized crime. The billions of dollars spent in law enforcement have been described as a "subsidy" for criminals.[103] A report by Wharton Econometrics for the President's Commission on Organized Crime identified the sale of illicit drugs as the source of more than half of all organized crime revenues.[104] The involvement of organized crime has led to well-publicized levels of violence that have become everyday fare in the drug trade. Black marketeers have no recourse to legal devices to enforce agreements and to settle disputes; they must resort to force more often than competitors in legitimate businesses. Some theorists predict that decriminalization will all but end the extraordinary violence associated with the

illegal drug trade. According to James Ostrowski: "The day after legalization goes into effect, the streets of America will be safer. The drug dealers will be gone. The shootouts between drug dealers will end."[105]

2. Enormous profits have made widespread corruption in law enforcement all but inevitable. One "conservative estimate" is that "at least 30 percent of the nation's police officers have had some form of involvement with illicit drugs since becoming employed in law enforcement."[106] The motivation for succumbing to corruption will remain overwhelming, as long as staggering sums of money are offered as an alternative to risking one's life in ineffective efforts to prevent relatively minor offenses.

3. Many drugs tend to be expensive not because of their production costs, but because of their illegality. According to one estimate, the price of heroin is approximately two hundred times greater than it would be under a free market of supply and demand,[107] and cocaine is perhaps twenty times more expensive.[108] As a result, many users commit property offenses in order to obtain money to buy drugs.[109] Legal drugs would be cheaper, so users would be less likely to commit crimes to purchase them.

4. Removal of the enormous profits in the sale of illegal drugs might motivate persons to better prepare themselves to make an honest living. Adolescents are not easily persuaded to gain an education or to learn a skill when they believe, whether correctly or not, that drug trafficking provides an easy opportunity for instant wealth and prestige. Obscene drug profits have made a mockery of the work ethic.[110] The existence of a lucrative black market for drugs may have contributed more to a deterioration in education than the effects of drugs themselves.

5. Illegality has had a pernicious impact on the supply and mode of ingestion of illegal drugs. According to what one commentator describes as the "iron law of prohibition,"[111] the potency of illegal drugs is increased to the greatest possible level in order to reduce the size of the container and the risks of interdiction. The average purity of a gram of

cocaine has allegedly increased from about 12 percent to 60 percent since 1980, at the same time that the potency of most alcoholic beverages in America has decreased.[112] The so-called cocaine and crack epidemics have been blamed on the government's modest success in interdiction. Less harmful drugs, such as marijuana, happen to be bulkier and easier to intercept than more harmful drugs, such as cocaine, so suppliers switched production in an effort to evade detection. In addition, illegal drugs are used in more harmful ways because they are so precious. According to John Kaplan, the injection of opiates is virtually unknown in Asian countries, where supplies are easily obtainable and less expensive.[113]

6. Prohibition may glamorize drugs by creating the "forbidden fruit" phenomenon. Illegality stimulates curiosity and desire, especially among persons who regard themselves as unconventional and rebellious. As Jon Gettman explains the decline in use after the de facto decriminalization of marijuana in the Netherlands, "Decriminalization of marijuana makes marijuana boring."[114]

7. The interest in minimizing availability has discouraged illegal drugs from being used for legitimate medical purposes. Lawyers for the National Organization for the Reform of Marijuana Laws (NORML) have failed to persuade the Drug Enforcement Agency to transfer marijuana to a higher schedule, so that doctors may prescribe it to patients suffering from debilitating diseases such as cancer, glaucoma, and multiple sclerosis. Some theorists suggest that the lack of opportunity to explore legitimate uses of controlled substances is among the greatest casualties of the drug war.[115]

8. The medical complications of drug consumption have been compounded by criminalization. As Nadelmann points out, "Nothing resembling an underground Food and Drug Administration has arisen to impose quality control on the illegal drug market and provide users with accurate information on the drugs they consume."[116] Thus persons have smoked marijuana sprayed with paraquat and mixed with even more dangerous substances, and heroin users have died after injecting unexpectedly potent or impure supplies. Many

55

of these fatalities are avoidable, but publicizing safe ways of using drugs is politically unacceptable during wartime.[117] In addition, drug users are reluctant to seek treatment because of the stigma of illegality. The night that basketball star Len Bias died of heart failure after using cocaine, his friends, fearing the police, waited until his third seizure before calling an ambulance.[118]

9. Courts and jails have become clogged as a result of "get-tough" policies toward drug offenders. The impact of drug offenses has led a number of commentators to speak of a collapse of the criminal justice system. Federal courts have become "drug courts," where narcotics prosecutions now account for 44 percent of all criminal trials, up 229 percent in the past decade.[119] In many jurisdictions, delays in criminal cases not involving drugs or in the adjudication of civil disputes have become intolerable. The number of Americans behind bars has recently exceeded the one million mark and sets new records every day. Prisons cannot be built fast enough to accommodate drug offenders. At last count, forty state prison systems were operating under court orders to reduce overcrowding or to improve conditions.[120] A report by the National Council on Crime and Delinquency concluded that "the current War on Drugs will overwhelm the nation's correctional systems over the next five years."[121] Mandatory sentencing under LAD may undermine efforts to combat violent crime. As a result of overcrowding by non-violent drug offenders, violent criminals are less likely to serve long prison terms.

10. Disrespect for law has been fostered among the millions of Americans who violate LAD annually. The long-term consequences of this disrespect are speculative and impossible to measure precisely, but no one should believe them to be trivial or unimportant. Hypocrisy and double standards are corollaries of disrespect.[122] Many drug prohibitionists have lost credibility after having been exposed as drug users. Yet President Bush downplayed the significance of the former drug use of Clarence Thomas, who he named to the

Supreme Court, only weeks after the Court upheld a sentence of life imprisonment without parole for the offense of drug possession.

11. A long history of misinformation and distortion about the dangers of drugs has led wary users to become skeptical of the accuracy of warnings conveyed by the medical establishment. Drug prohibitionists have felt a need to exaggerate the dangers of existing recreational drugs in order to justify their illegality. Commentators have noted an "irreparable credibility gap between users of drugs and drug experts" since the late sixties.[123] Consider the recent popularity of steroids, performance-enhancing substances used by perhaps a quarter million or more American youths. Despite ample warnings about their dangers, 82 percent of adolescent users disagreed with medical experts who said that steroids pose long-term health risks, such as liver and heart disease.[124] Perhaps the experts are correct, or perhaps they are mistaken. But this climate of distrust cannot be in the public interest. If a drug really is harmful, one would hope that users would believe doctors who sound the alarm. Decriminalization may help to produce more accurate information about the real hazards of drug use.

12. Among the more serious effects of prohibition is discrimination against the poor, who increasingly consume a higher and higher percentage of illegal drugs. Although two-thirds of weekly drug users in New York State in 1987 were white, 91 percent of the persons convicted and sentenced to state prison for drug-related offenses were either black of Hispanic.[125] Therapeutic treatment is frequently provided for middle- and upper-class users; prison is the preferred mode of "treatment" for the underprivileged.

13. The foreign policy of the United States has suffered untold damage from the war on drugs. In particular, our relations with Central and South American governments have been distorted by our drug policy.[126] All too frequently, both sides in foreign drug wars are funded by U.S. dollars.

14. The enforcement of LAD has diminished precious civil

liberties. Defense lawyers openly acknowledge the "drug
exception" to the Bill of Rights.[127] David Evans complains
that "martial law has been declared in our inner cities."[128]

15. Finally and most significantly, the war on drugs is
counterproductive in making criminals of tens of millions of
Americans whose behavior is otherwise lawful. Most drug
users are lucky to escape detection. Others are less fortunate.
Countless numbers of offenders have been forced to suffer
long terms of imprisonment for violating laws that may not
be morally justified. Even those who are eventually acquitted
spend tremendous sums of time and money defending themselves in court.

Many law enforcement officials who participate in this draconian system have become demoralized. The U.S. district
court judge J. Lawrence Irving resigned rather than continue
to impose harsh mandatory punishments on petty drug offenders. He lamented: "I can't continue to do it – I can't
continue to give out sentences that I feel in some instances
are unconscionable."[129] Another federal judge wondered
whether in years to come he and his fellow jurists will have
to assert the "Nuremberg Defense" – "I was only following
orders" – to justify the number of people they are sentencing
to prison for decades.[130]

Surely this sizeable litany of evils must trouble even the
most zealous drug prohibitionist. But do these harms outweigh the good that the war on drugs can be expected to
achieve in the foreseeable future? Commentators disagree
radically. Since an assessment of the cost and benefits of drug
policy requires clairvoyance as well as a willingness to balance incommensurables, reasonable minds can and do differ
about whether the war on drugs is worth its cost.

The perspective of these decriminalization theorists is a
valuable supplement to my own. However, I do not rely on
the conclusion that criminalizing the use of many drugs is
either ineffective or counterproductive. Critics who insist that
the war is futile would be silenced if some clever new strategy
could be devised to change the existing ratio of costs and
benefits. Would such a discovery persuade these critics to

shift their allegiance and join the crusades of drug prohibitionists? If not, why not?

These rhetorical questions indicate that a cost-benefit attack on LAD is necessarily incomplete. The preceding analysis fails to address the war on drugs from the perspective of the adult who wants to use drugs recreationally. The complaint of this individual is not that drug prohibition is ineffective and counterproductive, but that it violates moral rights. This issue is not simply *different*; it is *more basic* than that raised by an examination of costs and benefits. Few theorists prepare cost-benefit analyses of issues involving moral rights. For example, no one inquires whether television produces a net balance of costs over benefits, as part of a movement to make watching television illegal. Why not? Surely the answer cannot be that television obviously produces a net benefit to society. A better answer is that persons have a moral right to watch television, and cost-benefit analyses are compelling arguments for criminalization only for those activities unprotected by a moral right. If recreational drug use is protected by a moral right, cost-benefit analyses for criminalization are simply out of court.

In other words, the foregoing arguments lack the force of principle that philosophers should want. Even if victory were possible in the war on drugs, should victory be sought? This is the issue of principle I propose to address.

ARGUMENTS FOR CRIMINALIZATION

Defenses of and attacks against arguments for decriminalization have become so familiar that it is easy to forget that the burden of proof should be placed on those who favor the use of criminal penalties. When arguing about criminalization, most philosophers begin with a "presumption of freedom," or liberty, which places the onus of justification on those who would interfere with what a person wants to do.

Although it is helpful to be reminded of the existence of this presumption, I make no real use of it in what follows.

The case for or against LAD depends on which side has the better arguments; there is no need to resort to a burden of proof in assessing this controversy. In any event, a second and equally familiar presumption cuts in the opposite direction. A "presumption in favor of the status quo" allocates the burden of proof on those who oppose any change in current laws against the use of recreational drugs. No one has any clear idea about what weight to assign to these "clashing presumptions."[131] For this reason, it is probably unproductive to worry too much about who should bear the burden of proof on this issue.

Arguments for criminalization are important to review, if only to follow the advice of John Stuart Mill. Mill warned that even a true opinion becomes held "as a dead dogma, not a living truth," unless it is "fully, frequently, and fearlessly discussed."[132] Even those who believe that LAD is obviously justified can profit from a skeptical examination of their position. Unfortunately, many of those whose commitment to LAD is unwavering do not take Mill's recommendations to heart and are unwilling to be drawn into the fray. Several are unhappy when the issue of decriminalization is raised at all. In 1989, the Select Committee on Narcotics Abuse and Control solicited testimony from thirty-four witnesses who debated the pros and cons of LAD. Michael Oxley, a member of this committee, echoed the sentiments of several of his colleagues when he protested that "the idea of legalization should not even be dignified" with a hearing.[133] As Mill cautioned, the absence of debate is the best guarantee that a viewpoint will become a prejudice. Defenders of LAD have been spared the rigors of Mill's test for too long.

Why is LAD thought to be justified? Theorists who uphold the status quo in public debates seldom answer this question directly. Instead, they are fond of challenging their adversaries to describe specific and detailed decriminalization plans. Two of their more difficult questions are as follows. First, would the system of prescriptions for medical drugs survive the decriminalization of recreational drugs? Second, who would supply legalized recreational drugs, given the

60

extraordinary potential for tort liability?[134] These questions are important and troublesome. On the other hand, defenders of LAD have not been especially forthcoming in describing how victory in the war on drugs can be achieved at an acceptable cost. John Lawn, former administrator of the Drug Enforcement Administration, observes that "the real answer to the drug problem in the United States today is not legalization. Character reconstruction, not the dismantling of drug laws, is the answer."[135] Unfortunately, no one has the slightest idea how to reconstruct character in a free society. If put forward by decriminalization theorists, this sort of "solution" to the drug problem would be ridiculed as utopian and unrealistic.

A positive case for LAD is not equivalent to exposing weaknesses in the opposing point of view. If those who support existing drug legislation can be made to give a direct reply to the question of why they believe LAD to be justified, they are likely to provide different answers. The fact that several distinct responses are offered to a single question may be evidence of ambivalence and confusion. I am not especially interested in removing this confusion by playing the devil's advocate. I do not believe that the following discussion is useful only in producing better reasons than are currently available for what is already known to be true. I will conclude that a careful assessment of the moral arguments in favor of LAD reveals a number of serious defects. Reasonable minds will differ about whether LAD deserves support despite these defects. But I hope at least to shake the confidence of those who believe that the justification of LAD is straightforward and unproblematic.

How should one begin to decide whether a given criminal law is justified? There is a surprising dearth of sound theoretical literature on the issue of criminalization. Few commentators have attempted to describe the conditions that must be satisfied before an activity becomes eligible for punishment. In the absence of a sophisticated theory to govern the criminalization decision, solutions to almost every social problem are sought within the criminal justice system. No one has produced a theory to show why the criminal justice system should not be used to deal with any and all difficulties. An unwillingness to criminalize an activity is misconstrued as a denial that it is a problem at all. As a result, our state suffers from a crisis of overcriminalization. Drug use has long been cited among the best examples of the pernicious tendency to overutilize a penal approach to social problems.[136]

There is no agreement about even the most basic points involving criminalization. For example, it may seem obvious that the criminal law should not prohibit conduct that persons have a moral right to perform. Individuals cannot deserve to be punished for exercising their moral rights. Punishment is unjustified unless it is deserved. If these basic tenets are true, those (legislators and judges) who make the criminal law cannot afford to ignore moral debate. Yet few of the most distinguished figures in the long history of Anglo-American criminal theory have paid much attention to moral philosophy. They have been more anxious to downplay, rather than to develop, the connections between criminal law and moral philosophy.[137] Against such a historical background, moral rights are less likely to be respected by our criminal law. I fear that this lack of respect has been shown to adults who use drugs recreationally.

Another largely unexplored issue involves the degree of social consensus that must exist before criminal legislation is justified. Surely the criminal law should not be used if there exists a substantial difference of opinion among citizens about the propriety of the behavior to be punished. Perhaps the difficult question Whose morality should the criminal law enforce? cannot be answered, but it can be avoided by assuring that offenses are believed to represent immoralities by the vast majority of adults within a given jurisdiction. Reflection on the justification of punishment supports this conclusion. Punishment is and ought to be stigmatizing; it can succeed only if the conduct subjected to punishment is widely regarded as morally wrong.

The application of these principles to LAD produces some

disturbing results. Those who support the status quo frequently point to public opinion surveys that indicate that
somewhere between 80 percent and 90 percent of Americans
believe that illegal drug use should continue to be criminalized.[138] But these polls are even more useful to decriminalization theorists. By either figure, at least 10 percent of
Americans – upwards of twenty million – do not accept LAD.
Only 50 percent of high school seniors (admittedly, the largest percentage yet) agree that marijuana use "should be a
crime."[139] And the enthusiasm of those who support LAD is
not especially deep. In a recent survey, only 46 percent of
all respondents "strongly agree" with the statement that "all
drug use is immoral and should be illegal"; 15 percent "somewhat agree"; 17 percent "somewhat disagree"; and 18 percent "strongly disagree."[140] It is absolutely unthinkable that
surveys of attitudes about any other laws enforced by severe
punishments would reveal as high a percentage of Americans
who are not emphatic about whether the use of the criminal
sanction is justified. No movement exists to decriminalize
murder, manslaughter, rape, arson, armed robbery, or any
of the other handful of offenses that give rise to punishments
comparable to those imposed on drug offenders. Although
it is hard to know exactly where lines should be drawn, LAD
seems to lack the overwhelming public consensus needed to
justify the heavy hand of criminal punishment.

I assume without much argument that a respectable defense of criminal legislation must demonstrate that it is
needed to prevent *harm*. Everyone agrees that persons lack
a moral right to cause harm, so criminal laws that prohibit
harmful conduct do not violate the basic principles I have
described. Punishment of a person who causes harm can be
justified by reference to the offender's desert. But in the
absence of harm, criminal sanctions are undeserved and
unjustified.

The least controversial rationale in favor of criminalization
is that the conduct to be prohibited is harmful *to others*. Many
legal philosophers, following the lead of Mill, believe that
harm to others is a necessary condition that any criminal law

must satisfy in order to be justified. This position has been defended most ably by Joel Feinberg, from whose work I will borrow extensively.[141] I will consider in Chapter 3 whether and to what extent LAD can be defended on the ground that drug use is harmful to others. A more controversial rationale in favor of criminalization is that drug use should be prohibited because it is harmful *to users* themselves. Although a number of philosophers are unsympathetic to this rationale, paternalistic arguments in favor of LAD are frequently defended. I will take these arguments seriously in Chapter 2.

One common complaint about my strategy is misguided. Many philosophers are quick to point out that "no man is an island" and that whatever harms oneself also harms others or at least is capable of doing so. Perhaps there are no examples of "pure" or "unmixed" paternalism, that is, of an interference with liberty that is justifiable solely on the ground that the conduct to be prohibited harms the doer. I do not maintain otherwise. I do not suppose that a given activity can harm the doer but not others. The distinction between harm to oneself and harm to others is *not* a distinction between kinds of laws, but rather it is a distinction between *rationales* for laws. Any law might be defended by more than one rationale. I do not treat people as islands in using the distinction between harm to oneself and harm to others as an analytical device to help identify the best reasons for LAD. The paternalistic rationale for LAD may be stronger than the nonpaternalistic rationale, or it may be weaker. In either event, the distinction between harm to oneself and harm to others must be drawn in order to evaluate each of the arguments in support of LAD.

In the remainder of this section, I will briefly comment on two alternative rationales for LAD that I will not take very seriously in the following chapters. My premise that the use of the criminal sanction should require harm can be questioned.[142] Perhaps arguments can be marshaled in support of LAD that do not depend on harm, either to oneself or to others. According to *legal moralism*, the wrongfulness of con-

duct per se, apart from its harmful effects, is a sufficient
reason to impose criminal punishment.

Many drug prohibitionists resort to legal moralism in support of LAD. Bennett replies to the cost-benefit analyses of
decriminalization theorists as follows: "I find no merit in the
legalizers' case. The simple fact is that drug use is wrong.
And the moral argument, in the end, is the most compelling
argument."[143] There can be no doubt that popular objections
to illegal recreational drug use are often couched in the
strongest possible moral terms. Drug use is frequently portrayed as sinful and wicked.[144] Even an astute commentator
like Kaplan admits that "I cannot escape the feeling that drug
use, aside from any harm it does, is somehow wrong."[145]

For two reasons, however, I will have little to say about
legal moralism here. First, this principle is extremely problematic. No one has presented a compelling case in favor of
legal moralism; responses from philosophers have been almost entirely negative.[146] One recurrent theme of their attack
is that legal moralism might be used to enforce community
prejudice. The requirement that criminal liability presupposes a *victim* who has been *harmed* helps to assure that
persons will not be punished simply for doing what those
with political power do not want them to do.

Second, the application of legal moralism to LAD is utterly
baffling. Why would anyone believe that drug use per se is
immoral, apart from any harm it might cause? David Richards
is right to suggest that these beliefs are "entitled to a respect-
ful hearing."[147] The trick is to translate them into respectable
moral arguments that can provide the basis for criminal legislation in a secular state. As long as moral reservations about
drug use are presented as unsupported conclusions – or as
feelings – they will prove resistant to criticism. Arguments,
not conclusions, are the objects of philosophical evaluation.

What, exactly, do drug prohibitionists believe to be immoral about recreational drug use? Two alternatives are possible. Does the alleged wrong consist in the act of drug use
per se, or in the alteration of consciousness that drug use

produces? The former alternative seems unlikely. Suppose that the physiology of persons were altered so that a given drug no longer produced any psychological effect. Could anyone continue to believe that the use of that drug would still be immoral? In any event, contemporary Americans widely reject the view that the act of drug use is inherently wrong. Few condemn the moderate use of alcohol. The subdued moral opposition to alcohol heard today is light years away from the level of outrage expressed by zealots during the temperance movement.

The latter alternative seems no more attractive. Why should the alteration of consciousness produced by drug use be immoral, apart from any harm that might result? Some theorists have proposed that practices such as long-distance running and meditation can trigger natural neurological reactions that alter consciousness in respects that are phenomenologically indistinguishable from the effects of drug use.[148] No one has suggested that such practices are immoral, and for good reason. There is ample reason to doubt that harmless experiences are among the kinds of things that *can* be immoral.

Perhaps many Americans share a vague conviction that some but not all ways of altering consciousness, by the use of some but not all drugs, is immoral. If this conviction could be defended, the particular experience of alcohol intoxication might be upheld as morally permissible, whereas the experiences of intoxication produced by various illegal drugs could be condemned. As it stands, however, this conviction is a conclusion in search of an argument. Typically, persons appeal to harm, either to oneself or to others, in attempts to differentiate between intoxication from alcohol and intoxication from illegal drugs. In this guise, the argument should be taken seriously. What is less clear is how to understand a version of this argument that does *not* appeal to harm. The terrain here is so uncertain that no one should have any clear idea about how to proceed.

Arguments that illegal recreational drug use is immoral have been developed, if at all, almost exclusively by those who have rejected them. Richards may be the only philosopher to have addressed these arguments in detail.[149] According to Richards, moral objections to the experience of drug use originate in an "Augustinian philosophy of the self"; drug use is depicted as "degrading" because it frustrates "the competent exercise of certain personal abilities," which this tradition values.[150] The most important of these abilities is self-control.

Richards responds that drugs allow users to "regulate the quality and versatility of their experiences in life to include greater control of mood."[151] Alexander concurs: "Drugs, as they are normally used, increase people's autonomy and power. People use drugs to make themselves alert when they need to be alert, and to make themselves relax when they want to relax, and so on."[152] To this extent, the use of drugs expresses and increases self-control rather than undermines it. To be sure, the ability to control when to use or not to use a drug may be compromised by addiction. I will discuss the implications of addiction for the justifiability of LAD in Chapter 2. But both Richards and Alexander are persuasive in arguing that the use of recreational drugs by nonaddicts can increase rather than decrease their self-control.

Moral objections to drug use might also be derived from an ideal of human excellence. Drug use might not be conducive to the attainment of a particular conception of virtue. These arguments are frequently endorsed by drug prohibitionists. According to Bennett, "Drug use degrades human character, and a purposeful, self governing society ignores its people's character at great peril."[153] James Q. Wilson confines his virtue-based arguments to illegal drugs: "Tobacco shortens one's life, cocaine debases it. Nicotine alters one's habits, cocaine alters one's soul."[154] What conception of virtue is employed here? The Christian tradition, for example, identifies virtue with a personal imitation of Christ, emphasizing extraordinary sacrifice in the service of others. According to this tradition, drug use, like any other recreational activity, is suspect. Recreational activities are nonaltruistic and self-indulgent.

Richards rejects all such arguments on the ground that no particular conception of virtue will gain the universal assent of rational persons.[155] Suppose, however, that drug use were to conflict with whatever conception of human excellence is eventually accepted. What would follow from this concession?

The answer is that virtue-based arguments fail to support criminal punishment for recreational drug use. Bennett is correct that a society should not "ignore its people's character." But it does not follow that the protection of character is an appropriate objective of the criminal law. The prohibitions of the criminal law describe the minimum of acceptable behavior beneath which persons are not permitted to sink. Virtue-based considerations cannot be used to show that moderate self-indulgence, as well as any temporary impairment of rationality and autonomy brought about by most incidents of drug use, fall below this permissible level. The criminal law should not enforce a particular conception of human excellence, however attractive it may be. A theory of virtue might be applied to subject drug use to moral criticism. As I will emphasize in Chapter 4, opponents of LAD need not believe that drug use is beyond moral reproach. But no one should think that persons deserve to be punished as criminals because their behavior falls short of an ideal.

A second possible defense of LAD that does not appeal to harm is described by Zimring and Hawkins as *legalism*. They express the core of legalism as follows: "The taking of drugs prohibited by the government is an act of rebellion, of defiance of lawful authority, that threatens the social fabric."[156] According to legalists, the consumption of any illegal drug represents a "threat . . . to the established order and political authority structure."[157]

Legalism is not simply a logically possible position someone might adopt on behalf of LAD. Zimring and Hawkins allege that "the legalist perspective is the dominant orientation of the law enforcement community in the United

States."[158] They document how legalism is presupposed by the National Drug Control Strategy during Bennett's tenure in the Office of the National Drug Control Policy. These theorists endeavor to explain how legalism accounts for at least four of the most salient features of the war on drugs. First, it explains why illegal drugs, rather than alcohol and tobacco, are targeted. Second, it explains why all illegal drugs, such as marijuana and crack, are treated as equally objectionable. Third, it explains why harsh punishments are applied even to casual users. Finally, it explains why illegal drug use per se, rather than the harmful effects that drug use cause, is regarded as the main problem.

Zimring and Hawkins are anxious to demonstrate how legalism represents an unwise and inefficient premise for a rational drug control policy. They succeed admirably, subjecting each of these four characteristics of the war on drugs to penetrating criticism. What they fail to address is the total bankruptcy of legalism as a plausible justification for LAD. Surely it is possible to oppose a law without opposing the legitimacy of political authority itself. A legalist stance is not selective; it can be adopted toward any crime at all. The commission of any criminal offense can be likened to treason or insurrection. Legalism cannot justify why war is declared on some but not all offenses. Why not a war on shoplifting? The fact that an activity is against the law provides no answer to this and other normative questions. *Should* recreational drug use be criminalized? Legalism does not begin to address this issue, since it only describes the attitudes that we should have toward illegality once a law is already in place.

Perhaps I have not done justice to the legal moralist or the legalist. But in the absence of a more detailed and compelling argument for these positions, I will not further discuss whether these rationales can support LAD. In what follows, my general project is to attempt to identify whether there is any *harm* in recreational drug use that justifies its prohibition. I assume that if there is no substantial harm to be prevented by criminal punishment, LAD should be condemned as an unjustified interference in personal liberty. Two possible harms might support criminal punishment: harm to drug users themselves, and harm to others. I turn now to the first of these rationales.

Chapter 2

Drugs and harm to users

In this chapter I will assess whether criminal laws against the recreational use of drugs (LAD) are justifiable on *paternalistic* grounds.[1] In other words, I will evaluate attempts to defend or reject LAD solely because of the harm drugs cause to adult users themselves, quite apart from the harm they cause to nonusers. In Chapter 1, I proposed that the strengths and weaknesses of the case for LAD are best revealed by distinguishing the harm drugs cause to users from the harm they cause to others. I explore the separate issue of whether LAD can be justified by a "harm to others" rationale in Chapter 3.

With increasing frequency, drug prohibitionists have cited so-called moral harms to users in support of LAD. After conceding that a cost-benefit analysis is inconclusive, James Q. Wilson maintains that "the moral reason for attempting to discourage drug use is that the heavy consumption of certain drugs is destructive of human character . . . The dignity, autonomy, and productivity of many users, already impaired by other problems, is destroyed."[2] In citing this rationale for the prohibition of illegal substances, Wilson echoes the sentiments of former drug czar William Bennett: "Drug use – especially heavy drug use – destroys human character. It destroys dignity and autonomy, it burns away the sense of responsibility, it subverts productivity, it makes a mockery of virtue."[3]

It is doubtful that so-called moral harms should properly be regarded as harms at all.[4] In any event, the allegations of

71

Wilson and Bennett are grounded in an unidentified conception of human virtue. In Chapter 1, I described why virtue-based arguments cannot justify the heavy hand of criminal legislation, and I will not repeat these reasons here. For present purposes, what is noteworthy about these remarks is not that they depend on a vision of human excellence, but that they are unabashedly paternalistic. Drug users must be protected from themselves.

Physical and psychological harms are more commonly cited on behalf of LAD. The ubiquitous advertisements of the Just Say No campaign make a direct appeal to self-interest in attempts to persuade persons not to use illegal drugs. These ads do not seek to discourage illegal drug use by portraying it as antisocial. Nor do they stress the impact of drugs on human character. Their message is more blunt: Drugs can fry your brain like an egg; they can make you wreck your car. Drugs can kill you.

In combination, these various kinds of harms might form the basis of a powerful defense of LAD. Some commentators are quick to dismiss any defense that is nonpaternalistic. According to Vincent Bugliosi: "The *only* rationale for making the use of drugs illegal is that we want to protect people from themselves. *There is no other defensible justification.*"[5]

I will conclude that attempts to construct a paternalistic defense of LAD encounter formidable difficulties. The most plausible paternalistic arguments in favor of LAD suffer not only from theoretical defects but also from dubious empirical assumptions. I will appeal both to pharmacological studies about the effects of various drugs and, to an even greater extent, to sociological data about drug users. In light of the best available evidence, the paternalistic arguments for LAD will be shown to make unwarranted generalizations from worst-case scenarios that seldom conform to the reality of typical drug use. For example, notice that Wilson's defense of LAD mentions "heavy" consumption and "many" users. How does his argument support criminal penalties for moderate consumption by all adult users? Are the interests of "responsible" drug users to be sacrificed in order to prevent others from abusing drugs? What if the abusers are heavily outnumbered by the moderate users? I will argue that a more accurate profile of the paradigmatic drug user robs the paternalistic defense of LAD of much of its initial appeal.

At the same time, I will attempt to understand why the paternalistic argument in favor of LAD is so seductive. I will note the several points at which my critique of LAD is most vulnerable. Adults do not have an absolute moral right to use any imaginable recreational drug, whatever its effects on them may be. Nor does the state lack the authority to prevent adults from harming themselves by recreational drug use. I will describe what a drug would have to be like before adults would lack a moral right to use it recreationally, and the state would have the authority to prohibit it, in order to prevent self-inflicted harm. I am doubtful that such a recreational drug exists today. But someday a drug might be created that satisfies the description I will provide.

The most general problem in the attempt to construct a paternalistic defense of LAD is to decide whether and under what circumstances paternalism is *ever* justified. This topic has generated an enormous literature. Following John Stuart Mill, many philosophers categorically reject the idea that the desirability of preventing adults from harming themselves is ever a good reason to restrict their liberty. If their general antagonism toward paternalism is warranted, no "harm to self" rationale for LAD is possible. Harm to nonusers would become the only plausible basis to support LAD.

However, the supposed refutation of LAD that depends on the illegitimacy of all paternalistic legislation is too quick and easy. For several reasons, those who categorically reject paternalism would be hasty to move directly to the ensuing discussion of whether LAD can be justified on the ground that drug use is harmful to others. Virtually all commentators who support some degree of paternalism cite LAD among their paradigm examples. LAD represents a powerful challenge to the inviolability of anti-paternalistic sentiments. As one philosopher remarks, "If paternalism is justifiable anywhere, it is justifiable here."[6] If a wholesale rejection of pa-

ternalism cannot be sustained, it becomes important to identify any special problems in the defense of LAD over and
above the weaknesses of paternalism in general. In addition,
several of the misconceptions about drug use that I will discuss in this chapter undermine both a paternalistic as well
as a nonpaternalistic defense of LAD. Finally, suppose for
the sake of argument that support for LAD from nonpaternalistic sources is forceful although ultimately inconclusive.
If so, it would be crucial to understand the strengths and
weaknesses of the paternalistic case in detail. A plausible
though insufficient paternalistic basis for a law might combine with a plausible though insufficient nonpaternalistic basis for that law to produce a compelling case overall. The
issue of when two insufficient justifications, one paternalistic
and the other nonpaternalistic, combine to become sufficient
is unchartered philosophical territory.

In any event, I do not share this general hostility toward
paternalism. Disciples of Mill have not demonstrated that
adults should never be protected from self-inflicted harm.
The justifiability of instances of paternalism, including LAD,
depends upon a delicate balancing of several factors. Reasonable minds may weigh these factors differently. Nonetheless, I will conclude that a paternalistic defense of LAD
is weak.

CONSEQUENTIALISM AND DRUG USE

Two possible kinds of paternalistic arguments might be invoked to assess LAD. The first is *consequentialist*. The consequences of adopting LAD might or might not be preferable
for drug users than the consequences of not adopting it. The
second kind of argument is *nonconsequentialist*, or deontolog-
ical. A principle of autonomy that applies to and protects
adult drug use might be defended or critiqued. This principle
of autonomy might be used to show whether and under
what circumstances adults have or lack a moral right to use
drugs recreationally.

For several reasons, I will concentrate much more heavily on nonconsequentialist than on consequentialist arguments. As I will argue at greater length in Chapter 3, almost no philosopher should believe that consequentialism provides the proper moral framework for deciding where the boundary between state authority and individual liberty should be drawn. For example, few theorists are likely to suppose that the case for or against freedom of speech should be decided by balancing the consequences of protecting speech against the state interest in suppressing it. Instead, these sorts of debates should be fought on the battleground of moral rights, to which the consequentialist tradition is notoriously hostile. Why should the case for or against LAD be any different? Consequentialism is probably the wrong moral theory to help identify the moral rights, if any, of recreational drug users.

Thus consequentialists are unlikely to address the fundamental issue of principle that I raise: Does LAD invade the moral rights of adult recreational drug users? The Research Advisory Panel to the California State Legislature assumed that "we all remain prohibitionists to the extent that prohibition will work."[7] Members of this panel seemed to be unaware of objections to criminal sanctions against drug use, apart from whether they "work." Perhaps there are principled reasons why a war on drugs should not be waged, even if it could be won at an acceptable cost.

Here I will make only a few observations about the consequentialist case for or against LAD, in light of my conviction that this perspective is inappropriate. First, note that paternalists who support LAD on consequentialist grounds appeal to a special, restricted version of utilitarianism: They argue that legal proscriptions create more utility (or pleasure, happiness, preference satisfaction, or whatever else their theory identifies as good) than disutility for actual users. By contrast, real utilitarians who support LAD argue that legal proscriptions create more utility than disutility for users and nonusers alike. Their central contention is that punishing actual users deters (and perhaps educates) prospective users

75

from experimenting with illegal drugs. But this rationale is not paternalistic, and I will have little to say about it until Chapter 3.

The outcome of a consequentialist balancing might be favorable to LAD if everyone obeyed the law. If no one used illegal drugs, no one would have to be punished. But the point of a consequentialist analysis of legislation is to assess its impact in the real world. LAD is difficult to justify on paternalistic grounds when 28 million people disregard it, and our legal system must resort to punishment all too frequently.

Decriminalization theorists have pointed out that many of the bad consequences for drug users are actually effects of LAD rather than of drugs themselves. I have already described several of the ways that users are harmed by drug laws rather than by drugs. To repeat only one such example, illegal drugs are more likely to be contaminated by impurities. Legal drugs are subject to quality controls that are totally lacking for illegal substances. Paternalists can hardly recommend contamination on behalf of persons who use drugs.

An even more fundamental defect plagues a paternalistic defense of LAD. Consider the effects of drug prohibitions on users who are actually arrested and prosecuted. The harm they suffer from punishment almost certainly outweighs the harm they suffer by the conduct for which they are punished, especially if their punishment is severe. It is hard to believe that typical drug users are better off spending time in prison than in exposing themselves to whatever risks are involved in drug use. Drugs would have to be incredibly harmful before anyone could sympathize with the following remark made by Dr. Thomas Gleaton, director of the Parents Resource Institute for Drug Education: "If my child, my loved one, or my friend breaks the law by using illicit drugs, please arrest him or her."[8] Certainly one can imagine a drug so dangerous that virtually anything that is done to prevent a person from using it is less harmful to him than the drug itself. But I doubt that any existing recreational drug satisfies this description.

In addition, incarceration is hardly a guarantee that drug use will cease, given the ready availability of drugs in prisons. Estimates of the percentage of prisoners involved with drugs range between 40 percent and 90 percent.[9] The state cannot possibly justify harsh punishments for violations of LAD on the ground that they are in the best interests of the persons who are actually punished.

Offenders would have to be treated leniently before punishment could be justified on paternalistic grounds. Perhaps the risks faced by motorcyclists who do not wear helmets are sufficiently grave to justify the imposition of small monetary fines to induce them to take appropriate precautions. But as punishments increase in severity, any advantage in increased compliance to particular motorcyclists would soon be outweighed by the disutility of the punishment itself. From the perspective of the offender, the "cure" is worse than the "disease."

The punishments actually inflicted on drug users probably fail to satisfy this condition for justified criminal paternalism. For nonpaternalistic reasons, light sentences are unlikely to be imposed on drug offenders. No one believes that LAD can be effective as a deterrent unless punishments for illegal drug use remain relatively severe. The state can arrest and prosecute only a tiny percentage of the 28 million persons who violate LAD annually. Whatever reservations one may have about the deterrent effect of legislation in general apply more forcefully to LAD in particular, since the likelihood of apprehension and conviction is so low. For this reason, states tend to resort to exemplary punishments for the few unfortunates who are caught.

Even without the harm of punishment added to the scales, it is difficult to know whether drugs cause more good than evil for adults who use them. Both the positive and negative effects of drug use must be included in an honest consequentialist assessment. As I indicated in Chapter 1, the only positive effect on which I will rely is the increase in pleasure that results from recreational drug use. Any decriminalization debate is radically altered by including this factor. To return to an earlier example, no one would take seriously a proposal to prohibit television, despite the wealth of data about its undesirable effects on people who watch it. These data are not dispositive because they neglect the fact that consumers enjoy television. The prohibition of alcohol ultimately failed because the public continued to demand alcoholic beverages. Only a morality unresponsive to personal wants and desires could be blind to this consideration. Consequentialism is not such a morality, whatever else its defects may be.

Conspicuous by its absence, however, is a similar response to LAD. Why are the preferences of adult consumers not given comparable weight here? Neglecting the desires of recreational users allows critics of LAD to construe the war on drugs as a puritanical, antipleasure crusade. Many of the millions of Americans who use legal and illegal drugs apparently derive at least short-term pleasure from their experience. Once their euphoria is placed on the scales, no one has any clear idea whether drug use produces more utility than disutility for them. To insist that the users of any given drug *must* experience more evil than good is simple prejudice.

In the absence of empirical evidence, supporters of LAD might argue that the disutility of drug use *necessarily* outweighs the utility. This result could be guaranteed if the pleasure of drug use did not belong on the scales in the first place. But on what possible bases might it be excluded? I will discuss two reasons; neither deserves to be taken very seriously.

First, one might contend that recreational users do not *really* enjoy drugs. Many users of tobacco, in particular, report little pleasure from smoking.[10] Perhaps Bennett had such a result in mind when he described drug use as a "deceptive pleasure."[11] He contends, "A citizen in a drug-induced haze . . . is not what the founding fathers meant by the 'pursuit of happiness.' "[12] Those who do not consume a given drug find it nearly impossible to fathom how anyone could possibly enjoy it. Drug use is almost invariably depicted as leading to disaster, so that the vast majority of candid users, with hindsight, would admit that they had been wrong ever to have experimented with illegal substances. Those who dissent, and publicly proclaim that drug use is fun, are denounced as irresponsible.[13] Drug use is rarely explained in the same terms as other pleasurable activities but is widely attributed to peer pressure, boredom, alienation, immaturity, ignorance, depression, or some other human weakness.

This first ploy to disregard the pleasure of drug use will be dismissed by economists who take wants as given and make policy recommendations designed to maximize the satisfaction of existing consumer preferences. It will be rejected by philosophers familiar with the sleight-of-hand that results from positing an alleged "rational will" and then supposing that a person's "true wants" can be identified apart from his expressed desires. And it will be resisted by critics of paternalism, who caution that "where we disapprove of an activity, or cannot appreciate it, we tend to think that the agent himself derives little benefit from it. In these ways the practice of paternalism easily becomes a cloak for the imposition of our values on those who are coerced."[14]

Human weakness could not begin to account for the high incidence of drug use. Legal drugs are consumed by the vast majority of Americans, not all of whom could be weak. Insofar as generalizations are possible, the initial decision to experiment with a drug, legal or otherwise, is probably best explained by simple curiosity. But persistence in drug use cannot be attributed to curiosity. Many individuals continue to use drugs because they enjoy their experience. Policies to combat drugs will fail as long as the euphoria of use is discounted and consumption is explained solely in terms of some deficiency of personality.

A second and somewhat more sophisticated strategy for ignoring consumer preferences is to contend that the pleasure of drug use, although genuine, is *pathological*. Arguably, the pleasure derived from pathological activities should not be included in a consequentialist calculus. To cite an extreme example, no one would seriously attempt to balance the pleasure of rapists against the pain of their victims in order to assess the justifiability of laws against rape. Consequentialists are likely to denounce any pleasure rapists may gain as pathological and thus as immaterial to the issue of whether rape should be prohibited. A parallel (but mysterious and unexplained) tendency is to label the pleasure of recreational drug use as pathological and thus to dismiss it.

Of course, the chief difficulty here is to defend a theory to distinguish pathological from nonpathological pleasures. This obstacle is formidable. If any pleasure is pathological, the pleasure derived from violating rights, from inflicting suffering on another, surely qualifies. But there is less promise that a theory of pathological pleasure for self-regarding conduct is forthcoming. Why should some ways of gaining pleasure, not derived at the expense of others, be labeled as pathological? The pursuit of a pleasure that eventually leads to ruin might be regarded as pathological. But this is a reason to believe that a pleasure is outweighed, not that it should not be counted in the first place.

The pleasure of recreational drug use might be condemned as pathological if it were immoral to experience. As it stands, however, this belief is a conclusion in search of an argument. No such argument could be developed in Chapter 1, and I can fare no better here. This defense of LAD depends on legal moralism rather than on paternalism: Drug use is condemned not because of its harmful effects on users, but because it is wrong notwithstanding its effects.

With this realization, I propose to move beyond a consequentialist perspective on LAD. Instead of trying to determine how the euphoria of drug use might be discounted, it is preferable to reject theories that approach these sorts of issues by attempts to balance good against evil. I will discuss the pros and cons of a utilitarian analysis in more detail in Chapter 3. When the horizon is expanded to consider the effects on both users and nonusers, there is less need to pretend that drug use is not pleasurable. Any euphoria drug users experience might be outweighed by the harm they inflict on others. But in the remainder of this chapter, where

I focus on the effects of drugs on adult users themselves, I will confine my attention almost exclusively to nonconsequentialist arguments about LAD. I hope to encourage thought about drug prohibition as a matter of principle.

AUTONOMY AND DRUG USE

What is required is a *principled* assessment of LAD rather than a consequentialist analysis. By a principled assessment, I mean an attempt to show whether and under what circumstances adults have or lack a *moral right* to use drugs recreationally.

How might such an argument of principle be constructed? The best strategy would be to argue directly in favor of a general principle of *autonomy* that either does or does not apply to and protect the recreational use of drugs. I assume that the principle of autonomy is the basis (or at least one basis) for objecting to interference with activities that are protected by a moral right. Only totalitarians deny that there is a sphere of behavior beyond state interference, and (at least part of) this range of conduct is identified by the principle of autonomy. Someone violates my autonomy by prohibiting me from doing what I have a moral right to do, such as eating ice cream (or so I will tentatively suppose). If the principle of autonomy does not apply to or protect the decision to use recreational drugs, an important obstacle to justifying LAD will have been removed. But the first crucial step in an argument against LAD will have been taken if it can be shown that recreational drug use is autonomous and thus is protected by a (prima facie) moral right. LAD would infringe this moral right, whether the rationale for prohibiting recreational drug use is paternalistic or nonpaternalistic.

Unfortunately, this strategy encounters an immediate and insuperable difficulty. The exact formulation of the principle of autonomy is subject to enormous dispute.[15] Some versions of the autonomy principle protect drug use, others do not, and the application of still others to drug use is as controversial as the formulation of the principle itself. I am unable to provide a non-question-begging argument in favor of a version that clearly supports or does not support the existence of a moral right to use drugs recreationally. Someone who is antecedently convinced that persons have or lack a given moral right will use this conviction to reject arguments in favor of a general principle of autonomy that entails he is mistaken. For this reason, I will not commit myself to a particular conception of the principle of autonomy. In the absence of a commitment to a particular conception, no one can prove that recreational drug use is autonomous or nonautonomous. In much of the remainder of this chapter, I hope to identify the best reasons for believing that recreational drug use expresses an autonomous choice as well as the best reasons for believing that it does not. The better arguments, I think, are on the side that construes drug use as autonomous, although the case is ultimately inconclusive.

Perhaps progress can be made not by attempting to formulate the principle of autonomy itself, but by identifying the constraints that any acceptable principle must satisfy. I will discuss two possible constraints here. Unfortunately, the case in favor of either constraint is not decisive.

First, a plausible conception of autonomy may or may not allow for degrees. It seems to make sense to say that some decisions are more or less autonomous than others. A conception of autonomy that allows for degrees might better explain how nonautonomous beings can become autonomous. Infants and adolescents do not gain autonomy all at once; they progress gradually. Although autonomy itself may be colored in shades of gray, many of the uses to which the concept is put are either black or white. For most practical purposes, decisions must be deemed to be either autonomous or nonautonomous. Bright lines must be drawn. For any boundary along a spectrum of autonomous choice, persons whose decisions are close to this line will complain that they are not significantly different from persons whose decisions fall on the other side.

Autonomy resembles age in this respect. Most moral and

legal purposes for which age is needed are all-or-nothing, yet age itself admits of degrees. A line must be drawn to decide who is old enough to make a contract, to be eligible for a driver's license, to vote, or to collect Social Security benefits. Similarly, a line must be drawn to decide whether the decision to use a drug recreationally is or is not autonomous. If autonomy admits of degree, I would not anticipate that the choice to use a recreational drug is likely to be either the most or the least autonomous decision an adult will ever make. The ultimate issue is whether this choice is either sufficiently nonautonomous to allow a paternalistic interference or sufficiently autonomous to oppose a paternalistic defense of LAD.

Second, a plausible conception of autonomy may or may not be purely formal. According to a purely formal conception, any given decision, regardless of its content, can qualify as autonomous, as long as it is made in the appropriate way. But other philosophical traditions favor a nonformal or substantive conception of autonomy, so that some particular decisions cannot qualify as autonomous, no matter how they are made. If a formal conception of autonomy is preferable, there is almost no reason to doubt that the decision to use recreational drugs is protected by the principle of autonomy, however it is formulated. Unfortunately for opponents of LAD, arguments in favor of a formal conception of autonomy are indecisive.

Arguments in favor of a formal conception have been offered by Gerald Dworkin. He contends that behind each of the several versions of the principle of autonomy that philosophers have defended "is a shared conception of what a person is." The pursuit of autonomy is the means by which an agent "shapes one's life" and "gives meaning to his life." From these premises, Dworkin concludes that autonomy must be "contentless." For persons "can give meaning to their lives in all kinds of ways: from stamp collecting to taking care of one's invalid parents. There is no particular way of giving shape and meaning to a life." Moreover, "any feature that is going to be fundamental in moral thinking must be a feature that persons share," and "any substantive conception of autonomy is not likely to be shared."[16]

But those philosophers who believe that the content of some decisions could not possibly qualify as autonomous are unlikely to be persuaded by these reasons. They might concede that "shape and meaning" can be given to a life in a wide variety of ways, but they would disagree that *any* decision is capable of conferring such value. Primary ambitions for genocide and world domination might not give genuine "shape and meaning" to one's life. If Hitler would not concur, so much the worse for him.

Perhaps additional support for a formal conception arises by interpreting autonomy as a *capacity* possessed by persons. If individuals can exercise this capacity to make any choice whatever, this interpretation supports a formal conception of autonomy. This result conforms to Dworkin's own formulation of the principle of autonomy: "Autonomy is conceived of as a second-order capacity of persons to reflect critically upon their first-order preferences, desires, wishes, and so forth and the capacity to accept or attempt to change these in light of higher-order preferences and values."[17] Presumably this conception is designed to describe autonomous *persons*; a *choice* is autonomous when this capacity is exercised. Thus a decision is autonomous when a person's second-order preferences are congruent with his first-order desires.[18] This conception of autonomy closely resembles Harry Frankfurt's conception of free will. According to Frankfurt, "It is in securing the conformity of his will to his second-order volitions that a person exercises freedom of the will."[19] According to these formal conceptions, any particular decision, including the decision to use drugs recreationally, can qualify as autonomous and free. Drug users can, and frequently do, have second-order desires to act according to their first-order desires to use drugs recreationally. In other words, adults who want to use drugs can, after critical reflection, want to want to use drugs. If so, their drug use is autonomous and free.

This result is not automatically altered by supposing that the adult user is addicted to drugs. If a person who wants to use drugs wants to use drugs, I see little reason to deny that her drug use is autonomous and free, even though she is an addict. To be sure, a person may have a second-order desire to want not to want to use drugs. If this person is an addict, she might encounter great difficulty in bringing her first-order desire to use drugs into conformity with her second-order desire not to want to use drugs. Many addicts succeed in changing their drug-using behavior in this way. But others fail. There is good reason to suspect that the drug use of an addict who has a second-order desire not to want to use drugs is less autonomous and free than that of a casual user. Later in this chapter, I will return to the difficult question of whether and to what extent addiction renders drug use nonautonomous and unfree.

Even if autonomy is construed substantively rather than formally, philosophers must face the overwhelming difficulty of distinguishing those choices that can qualify as autonomous from those that cannot. If autonomy protects only some choices, it is not a foregone conclusion that recreational drug use is not among them. Many substantive formulations of the autonomy principle defended by philosophers apparently apply to and protect recreational drug use.

For example, the principle of autonomy as construed by Joel Feinberg comes close to explicitly protecting recreational drug use. Feinberg observes that

> the kernel of the idea of autonomy is the right to make choices and decisions – what to put into my body, what contacts with my body to permit, where and how to move my body through public space, how to use my chattels and physical property, what personal information to disclose to others, what information to conceal, and more.[20]

Apparently this formulation is substantive. Unless the final words "and more" should be construed to apply to *all* choices, some decisions are not protected by the principle of autonomy.

Despite this implicit limitation, recreational drug use is clearly included within the scope of this conception of autonomy. The first decision mentioned by Feinberg – the choice to put a substance into one's body – is incompatible with LAD. This substantive conception of autonomy offers as much protection to the decision to use a recreational drug as to the decision to eat ice cream. If autonomous behavior expresses a (prima facie) moral right, adults have as much right to use a drug recreationally – *any* drug – as to eat ice cream. Thus Feinberg's formulation of the autonomy principle supports my suspicion from Chapter 1 that the general right from which the more specific right to use recreational drugs is derived is important and fundamental in a free society.

Other substantive conceptions of autonomy may or may not apply to and protect recreational drug use. John Rawls follows Immanuel Kant in linking autonomy with rationality. In this tradition, autonomous choices are those that persons would make when fully rational or under idealized conditions. According to Rawls, these ideal conditions include ignorance about one's preferences, biases, and the like. Against this background, Rawls contends that

> it is rational for [the parties] to protect themselves against their irrational inclinations by consenting to a scheme of penalties that may give them a sufficient motive to avoid foolish actions and by accepting certain impositions designed to undo the unfortunate consequences of their imprudent behavior.[21]

Some choices are irrational, are not protected by the principle of autonomy, and may be prohibited for the good of the agent.

Which recreational, imprudent activities are sufficiently "foolish" to fall outside the scope of autonomy? Would persons consent to prohibitions against boxing? Hang gliding? The consumption of alcohol? How should "foolish" recreational activities be distinguished from those that are legitimate? From the lofty perspective of rationality, all

recreational pursuits appear somewhat frivolous and suspect. But surely rationality would not endorse a sweeping
condemnation of every dangerous recreational pastime.
Clearly, distinctions would have to be drawn on the basis of
empirical evidence about the activity. But what empirical data
are relevant?

The importance of these questions is obvious, whether or
not one accepts a Rawlsian approach to the justifiability of
political authority. Much of the remainder of this chapter can
be construed as an attempt to answer them. A general issue
is whether drug use is sui generis and should be differentiated from other kinds of recreational activities. I ask again,
Are drugs different? The criteria to identify foolish, irrational,
nonautonomous choices from which the agent requires protection may or may not differ depending on whether that
choice involves the use of a drug.

Of course, the paternalistic case for LAD does not crumble
even if the principle of autonomy applies to and protects the
recreational use of drugs. Autonomy is not the ultimate
trump in moral and political debates; perhaps this principle
is outweighed by competing moral considerations that mil-
itate against the prima facie right to use drugs recreationally.
In attempting to shift the focus of debate to issues of principle, I do not mean to suggest that principles are all that
matter. Rights are not absolute; principles do not exhaust
moral and legal argument.

In this respect, my approach to recreational drug use differs from that of the libertarian, who holds that "the use of
mind-altering substances is never a proper subject of public
policy and should always be left to individual choice."[22] Some
libertarians go as far as to advocate decriminalization despite
their belief that drugs "are a horror,"[23] as though the best
moral and political theory disables the state from coping with
social problems that are truly horrendous. No one should
want to live in the libertarian state that lacks the authority
to deal with a plague, scourge, epidemic, or any of the other
colorful names that have been used to describe recreational
drug use. If drugs were accurately described by these terms,

87

principles would have to yield to the compelling state interest in prohibiting drug use.

If autonomy is construed as a purely formal conception, it must be outweighed by competing moral considerations on numerous occasions. Only an anarchist would believe that persons have an absolute, that is, a nonoverrideable, right to act according to any autonomous decisions they have made.[24] The most widely accepted reason to interfere with an autonomous choice is that it causes harm to others. But perhaps harm to oneself is sometimes a good reason as well. In other words, the paternalist is not defeated simply because a person causes harm to himself autonomously; in addition, no competing moral consideration must override his autonomy to justify interference.

The importance of the following distinction is easily missed:

a. A decision is *not* protected by the principle of autonomy, so persons lack a prima facie moral right to engage in it.
b. A decision *is* protected by the principle of autonomy, so persons *have* a prima facie moral right to engage in it, but that right is overridden by a competing and more stringent moral consideration.

The distinction between (a) and (b) can be crucial. If rights have any special significance at all, they are valuable in protecting a person from interference purportedly justified by ordinary utilitarian reasons. In other words, ordinary utilitarian reasons are insufficient to justify prohibiting a person from performing an action he has a right to perform.[25] An almost catastrophic extent of disutility is required to override the exercise of a moral right. If this view about the significance of moral rights is correct, ordinary utilitarian reasons cannot be used to justify interference with an activity that is protected by the principle of autonomy. But ordinary utilitarian reasons can be used to justify interference with an activity that is not protected by the principle of autonomy in the first place. For this reason, it is crucial to decide whether the principle of autonomy (a) does not protect drug use at all, or (b) protects drug use, although that protection can be overridden. Only if (a) is true are ordinary utilitarian reasons sufficient to justify interference with drug use.

Which moral considerations can override my exercise of rights and autonomy, if ordinary utilitarian considerations cannot? As I have indicated, a horror, or near catastrophe, will suffice. A conflicting, more stringent right will suffice as well; for this reason, the need to protect others from harm I would cause them is a good reason to override my exercise of rights and autonomy. Other persons have a competing, more stringent right not to be harmed by my exercise of rights and autonomy. But can the need to protect me from harm I would do to myself ever outweigh my exercise of rights and autonomy? Radically different answers might be given.

Feinberg's position on this issue is uncompromising. He claims that "a person's right of self-determination, being sovereign, takes precedence even over his own good."[26] Feinberg rejects the alternative that "we must balance the person's right against his good and weigh them."[27] He does not, however, claim to provide a decisive argument for this "absolutist" position about the priority of the right over the good. Can Feinberg really believe that "paternalistic reasons never have *any* weight on the scales at all?"[28] Is the interest in preventing persons from harming themselves totally irrelevant to the case for legislation? Many philosophers will find Feinberg's antipaternalism to be extreme.

Clearly, further argument is required to decide whether and under what conditions a principle of autonomy that provides prima facie protection to recreational drug use by adults can be overridden by paternalistic considerations. Much of the remainder of this chapter will discuss the complexities that arise in attempts to balance the importance of autonomy against the desirability of preventing persons from harming themselves. I will conclude that a paternalistic defense of prohibitions against the use of existing recreational drugs is not compelling, even if a person's good occasionally takes priority over his rights.

The attempt to evaluate LAD by formulating a principle of autonomy has encountered enormous problems. Neither the exact formulation itself nor the constraints that any acceptable formulation must satisfy are sufficiently clear to be of much help in deciding whether the recreational use of drugs by adults expresses an autonomous choice and is protected by a moral right. In addition, the weight to be assigned to autonomy in its competition with other values is difficult to measure. For these reasons, I will pursue a different and less direct strategy to assess a nonconsequentialist defense of LAD on paternalistic grounds.

ANALOGIES

A second strategy to provide a principled assessment of LAD does not attempt to explicitly formulate the principle of autonomy, but proceeds by analogy. The paternalistic case for LAD can be compared and contrasted with the paternalistic case for other recreational activities that pose significant risks to adults who engage in them. These activities include boxing, mountain climbing, race car driving, skiing, eating fatty foods, playing football, driving a car with or without a seat belt, riding a motorcycle with or without a helmet, sunbathing, playing "Russian roulette," consuming saccharin, participating in rodeos, bungee-jumping, and a host of others. At present, some but not all of these activities are and ought to be prohibited by law. Does the principle of autonomy apply to and protect the decision to engage in any of these risky behaviors? If so, defenders of LAD can be asked to point to a morally relevant difference between drug use and the recreational activities that autonomy protects. But if the principle of autonomy does not apply to or protect the decision to engage in any of these risky behaviors, this strategy fails to offer much insight into the justifiability of LAD. All analogical arguments are limited in this respect.

Suppose that autonomy does not apply to or protect any of these recreational activities. According to this school of thought, represented in the previous section by alternative (a), adults do not have a moral *right* to eat ice cream after all. Instead, adults are merely *permitted* to eat ice cream, but their behavior is unprotected by a right derived from the principle of autonomy. Again, rights are important because they cannot be defeated by ordinary utilitarian reasons. In other words, a utilitarian rationale would be sufficient to justify prohibiting eating ice cream, if persons were merely permitted to do so. A utilitarian rationale would be insufficient, however, to justify prohibiting eating ice cream, if this behavior were protected by a right. If this account of the significance of rights is correct, it would be crucial to decide whether persons have a moral right to eat ice cream, in the event that its consumption turned out to cause a substantial risk to health and a net balance of disutility.

Examples of behavior that is and is not protected by a moral right are easy to provide. The behavior governed by most traffic regulations is unprotected by a right. Suppose that persons are initially permitted to drive in either direction along Euclid Avenue but that subsequent studies conclude that highway safety would be facilitated, and congestion relieved, by making the avenue one-way east. Almost everyone believes that these ordinary utilitarian reasons would be sufficient to prohibit persons from driving west along Euclid Avenue. But many other examples are not comparable to traffic regulations. Suppose that the practice of a religion or the exercise of speech produced a net balance of disutility. This supposition would not justify prohibiting them. Unlike the behavior governed by traffic regulations, speech and religious expression are protected by moral rights.

Although clear examples can be described on each side of the distinction, there is a great deal of controversy about how to categorizé any number of cases. Recreational activities fall squarely within this gray area. The claim that adults do not have a moral right to engage in any recreational activity, but are merely permitted to do so, is among the best reasons to deny that they have a moral right to use drugs recreationally.

If all recreational activities fall outside the scope of the protection of autonomy, the state may resort to utilitarian reasons in deciding whether to prohibit them.

Of course, the drug prohibitionist cannot claim victory in supporting LAD simply by arguing that all recreational activities are nonautonomous and unprotected by moral rights. In addition, there must be a morally relevant difference between those recreational activities that should be permitted and those that should be prohibited. One candidate for such a difference is that permitted recreational activities cause a net balance of utility, whereas recreational drug use does not. Does the use of a particular drug, or recreational drug use in general, really cause a net balance of disutility? I will suggest in Chapter 3 that utilitarian arguments about LAD are inconclusive. But LAD will have been given an impressive defense *if* recreational drug use produces a net balance of disutility *and* persons lack a moral right to engage in any recreational activity.

How plausible is (a) when applied to all recreational activities? Most adults believe that their autonomy would be infringed, and their rights violated, if the state prohibited a great many recreational activities that are currently permitted. They are not likely to believe that the case for or against allowing some or all of the recreational activities already mentioned depends solely on the outcome of a utilitarian balancing. They would probably concede, for example, that society would gain a net increase in health and utility if persons were required to buckle their seat belts while driving. But this concession does not entail that laws requiring seat belts do not infringe their rights and autonomy. If mandatory seat belt laws do not infringe rights and autonomy, it is not because they promote utility. The same point is true of LAD. Does LAD infringe moral rights and autonomy, notwithstanding its supposed tendency to promote health and utility?

If autonomy and rights are indeed at stake in many recreational activities, as seems likely, ordinary utilitarian reasons should not be employed to dismiss these analogies. Of course, both theorists and politicians have been known to disagree. They frequently offer utilitarian reasons in response to a challenge to explain why the recreational use of some drugs, but not others, is illegal. Mark Kleiman and Aaron Saiger contend, "From a public health standpoint, creating a cocaine problem the size of the current alcohol problem would be a major disaster."[29] William Bennett quotes Charles Krauthammer in rephrasing the issue as follows: "The question is not which is worse, alcohol or drugs. The question is can we accept both legalized alcohol *and* legalized drugs? The answer is no."[30]

These responses do not address the question in principled terms. The "public health standpoint" or the "we" in these retorts indicate that neither Kleiman and Saiger nor Bennett are adopting the nonconsequentialist perspective of the individual. No one should be persuaded that she lacks a right to use the drug of her choice because the state cannot simultaneously allow others to use the drug of their choice. Even if disutility is caused by accommodating both choices, the person whose preference is unsatisfied should demand to know: Why *his* preferences and not *mine*?

To be sure, a majority of Americans condone the use of alcohol and tobacco, whereas they oppose the use of marijuana, cocaine, and heroin. Few call for the reintroduction of alcohol prohibition, yet the decriminalization of illegal drugs is opposed by as many as 90 percent.[31] As I argued in Chapter 1, this statistic cannot be used to support the conclusion that is ordinarily drawn from it. LAD probably lacks the consensus required of justified criminal legislation. Here my point is different. This resort to democratic theory cannot be used to justify the legalization of some drugs but not others, even if "we" cannot "accept" them all. This crude appeal to majoritarianism disregards individual rights, which should not be extended or withdrawn by democratic procedures. Even if only one person wanted to use LSD, and no one else wanted to allow him to do so, its prohibition would require a justification. The only acceptable answer to the "why his preferences and not mine?" question requires a principle that cites a morally relevant difference between the permissible and the prohibited. This principle must explain why the decision to use some drugs is nonautonomous and unprotected by a moral right, whereas the decision to use other drugs, or to participate in other selected recreational activities, is autonomous and protected by a moral right.

Perhaps the most familiar reason that will be given to differentiate the use of illegal drugs from many other recreational activities is that drug use is *more* risky than members of the comparison class that are and ought to be permitted. According to version (a) of this response, the principle of autonomy applies to and protects the decision to take a risk, unless the extent of this risk exceeds a given critical threshold. No protection is afforded after the amount of a risk exceeds this threshold. According to version (b) of this response, the principle of autonomy applies to and protects the decision to take any risk, however great. But after the extent of a risk exceeds a given critical threshold, the protection afforded by the principle of autonomy is outweighed by the need to prevent persons from harming themselves.

Neither strategy to exempt very risky behavior from the scope of protection by the principle of autonomy is very plausible. One would anticipate that the principle of autonomy would allow adults to decide for themselves what extent of risk to assume. Still, the perception that drugs are especially harmful to users has contributed greatly to public hostility toward them. At least two questions must be confronted if this defense of LAD is to have any prospects for success. First, how should this critical threshold of risk be characterized? Second, which drugs, if any, create risks to users that exceed this critical threshold? These questions cannot be answered with any precision. But enough progress can be made to indicate that this strategy is unlikely to support anything remotely resembling the status quo about LAD.

A common standard to compare the extent of risk of very different kinds of activities is not easily constructed. Some risky activities result in broken bones that usually heal; others cause a deterioration in mental functions that may or may not be reversed; still others progressively damage soft tissue. No single statistic can reduce the extent of risk to a common denominator, and I do not pretend to do so here.

Yet insight can be gained by a quick comparison of the fatality records for legal and illegal drugs. These data, long available, should surprise only those who have succumbed to drug hysteria without bothering to examine the empirical evidence. There seems to be no correlation (except perhaps an inverse one) between the illegality of a drug and the likelihood that it will cause death. Nicotine causes many more deaths (between 350,000 and 430,000 annually) than all other drugs combined, both legal and illegal, and the toll is still rising.[32] Next highest in number of fatalities is alcohol (between 50,000 and 200,000 annual deaths). These data become only slightly less alarming when adjusted for the fact that nicotine and alcohol are used more widely than illegal drugs. When the risk of a given drug is expressed as a ratio of the number of fatalities per weekly users, nicotine (83.3 deaths per 10,000 weekly users) is still far and away the most deadly drug. About 25 percent of all adolescents who smoke a pack of cigarettes daily lose, on average, ten to fifteen years of their lives.[33] Illegal drugs seem benign by comparison, although the data on their long-term effects are less reliable. Significantly, no known fatalities have ever been attributed to the consumption of marijuana, despite its use by 51 million Americans in the past fifteen years. Cocaine, even when smoked in the form of crack, was cited as the primary cause of death in only 2,496 cases in 1989,[34] and there is reason to suspect that this figure may be exaggerated.[35] Since 862,000 Americans reported using cocaine weekly in 1988, the number of deaths per 10,000 weekly users is about 29. This figure is roughly comparable to alcohol (perhaps 20.6 deaths per 10,000 weekly users).[36]

If the rationale for LAD is to prevent persons from killing themselves, it seems apparent that the state has made the wrong recreational drugs illegal. Any number of commentators have concluded that "the data demonstrate that for

the population as a whole, the health problems caused by
the currently legal recreational drugs are far more serious
than those caused by the currently illegal recreational
drugs."[37]

It is unlikely that anyone would react to these statistics by
demanding that the use of both nicotine and alcohol should
be punished. Even though some historical revisionists have
begun to pronounce the country's past experiment with the
prohibition of alcohol as "a success,"[38] no leading figure has
recommended a return to that era. What is less clear is
whether the universal unwillingness to reinstate the prohibition of alcohol is based on the perception that the experiment "failed" as social policy or is due to the conviction that
adults have a moral right to drink. Many theorists would
adopt both positions. After all, a constitutional amendment
was required to ban alcohol in 1919, suggesting that prohibition could not be implemented by ordinary democratic
procedures.

When placed in perspective, illegal drug use is not an
extraordinarily dangerous recreational activity. The risk of
fatality encountered by users of illegal recreational drugs is
not unlike that faced in many permitted recreational pursuits.
About 4,200 Americans died in motorcycle accidents in 1987,
even though there are fewer motorcycles than cocaine
users.[39] The risk of recreational drug use may be roughly
comparable to that of mountain climbing in general, but it is
far smaller than the risk of an assault on the Himalayas in
particular (which killed 47 of the 1,609 non-Nepalese who
attempted it).[40] Furthermore, illegal drug use is probably a
good deal less hazardous than race car driving or boxing.

Surely it is possible to imagine a recreational drug that
poses a greater risk of death to users than any of these activities. Sometimes drugs are likened to the Sirens described
in Homer's *Odyssey*, who lured all sailors to their doom until
Odysseus devised a clever scheme to listen to their songs
while avoiding harm. But no such drug exists today. If such
a recreational drug were to be created, and the principle of
autonomy did not apply to or protect activities that exceed

a given critical threshold of risk, prohibitions of such a drug would be justifiable.

Although fatalities provide a dramatic basis to compare the relative risks of various recreational activities, death is not the only kind of harm alleged to be caused by drug use. The risks of nonfatal disease or illness might be increased as well. Steven Jonas has contrasted the health risks of legal and illegal drug use. He writes that tobacco "is a major cause of coronary artery disease, peripheral vascular disease, cerebrovascular disease, lung, laryngeal, oral, esophageal, bladder, pancreatic, and kidney cancers, and of chronic obstructive pulmonary disease."[41] Alcohol use has been linked "with about 75 different human diseases and conditions."[42] However, "there is no present evidence that long-term cocaine use is a risk factor for any major physical diseases."[43] And heroin use causes "relatively little physical harm to the human body."[44] Finally, "there is little evidence that the occasional smoking of marihuana inflicts much harm on the consumer."[45]

Recreational drug users have also been alleged to suffer psychological harm.[46] This claim is hard to evaluate, and not simply because of the difficulties in defending criteria of psychological health. A greater obstacle in assessing this claim is that few longitudinal studies of the psychology of drug users have been conducted. The existing evidence, however, provides no cause for great alarm. One such study concluded that adults who used moderate quantities of recreational drugs as adolescents (and who outnumber either heavy drug users or total abstainers) are "the psychologically healthiest subjects, healthier than either abstainers or frequent users."[47] The authors seem almost apologetic in concluding that "some drug experimentation, in and of itself, does not seem to be psychologically destructive."[48]

Thus existing illegal recreational drugs should probably not be prohibited because they pose an unacceptable magnitude of risk of harm to users relative to permissible recreational activities. But suppose that I underestimate the risks of illegal drug use. What would follow from conceding that the use of a given drug is extremely risky? No one should believe that the extent of risk of a recreational activity is the only factor that governs whether it is ultimately protected by the principle of autonomy. Surely the importance of that activity is significant as well. Important risky activities have a claim to protection that unimportant risky activities do not.

From whose perspective should importance be assessed? No social criteria are readily available to distinguish important from unimportant recreational activities. After all, society would continue to function without allowing any particular recreational activity. More likely, these criteria must be supplied by the agent. Deciding which activities have or lack importance should itself be encompassed by the principle of autonomy. Many philosophers resist paternalism partly in order to avoid surrendering to others the authority to decide that an activity deemed important by the agent is really unimportant, so that its curtailment should not be regarded as a significant loss.

LAD is hard to support if adults are the ultimate authorities about the significance of given activities. Many persons are likely to describe their recreational use of drugs as important in their lives. In fact, one of the most common complaints about recreational drug use is that adults frequently regard it as *too* important. Individuals readily identify themselves as smokers, drinkers, or, in their more candid moments, as users of an illegal recreational drug. The same is true of any number of recreational activities people become passionate about, such as scuba diving or skiing. But not all risky activities are on a par. Driving without a seat belt is identified as important by almost no one. Even persons who have campaigned to repeal mandatory seat belt laws in Nebraska and Massachusetts are unlikely, without prompting, to include riding without a seat belt among the activities that matter most to them. If the importance of the activity to the agent is a substantial factor in deciding whether it is protected by the principle of autonomy, it is coherent to believe that the choice to use a recreational drug is protected, whereas the choice to drive without a seat belt is not.

A few additional considerations might be relevant in deciding whether the principle of autonomy applies to and protects a given recreational activity, or whether any such protection is ultimately outweighed. One such consideration is whether the risky activity can be replaced by a less dangerous alternative. This principle seems to explain the extraordinary degree of paternalistic restriction placed on food additives. Although the state has vast authority to regulate food safety under the much-amended Food, Drug, and Cosmetic Act of 1938, the "natural constituents of unprocessed agricultural commodities" are almost never prohibited.[49] Food additives, on the other hand, are subject to very stringent regulations. Additives are differentiated from foods for a variety of reasons. Perhaps the main difference is that no particular food additive is unique. If one additive is harmful, another can be developed that is safe, and the consumer will barely notice the difference. Paternalistic considerations might outweigh the protection that autonomy affords to a harmful decision if the agent could achieve the same objective by a less risky alternative. As one commentator asks, "Why take a risk when you can get the benefit (fulfill the need) in some other way?"[50] If two recreational drugs were indistinguishable from one another, the more harmful could be prohibited. However, recreational drugs are probably more like foods than like food additives in this respect.[51]

In addition, all commentators on the use of the criminal law construe punishment as a last resort. Whenever possible, the objectives of a social policy should be achieved by means less drastic than a total prohibition. No state has banned motorcycles, but many have made motorcycle riding safer by requiring the use of a protective helmet. As a result, the autonomy of motorcyclists is infringed less severely than by prohibiting motorcycles altogether. Unfortunately, almost no comparable measures to reduce the risks of illegal drug use have been implemented. For example, many of the risks of marijuana are due to the fact that the substance is usually smoked. Allowing marijuana to be consumed in the form of a pill or tablet would minimize its risks while showing some degree of respect for the autonomy of users. Such proposals are typically resisted on the ground that they appear to condone drug use. But this objection may not offset the respect for autonomy that such regulations would demonstrate. In short, paternalists who insist that the use of given drugs should be prohibited altogether must be prepared to argue that less restrictive alternatives would not go far enough toward ensuring safety.[52]

On the basis of these analogies, it becomes possible to describe a recreational drug that the state would have good reason to prohibit on paternalistic grounds. First, this drug would have to create significant harms to a great many persons who use it. Second, few persons would regard the use of this drug as especially significant in their lives. Finally, attempts to minimize the health hazards of this drug below the tolerable threshold must be deemed unsuccessful. It is best not to be too dogmatic about whether any existing recreational drugs satisfy these conditions, although I make no attempt to conceal my skepticism.

But perhaps these analogies fail. Maybe drugs are different after all. There may be sound paternalistic reasons to prohibit drug use that do not pertain to the other recreational activities with which I have compared it. I now turn to the most compelling reason to believe that these analogies misconstrue the rationale for LAD.

ADDICTION AND AUTONOMY

In this section, I will evaluate a much more plausible response to the preceding analogies. Perhaps the most important potential difference between recreational drug use and the other activities with which it has been compared is that drugs, unlike these other activities, can be *addictive*. Many theorists have indicated that addiction is the crucial factor that undermines the application of the principle of autonomy to drug use and that blocks comparisons between the risks involved in drug use and the risks involved in other recreational activities. Robert Goodin expresses this point in his powerful indictment of nicotine:

> If it is autonomy that we are trying to protect in opposing paternalistic legislation in general, then the same values that lead us to oppose such legislation in general will lead us to welcome it in those particular cases where what we are being protected from is something that would deprive us of the capacity for autonomous choice.[53]

Goodin goes on to argue that the use of addictive drugs deprives persons of their capacity for autonomous choice. If his argument is sound, the autonomy that is sacrificed by the enforcement of LAD is justified in order to protect autonomy itself. For this reason, Goodin concludes that the principle of autonomy opposes rather than protects the decision to use addictive drugs.

Is this argument sound? Before assessing this argument directly, notice a few troublesome features. First, it presupposes a substantive rather than a formal conception of autonomy. This argument seemingly accuses persons of inconsistency when they try to invoke the principle of autonomy to protect their decision to use addictive substances. The accusation is not simply that they have made a bad choice. Yet consistency is a formal constraint; it does not preclude any particular decision, but only combinations of decisions. This argument does not condemn two or more decisions, but only the decision to use addictive drugs. Depriving oneself of autonomy cannot really be inconsistent. Electing to deprive oneself of autonomy may be unwise, but it does not exhibit a defect of logic. If the best conception of autonomy is formal, this attempt to differentiate recreational drug use from other risky activities is unsound.

Moreover, I have used Dworkin's conception of autonomy and Frankfurt's conception of freedom to raise doubts about whether the drug use of an addict is nonautonomous or unfree. If these conceptions are adopted, the judgment that persons use addictive drugs nonautonomously or unfreely applies at most to only a subset of addicts. A drug addict might experience no conflict between his first-order desire to use drugs and his second-order preferences. In the absence of such a conflict, I see little reason to conclude that his behavior is nonautonomous or unfree. Philosophers who persist in believing that addiction undermines autonomy must describe the sense of autonomy on which they rely.

In addition, conceding that a substance is used nonautonomously cannot be a sufficient condition for paternalistic interference; a law is not justified simply because it protects persons from decisions that result in deprivations of their autonomy. Despite Goodin's curious stipulation that addictions are "unambiguously bad,"[54] a rational person might well decide that the advantages of using a drug outweigh the disadvantages, even though he will become addicted to it. Presumably many coffee drinkers agree. The use of caffeine is certainly addictive and apparently creates minor health risks. Yet no one should conclude that the decision to drink coffee is unprotected by the principle of autonomy, so that it should be prohibited for the sake of those who drink it. Why not?

The simple answer is that the risks of caffeine are too trivial to warrant paternalistic intervention. Evidently, the fact that a recreational drug is both unhealthy and addictive does not justify its prohibition. In addition, a given threshold of risk must be crossed before prohibition is warranted. Conceivably, other addictive recreational drugs may resemble caffeine in not exceeding whatever threshold of risk is required.

Despite these difficulties, the addictive nature of drugs might provide a plausible means to differentiate their use from other risky recreational activities. Intuitively, the use of addictive substances seems to undermine autonomy in a way that nonaddictive activities do not. For this reason, addictive behavior may have less claim to protection in the name of autonomy. The remainder of this section (and much of the following section) explores this apparent difference. I conclude that this argument offers only minimal support for LAD. Existing recreational drugs would have to possess properties they almost certainly lack before this argument would be compelling.

A serious attempt to apply this argument to LAD would begin by sorting drugs into two categories – those that are addictive, and those that are not. This strategy would not yield results that coincide with existing statutes. Some legal drugs, for example, nicotine, are highly addictive, whereas some illegal drugs, for example, LSD, are not addictive at all. Are paternalists who contend that the protection of autonomy provides the only acceptable basis to prohibit risky decisions really prepared to decriminalize the use of non-addictive drugs like LSD? This question might make paternalists reluctant to rely on the phenomenon of addiction as the sole basis to uphold LAD.

A deeper evaluation of this argument must address the nature of addiction itself. Whether and under what circumstances autonomy is protected by preventing persons from using addictive substances cannot be assessed without invoking a conception of addiction. Unfortunately, the nature of addiction is no more clear than that of autonomy, and it raises "a monstrous tangle of social, psychological, and pharmacological issues."[55] Few concepts are used as loosely. Norman Zinberg observes, "It is clear that the concept of addiction, like the concept of drug abuse, has long been approached in an unscientific or pseudoscientific way."[56] Some theorists use the concept broadly, encompassing "any pleasurable behavior that turns out compulsive."[57] By an alcohol analogy, persons are said to be "sexaholics" or "workaholics." Other theorists seemingly deny that addiction exists at all. According to Thomas Szasz, "Addictive drugs stand in the same relation to ordinary drugs as holy water stands in relation to ordinary or non-holy water."[58] At the very least, the concept of addiction is "in a preparadigmatic period."[59] Scholars in various disciplines continue to debate two fundamental issues: First, what addiction is; and second, what causes addiction, insofar as the phenomenon is genuine.[60] Psychological, social, and biological models of addiction compete, and hybrid accounts and new alternatives proliferate

103

in journals. A philosopher would be unwise to stake a definitive position on these extremely controversial issues. I hope to avoid a firm commitment about what addiction "really is."

The more promising contribution a philosopher might make is to identify what addiction would have to be like in order for the preceding argument to be persuasive. What properties would a hypothetical drug have to possess before its use would not be protected by the principle of autonomy? What is it about addiction that weakens ordinary resistance to paternalistic intervention? How might the phenomenon of addiction play a role in a premise of a sound argument to conclude that the use of an addictive substance is not protected by the principle of autonomy? Answers to these questions identify the direction in which empirical investigation becomes morally relevant. Empirical research is instrumental to decide whether given drugs satisfy whatever criteria are philosophically important.

A conception of addiction that is useful to the paternalist who hopes to support LAD must satisfy the following basic requirement. Drugs must be addictive in a different sense from most or all other recreational activities. The whole point of invoking the concept of addiction is to block comparisons between drug use and most other risky recreational activities, in order to provide a reason to believe that the principle of autonomy protects the latter but not the former. The phenomenon of addiction provides the best reason to believe that drugs are different. But if most other recreational activities that create equivalent risks are addictive in the same respect(s) as drug use, addiction will not serve to differentiate them from one another. For this reason, paternalists who defend LAD and hope to resist my analogies have reason to hope that Zinberg is wrong to conclude that "the inference that the use of illicit drugs is more addictive than the use of socially accepted substances is incorrect. The users of sugar and salt . . . are no less controlled by their need for these substances than are the users of marihuana, LSD, and cocaine."[61] Although persons might claim to be "addicted" to reading, eating chocolate, playing video games, skiing, or skydiving, the paternalist who hopes to support LAD must treat such claims as metaphorical, unless these activities are also to be subject to prohibition in the name of autonomy. Perhaps a few risky recreational activities will turn out to be addictive in the same respect(s) as drugs. Gambling, for example, is sometimes described as a "true" addiction.[62] If so, the case for prohibiting these activities in the name of autonomy is, ceteris paribus, as strong as the case for prohibiting the recreational use of drugs.

Since there is radical disagreement about the nature of addiction, it is best to employ a broad definition that includes several different criteria, without commitment to which criterion is more or less essential to the concept. I will borrow the following characterization of addiction (or of "the dependence syndrome," said to be "likely [to] replace the term addiction.")[63] The following seven factors identify this syndrome:

1. A subjective awareness of compulsion to use a drug or drugs, usually during attempts to stop or moderate drug use.
2. A desire to stop drug use in the face of continued use.
3. A relatively stereotyped pattern of drug-taking behavior.
4. Evidence of neuroadaptation (that is, tolerance and withdrawal symptoms).
5. Use of the drug to relieve or avoid withdrawal symptoms.
6. The salience of drug-seeking behavior relative to other important priorities.
7. Rapid reinstatement of the syndrome after a period of abstinence.[64]

One important consequence of this definition is that addiction is a matter of degree. Persons might be said to be more or less addicted, depending on how many criteria they satisfy and the extent to which they satisfy them.

Which of these seven criteria, if any, is relevant to the issue of whether addiction deprives persons of autonomy and thus is potentially useful to the paternalist? In what follows, I will attempt to answer this question by focusing on several of these criteria.

The sixth criterion, which describes a phenomenon some-times called "psychological dependence," does not support the conclusion that the use of an addictive substance is non-autonomous. The fact that users elevate drugs to a significant status relative to their other interests does not by itself dif-ferentiate drug use from any number of other dangerous activities that are not candidates for paternalistic intervention in the name of autonomy. For example, some persons devote an extraordinary amount of time and energy to mountain climbing. This hazardous obsession may seem peculiar and objectionable to persons who do not share or comprehend it. The notorious "because it's there" explanation of moun-tain climbing would seem pathetic and ludicrous if offered as an explanation of recreational drug use. But intervention cannot be justified on this ground alone. As I have indicated, one of the central themes among philosophers who oppose paternalism is their refusal to allow others to decide what the priorities of an adult should be. Quite simply, the phe-nomenon of psychological dependence cannot be employed as a premise in a plausible argument to conclude that drug use is nonautonomous and subject to prohibition. Any such argument would prove far too much.

The irrelevance of psychological dependence per se may require further defense. As long as the adult has the ability to choose not to persist in drug use, or not to continue to afford drugs a high priority relative to his other pursuits, the fact that he attaches an extraordinary amount of significance to drugs is not a reason to believe that his use is nonauton-omous. Of course, the contrary supposition that the drug user lacks this ability casts the situation in an entirely dif-ferent light. But even in those cases in which the user does not have the ability to stop using drugs, psychological de-pendence is unimportant to the argument for prohibition. Suppose that two users, Bob and Steve, are equally unable to discontinue their use of drugs, but drug use has a much greater significance in Bob's life than in Steve's. Is there any reason to conclude that Bob's drug use is less autonomous than Steve's? If not, the relevant variable is not the psychological dependence of the drug user.

Even more clearly irrelevant to the issue of autonomy is the phenomenon of tolerance, as contained in the fourth criterion. The fact that progressively greater dosages of a given substance are required to produce the same effect provides no reason to believe that the use of that substance is nonautonomous. No one should be entirely clear about whether two stimuli produce "the same effect." But a skier who is confined to a beginner's slope would not continue to experience a comparable degree of thrill and satisfaction as he gains greater skill and expertise. Again, an attempt to employ the phenomenon of tolerance as a premise in a plausible argument to conclude that drug use is nonautonomous and subject to prohibition would prove far too much.

The seventh and final criterion is immaterial as well. Persons who engage in any number of recreational activities undergo periods of "abstinence," only to "rapidly reinstate" their initial behavior. Many recreational activities are seasonal. The fact that conduct conforms to this pattern provides no indication that autonomy is lacking and does not weaken the resistance to paternalistic intervention.

But a dimension that is implicit in several of the remaining criteria is more relevant to the issue of whether behavior is autonomous. According to this criterion, addicts experience a "compulsion" to engage in an activity, especially during a period in which they "desire to stop" or "attempt to stop or moderate" their behavior. Many addicts report that they are powerless to discontinue their drug use, despite their best efforts to do so. Addiction seems to undermine the autonomy or freedom of these persons in the sense described by Dworkin and Frankfurt. An addict would be unable to effectively exercise his second-order desire, his desire not to want to use drugs, to prevent him from further drug use.

More needs to be said about how this criterion of addiction is relevant to the issue of whether drug use is autonomous.

Two questions must be answered. First, what does it really mean to say that an addict is powerless to stop using drugs? The addict cannot be powerless to stop in the same way that a person who is pushed from a cliff is powerless to stop his fall. Nor is the addict powerless to stop in the same way that a person is powerless to stop his breathing. Nor is the addict powerless to stop in the same way that a robot is powerless to depart from its program. In what way *is* the addict powerless to stop using drugs? Second, why is the inability to stop a reason to doubt that an activity is fully autonomous? Habits are notoriously difficult to break, but it is not obvious that habitual behavior is nonautonomous. A devoted enthusiast of a soap opera might experience an inability to stop watching his favorite show. Does this inability automatically render his behavior nonautonomous? Answers to these questions invite further clarification of *why* persons are unable to change their behavior. I will argue that only some reasons for persisting in drug use might make that behavior non-autonomous and subject to paternalistic intervention.

I propose that the best way to understand the addict's plea that he is powerless to stop and that his drug use is non-autonomous is that his attempts to quit trigger severe withdrawal symptoms that can be relieved only by further drug use. The addict becomes *physiologically dependent;* his body requires periodic dosages of the drug to maintain physiological homeostasis. I am not altogether confident that a choice becomes nonautonomous simply because it is made in order to relieve severe withdrawal symptoms; I do not endorse without reservations the argument I will now develop. However, I see no other reason to conclude that the addict is powerless to stop using drugs or that his drug use is non-autonomous. The remainder of this section explores whether and to what extent a choice made to avoid severe withdrawal symptoms is nonautonomous and thus is subject to paternalistic intervention.

The mere fact that a person is physiologically dependent and uses a drug to relieve withdrawal symptoms does not entail that his use of that drug is nonautonomous. In addition, the pain of withdrawal must be sufficiently severe so that it is unreasonable to expect him to endure it. Only then might it be said that an addict is powerless to quit. Consider again the addictive properties of caffeine. Many regular drinkers experience mild withdrawal when they are deprived of coffee. By the afternoon of a morning in which they have not had coffee, they suffer minor headaches, are somewhat lethargic, and become relatively irritable. These discomforts can persist for a few days, until the addiction is finally overcome. But apart from the minimal risks caffeine involves, I doubt that these symptoms are sufficiently severe to warrant the judgment that caffeine addicts are powerless to stop drinking coffee. Each morning, they have the ability to choose to continue or to decide to quit. The pain of overcoming their addictions is not so enormous that they could not reasonably be expected to undergo it, if they had good reason to stop. Persistent use is autonomous; caffeine addicts can quit.

Social conventions create a vague and imprecise threshold of pain or discomfort that adults should be able to withstand for the sake of avoiding an evil. If this evil occurs as a result of a choice that is made in order to avoid a pain or discomfort less intense than this threshold amount, adults will be said to have chosen this evil autonomously and will be subject to blame. This standard operates throughout the criminal law. Consider the excuse of duress. Modern statutes create a defense of duress if a person commits a crime "under a threat of unlawful force that a person of reasonable firmness in his situation would have been unable to resist."[65] This defense includes both an "objective" and a "subjective" component. Objectively, the defense is unavailable unless persons of reasonable firmness would succumb to the threat. A person cannot plead duress on the ground that he has a special aversion to pain. Subjectively, the defense is unavailable unless the threat actually motivates the person to commit the crime. A defendant cannot plead duress as an excuse if the threat did not induce him to act, even though it may have been sufficient to move a person of reasonable firmness to commit the crime.

Why does a humane system of criminal law recognize duress as an excuse? The best answer is that persons should not be required to suffer unreasonable hardship as the price of conformity to law. Adults should not be blamed for their willingness to do wrong, when their only alternative is sufficiently unattractive that persons of reasonable firmness would have behaved similarly. We do not condemn individuals who are unwilling to suffer a great amount of pain or discomfort in order to avoid an evil. When persons choose an evil under duress, it might be said that their behavior is nonautonomous.

In this sense, a person has "no choice" when confronted by the robber who demands either the money or the life of the victim. Literally, of course, the victim *has* a choice; but the only alternative to surrendering his purse is so painful that "persons of ordinary firmness" would succumb. In having "no choice," the victim might be said to act nonautonomously.

No one should extend this rationale to include cases in which the agent commits an offense in order to attain a benefit. The avoidance of evil and the pursuit of good are not symmetrical bases for creating an excuse. The threat to inflict pain might support the conclusion that an agent was powerless not to commit a blameworthy act, but the offer to provide pleasure does not. This conclusion is important, since drugs may act as positive reinforcers of subsequent use either by inducing pleasure or by blocking pain. No adult acts under duress by using drugs to attain great pleasure rather than to avoid severe pain.

Consider an example involving neither drugs nor criminal behavior. Suppose that a soldier is determined to keep his hand in a bucket of very hot water. He will avoid a terrible evil the longer he is able to keep his hand submerged. His sadistic enemy will spare the life of one additional comrade for each second he is able to endure the pain. The temperature of the water becomes hotter and hotter; eventually, the soldier can stand it no longer, and he pulls back his hand. If the water is hot enough, the soldier should not be blamed. He is powerless to persist; he had no choice; he removed his hand nonautonomously. The severity of the pain excuses conduct that otherwise would be blameworthy.

In this example, criticism seems inappropriate regardless of whether the water is heated because of the deliberate choice of the enemy or from a natural occurrence. The extent of the pain avoided, and not its source, should give rise to the excuse. If so, why does the criminal law make the excuse of duress available only when a person commits a crime in response to a human threat? Suppose that a person commits the same crime in order to avoid a comparable degree of pain not inflicted by a human being. Shipwrecked sailors and trapped miners should be excused on the ground of duress for committing what would otherwise be criminal acts.[66]

Suppose that the law of duress were expanded to include "threats" other than those from external agents. If so, should this defense be available to a defendant who has committed a crime in order to avoid the pain of withdrawal from an addictive drug? Consider an addict who is charged with the crime of possession and use of a controlled substance. He protests that the pain of withdrawal is too high a price to pay for conformity to law. Should this plea be recognized as a defense? Is the pain of withdrawal comparable to scalding water in the previous example, so that an addict should not be blamed for refusing to endure it? Or is there a moral basis for not excusing him?

At least three reasons not to excuse the addict might be given. First, one might reply that the addict is responsible for his own condition and that the excuse of duress should not be available in circumstances in which the defendant has culpably caused the predicament that leads to his need for a defense. Perhaps addicts should not be excused for their use of drugs when addiction was a foreseeable consequence of their earlier autonomous choices. Modern statutes typically withhold the defense of duress when "the actor recklessly placed himself in a situation in which it was probable that he would be subjected to duress."[67] If persons should not be excused for refusing to suffer pains they are culpable for having caused, even an extended principle of duress will not exempt addicts from blame for drug use.

A second reply is that the pain of withdrawal is not the only alternative to drug use for many addicts. The severe withdrawal symptoms of some drugs, most notably heroin, can be blocked by treatment, which typically requires administration of yet another addictive drug. If the severity of withdrawal can be lessened without resorting to further use of the drug, the desire to avoid such pain may not excuse subsequent episodes of drug use. The failure to pursue alternative means to avoid withdrawal might render continued drug use autonomous.

A third and final reply is that the pain of withdrawal is not sufficiently severe to function as an excuse. Adults of "reasonable firmness" can be required to suffer the hardships of withdrawal rather than to commit crimes in order to be spared them. Although no one should be expected to endure the agony of water that is nearly boiling, the pain of withdrawal from any existing drug is not at all comparable. The plausibility of this third response requires empirical data about the severity of withdrawal from various drugs.

How is it possible to measure the pain involved during withdrawal from drugs? One approach is to ask persons who use both legal and illegal drugs to compare and contrast the relative hardships of quitting. Many Americans have stopped smoking and appreciate the difficulties of overcoming their addictions to nicotine. In one study, 74 percent of persons who both smoked and used one or more illegal drugs, and who sought treatment for drug dependence, reported that cigarettes would be at least as hard to give up as the substance for which they sought treatment, whereas 57 percent said that cigarettes would be even harder to give up.[68] The authors of this study attributed skepticism about their results to the "exaggerated but popular notions of the addictiveness of heroin and other drugs."[69]

Comparisons with familiar hardships not involving drugs may help to gain a perspective on the severity of withdrawal. Consider heroin withdrawal, which involves notoriously severe symptoms. One author likens the pain of withdrawal from a bad case of heroin addiction to a one-week flu.[70] Herbert Fingaratte and Anne Hasse conclude that the "fatal flaw" in arguments that purport to show that "addictive conduct is legally involuntary" is "profound factual misapprehensions about the assumed horrors of withdrawal symptoms."[71] If they are correct, it seems unlikely that an expanded defense of duress should excuse addicts from drug use.

Courts have reached a similar conclusion. In *U.S. v. Moore*, the defendant challenged his conviction for heroin possession on the ground that his addiction rendered his conduct "nonvoluntary."[72] Without denying that voluntariness is a prerequisite of legal responsibility, the court rejected this plea on a number of grounds. In part, the court feared that an excuse for the crime of drug possession would be extended to include criminal behavior to procure drugs, such as robbery and burglary. But the court cited an additional ground that is more germane to the present issue. The court acknowledged "the appreciable number of narcotics 'addicts' who do abandon their habits permanently, and much larger number who reflect their capacity to refrain by ceasing use for varying periods of time."[73] The court found no reason to believe that those many addicts who had stopped using heroin possessed greater self-control or discipline than "a person of reasonable firmness." The court was not persuaded that the defendant was powerless to discontinue his use of drugs, when so many other addicts had managed to overcome their conditions. In so many words, the court held that the heroin addict uses drugs autonomously.

The following hypothetical should help to decide whether *Moore* was decided correctly. Suppose that a terrorist invented several "withdrawal pills" that caused persons to suffer symptoms identical to those experienced by addicts during withdrawal from various drugs. These symptoms included vomiting, diarrhea, chills, nausea, irritation, headache, and the like. The terrorist threatened to force a person to take one of these pills unless he committed a crime. Should the state allow the person who chose to commit the crime rather than to take the pill to be excused from criminal liability? Reasonable minds might answer this question differently. In part, the answer depends on the seriousness of the offense to be committed. But if the offense were sufficiently serious, our criminal justice system almost certainly would not recognize an excuse of duress. The "threat of unlawful force" required to excuse criminal behavior typically involves serious bodily injury. Persons of "reasonable firmness" should be required to endure lesser pains in order to remain law-abiding. The discomfort of withdrawal is not comparable to serious bodily injury. Thus the desirability of avoiding withdrawal should not be a defense from liability for many crimes, including, perhaps, the crime of drug use.

The use of illegal drugs to alleviate the symptoms of various diseases is seldom held to excuse such behavior. For example, patients who suffer from the chronic disease of scleroderma experience nausea, fatigue, loss of appetite, weight loss, diarrhea, constriction of the esophagus, extreme difficulty and pain in swallowing, painful joints, and great sensitivity to cold in their hands and feet. Many doctors believe that the use of marijuana will help to relieve these symptoms. However, courts typically affirm the convictions of persons who use marijuana for this purpose.[74] Courts would be expected to become more sympathetic as these pains increased in severity. At some point, defendants would have "no choice" but to resort to illegal drug use to avoid these symptoms.

If the pain of withdrawal from heroin addiction is insufficient to support the judgment that sustained heroin use is nonautonomous, the prospects for concluding that the continued use of other existing illegal drugs is nonautonomous are even more remote. No one has ever suggested that anyone uses marijuana to avoid the discomfort of withdrawal. The same is true of cocaine. Unquestionably, persons who use great quantities of cocaine for long periods of time experience unpleasant withdrawal symptoms when the drug becomes unavailable. According to one commentator,

> Researchers have identified a number of cocaine withdrawal reactions, including (1) apathy, depression, and exhaustion following short, high dosage binges; (2) agitated depression, lethargy, insomnia, and irritability following high dosage usage; (3) a marked psychological depression upon discontinuance and (4) a craving for cocaine, prolonged sleep, general fatigue, lassitude, hyperphagia, ... depression, and suppression of REM sleep after abrupt cessation of chronic administration.[75]

These experiences can hardly be described as agonizing and do not warrant the judgment that the sustained use of cocaine is nonautonomous. Withdrawal symptoms from cocaine addiction "fluctuate and are neither constant nor severe enough to meet psychiatric diagnostic criteria for major mood disorders."[76] Quite simply, users do not continue their involvement with cocaine primarily in order to avoid withdrawal.[77] If so, the case for supposing that cocaine users are powerless to stop, and that their continued use of cocaine is nonautonomous, is much weaker than for heroin addicts.

My position is easily misinterpreted. Many theorists hailed the discovery of withdrawal symptoms as evidence that cocaine is addictive, a conclusion that others dispute. Still others insist that the recent tendency to classify cocaine (and crack) as addictive is not based on new evidence about the drug, but results from ideological concerns. According to this school of thought, researchers who denied that cocaine is addictive were accused of being "soft on drugs," as though a denial that a drug is addictive is tantamount to condoning its use. Many researchers succumbed to political pressures by simply crafting a new and more expansive definition of addiction that applies to cocaine.[78]

Who is correct in this dispute? I am inclined to think that "a yes or no reply [to the question of whether cocaine is addictive] does not do justice to the tangle of medical definition, folk wisdom, legal classification and social recrimination that is summarized by the word 'addictive.' "[79] Fortunately, I need take no firm stance on this question. My interest is in the moral and legal uses of the concept of addiction. I have suggested that this concept might be employed in an argument to conclude that the persistent use of an addictive drug is nonautonomous because the pain of withdrawal might be so severe that users have "no choice" but to consume that drug repeatedly. This argument, however, fails on empirical grounds. Unless some basis other than the pain of withdrawal can be used to explain why addicts are powerless to stop, I conclude that their continued use of cocaine is autonomous. If the justifiability of a paternalistic interference requires that the choice of the agent is nonautonomous, users should not be prohibited from consuming cocaine for their own good.

It is time to take stock. The phenomenon of addiction seemed to provide a promising basis for differentiating recreational drug use from other risky activities that are not candidates for paternalistic intervention. The habitual behavior of persons who watch soap operas, it might be said, expresses autonomy, whereas the drug use of addicts does not. The greatest difficulty in developing this argument is to provide a reason to believe that the drug use of addicts is nonautonomous. The only criterion of addiction that arguably creates a basis for this judgment is that addicts are powerless to stop their drug use. The best reason to believe that addicts are powerless to stop using drugs is that they suffer from severe withdrawal symptoms when they try to quit. Persons might be deemed powerless to stop whatever behavior allows them to avoid extreme pain. Thus they might be said to be acting under an expanded rule of duress and to be behaving nonautonomously. But there are formidable difficulties in concluding that the desire to avoid withdrawal makes persistent drug use nonautonomous. Chief among these difficulties is that the pain of withdrawal from even the most highly addictive drugs is insufficient to support the judgment that the addict has no choice but to continue using drugs. Although hardly a paradigm of autonomous choice, the better argument supports the conclusion that addicts use drugs autonomously. If so, paternalistic interference with the use of addictive drugs cannot be defended in the name of autonomy.

At the same time, it is possible to describe how the use of a hypothetical drug by an addict would *not* be autonomous, so that paternalistic intervention might be justifiable. The pain of withdrawal from such a drug would have to be severe, roughly comparable to the bodily harm that results from scalding water. Addicts would not be culpable for becoming addicted, perhaps because they were forced to use the drug until they became powerless to resist, or because they had no reason to suspect that the drug possessed addictive properties. And no alternative preferable to drug use would be available to allow addicts to quit. If the use of this hypothetical drug exposed persons to substantial risks, paternalists would have good reason to prohibit it in the name of autonomy.

It is best not to be too dogmatic about whether such a drug actually exists. In any event, it is logically possible that such a drug might be created. I do not insist a priori that the repeated use of any conceivable drug is inevitably autonomous. Fortunately, however, I think it is unlikely that any existing drug satisfies this description.

ADDICTION, SLAVERY, AND AUTONOMY

Prohibitions of addictive substances that give rise to severe withdrawal symptoms are not the only instances in which philosophers have argued that the need to protect autonomy justifies paternalistic interference. John Stuart Mill denied that a voluntary agreement to sell oneself into slavery should be enforceable, because it would involve a total forfeiture of autonomy. Mill concluded that

> by selling himself for a slave, [the individual] abdicates his liberty. . . . He therefore defeats, in his own case, the very

purpose which is the justification of allowing him to dispose of himself. . . . The principle of freedom cannot require that he should be free not to be free. It is not freedom, to be allowed to alienate his freedom. These reasons, the force of which is so conspicuous in this peculiar case, are evidently of far wider application.[80]

Mill's example of voluntary slavery has generated far more theoretical discussion than is warranted by its practical significance. To the best of my knowledge, no one has ever attempted to enforce such a bizarre agreement. Yet this example is important because it is "of far wider application." Even the most confirmed critics of paternalism might balk at enforcing this agreement. If paternalistic interference with a voluntary choice is ever justified to protect autonomy, it is justified here.

For present purposes, voluntary slavery agreements are significant because of their alleged affinities with decisions to use addictive drugs. According to Goodin,

If the product is truly addictive, then we have no more reason to respect a person's voluntary choice (however well-informed) to abandon his future volition than we have for respecting a person's voluntary choice (however well-informed) to sell himself into slavery.[81]

Goodin concludes that the desirability of safeguarding autonomy provides no reason to protect either decision.

In this section I will argue that the case for prohibiting the use of addictive drugs is much weaker than the case for prohibiting voluntary slavery. If I am correct, those who are persuaded by Mill's example might still reject LAD, in virtue of their several differences. And those who are unpersuaded by Mill's example should be even more resistant to LAD.

It is helpful to make the examples that I will contrast more believable. First, suppose that a wealthy Legree offers Smith one million dollars to become his slave. Smith, a person of moderate means, is inclined to accept this offer because of his beneficence and generosity; he would like to provide a first-rate education and upscale life-style for each of his several children. If it is clear that Smith is sane and that his consent is truly voluntary, should the state prevent him from binding himself for his own good? The second example, to be contrasted with the first, is more familiar. Jones would like to use an addictive recreational drug. If he is sane and his consent is truly voluntary, should the state prevent him from using the drug for his own good?

Feinberg would not create an exception to his opposition to paternalism in the case of the voluntary slave. According to Feinberg, the fact that a voluntary decision to become a slave involves a permanent, irrevocable, and total forfeiture of autonomy is not a sufficient reason to prohibit it. He observes, "If one is not in principle 'free not to be free' then he does not enjoy de jure autonomy."[82] Analogously, the supposed loss of autonomy involved in addiction is not a sufficient reason to support LAD.

Feinberg may be correct. But I am less interested in addressing the more basic question of whether the law should enforce the agreement between Legree and Smith than in differentiating this issue from the justifiability of LAD. The point of this section is to describe both the conceptual and empirical differences between these two examples. I will argue that addiction and voluntary slavery seem comparable only when the addictive process is misdescribed. I will attempt to characterize what addiction would have to be like before the two examples become relevantly similar. In other words, I will attempt to identify the properties a drug would have to possess before the reasons to prohibit it are as strong as those against voluntary slavery. Alternatively, I will modify the slavery example to make it more like addiction. When the slavery example is modified in these respects, reservations about enforcing Smith's agreement are weakened. Whatever is said about the justifiability of preventing Smith from enslaving himself, I will conclude that the case against allowing Jones to use an addictive drug is much weaker.

Notice that this argument again presupposes that drugs are addictive in a sense in which other recreational activities

119

are not. Although a few other recreational activities are said to be addictive, they are never portrayed as reducing participants to a state of slavery. No one suggests that skiing should be prohibited because, if permitted, it would enslave many adults who tried it. Anyone who endorses this argument as a justification for LAD must describe what is unique about drug addiction that makes the slavery metaphor so compelling.

Feinberg notes two significant differences between the slavery example and *any* instance of criminal paternalism. First, the slavery example does not involve criminal penalties. Neither Smith nor Legree is punished for having made their agreement. Instead, the state simply refuses to enforce their promise in the event of a breach. Jones, in contrast, is punished for his choice. Surely a much higher standard of justification is required to warrant the use of the penal sanction than to make contractual remedies unavailable. Second, the failure of the state to enforce their agreement does not prevent either Smith or Legree from acting according to his preferences by establishing a de facto arrangement of slavery. Smith is free to obey Legree's orders, and Legree is free to command him. However, the state will not compel Smith to continue as a slave should he change his mind. Jones, in contrast, is prohibited by LAD from acting according to his preferences.

Other important differences between these two examples are not common to each instance of criminal paternalism. I will explore six of these differences at greater length. The first difference has already been discussed, and I will only summarize it here. Many of the evils of addiction that invite comparisons with slavery are a product of the illegality of drugs and not of their pharmacology. Persons addicted to illegal drugs deplete their bank accounts to pay for their supplies, go to extraordinary lengths to locate dealers, and avoid whatever medical treatment they might need for fear that their condition will come to the attention of authorities. If drugs were readily available, no one would think of addicts as enslaved to them.

The second significant difference between these examples is that the decision to sell oneself into voluntary slavery involves an *immediate* surrender of autonomy. In other words, autonomy is lost at the instant the agreement becomes effective. Smith is not given the opportunity to experiment with slavery for a while and postpone his final decision about whether to become enslaved. If Smith were afforded this opportunity, and allowed to enter into slavery gradually, there would be somewhat less reason not to enforce his agreement.

But addiction is not similarly instantaneous. Jones will not become addicted upon his initial use of a drug. This point is both conceptual and empirical. Many criteria of addiction (or of the "dependence syndrome") as construed in the preceding section cannot be satisfied by a single incidence of drug use. A drug user cannot "desire to stop drug use in the face of continued use," or display "a relatively stereotyped pattern of drug-taking behavior," or "[reinstate] the syndrome after a period of abstinence" by using a drug for the first time. A person might exhibit a few of the remaining criteria of addiction after a single exposure to a drug. Jones might immediately acquire a tolerance, afford drugs a psychological centrality relative to his other interests, or experience withdrawal after the effects of the drug recede. He would probably be unaware that he has developed a tolerance, or is prepared to make great sacrifices to obtain the drug again, or is undergoing withdrawal. Nonetheless, each of these criteria might be satisfied.

I have argued that most of the criteria of addiction that can be present after a single episode of drug use are irrelevant to the question of how the use of an addictive drug affects autonomy. The phenomena of tolerance and psychological dependence are not grounds for concluding that behavior is nonautonomous. However, there is no conceptual reason why the pain of withdrawal could not be so severe after a single incident that persons would be powerless to resist further use. If so, addiction would be immediate.

As a matter of fact, however, no existing recreational drug

creates such extreme withdrawal symptoms so quickly. I have already expressed doubts that withdrawal symptoms from drugs that have been used over long periods of time are sufficiently severe to warrant the judgment that continued use is nonautonomous. Withdrawal symptoms after a single episode of drug use are practically nonexistent. If a new drug were created that triggered terrible withdrawal symptoms after a single use, the case for prohibiting Jones from taking it would be comparable, ceteris paribus, to the case for not enforcing Smith's agreement. However, existing recreational drugs addict persons much more slowly.

Many persons try drugs and conclude that they do not want to try them again. Some persons do not enjoy their experience enough to repeat it. Others have satisfied their curiosity and have no further motive to persist. Still others abstain from additional experimentation because they enjoyed their initial exposure too much and do not want to run the risk of addiction. But whatever their motives for failing to continue, no comparable opportunity is available to Smith.

Goodin appears to recognize this difference between Jones's choice and Smith's agreement. He concedes that the initial decision of the recreational drug user might be autonomous. Subsequent decisions, however, are said not to be comparable. Goodin contends: "The real force of the addiction findings . . . is to undercut the claim that there is any *continuing* consent to the risks involved. . . . Once you were hooked, you lost the capacity to consent in any meaningful sense on a continuing basis."[83]

But Goodin has overlooked a crucial series of points. Admittedly, Smith and Jones are similarly situated at the time that they decide whether to take their initial steps. Suppose also that their positions are comparable after Smith has become enslaved and Jones has become "hooked." But what about the intermediary stages, when Jones decides whether to use a drug for a second, ninth, or twentieth time? Notice that the same question cannot be raised about Smith; there *are* no intermediary stages to examine. One simply cannot compare the beginning point, at which the agent contemplates becoming a slave or using an addictive substance, with the end point, at which he has become a slave or an addict, and conclude that there are no important differences between the two. The crucial difference is that there are any number of intermediate points in the drug example but not in the slavery case.

A third important difference between LAD and the prohibition of voluntary slavery is that Smith's decision is *irrevocable*. This fact is crucial to the unwillingness to enforce his promise. If Smith were able to reconsider his decision and resume a normal life, reservations about allowing him to be enslaved would all but vanish.

Addiction, however, can be temporary. Although addictions are notoriously difficult to break, persons can and do overcome them every day. Few individuals who are addicted to an illegal drug remain addicts for the duration of their lives. Many heroin addicts permanently give up heroin after a relatively brief period of addiction.[84] Even the most committed heroin users frequently "mature out" of addiction after a few years.[85] Many crack addicts quit because they do not want to lose their jobs, alienate their friends, neglect their children, or ruin their social status.[86]

The fact that many addicts "kick" their habits is well-known. Why, then, would anyone compare addiction to a permanent state of slavery? Perhaps there are misconceptions about the difficulty in overcoming addiction. It might be thought that just as slaves can be emancipated, so too can addiction be overcome, but only with the help of treatment.[87]

This preconception cannot withstand empirical scrutiny, however. Because of their concern with health, the importance of a personal relationship, or their perception that they have "hit bottom," large numbers of addicts succeed in quitting even the most addictive drugs. Many persons "revoke" their addiction without the benefit of a treatment program. "Spontaneous" recoveries from addiction to opiates, alcohol, tobacco, and cocaine are well documented.[88] Some of the more spectacular examples were provided by Vietnam War veterans who had been heroin addicts during the war. The vast majority of these addicts did not continue their use of heroin upon returning home, and only a handful required treatment to quit.[89] In addition, only a tiny percentage of hospital patients who regularly receive more powerful doses of opiates than those available on the streets ever become addicted or remain addicted after release.[90] Quite simply, addiction need not be a permanent condition.

A fourth important difference between slavery and addiction involves the probability of the undesirable outcome in each example. The use of addictive substances does not create a certainty of addiction. Many studies have shown that persons (sometimes called "chippers") are able to use addictive drugs over long periods of time in a controlled, non-abusive way, without ever becoming addicted.[91] Although the percentages differ for various drugs, most users of what are generally considered to be the most addictive and dangerous substances do not become addicts. A majority of the persons who have ever tried *any* illegal drug have stopped using it.[92] Perhaps these facts have not been widely publicized because of a fear that knowledge among prospective users would reduce their inhibitions against experimentation.[93]

Consider cocaine. Empirical studies indicate that most persons control their intake, using cocaine during leisure hours or on special occasions.[94] Statistics reinforce this finding. Few of the 21 to 25 million Americans who have tried cocaine have become addicts. Although 8 million people reported using cocaine at least once in 1988, only 862,000 used the drug at least once a week, and a mere 320,000 reported using it daily.[95] Thus, daily users of cocaine constitute less than 5 percent of all persons who use it annually and less than 2 percent of persons who have ever tried it. These are not the statistics one would expect if cocaine addicted everyone who sampled it.

These figures do not seem to differ radically when cocaine is smoked in the form of crack. According to one estimate, approximately one of every six persons who tries crack becomes a crack addict.[96] According to another survey, about

9 percent of current crack users (persons who have used crack in the last month) are heavy users (persons who have used crack twenty or more times in the last month).[97] Some theorists contend that at any given time about 10 percent of cocaine and heroin users can be classified as addicts, that is, about the same percentage as drinkers of alcohol who can be classified as alcoholics.[98] Nicotine is the drug with the highest percentage of current users who are addicts; the figure may be as high as 90 percent.[99] The exact ratio of addicts to users, however, is less important than the general conclusion to be drawn from this figure. The use of addictive recreational drugs creates only a possibility, not a probability, and clearly not a certainty, that addiction will result.

Mark Kleiman and Aaron Saiger reach a more pessimistic conclusion from these same data. They maintain that the ratio of one crack addict for every six users is "about as bad as it could be."[100] They reason that if the ratio were higher, fewer persons would experiment and run the risk of addiction; if the ratio were lower, crack would be less socially disruptive. But whether this figure is "as bad as it could be" depends on the argumentative purpose for which it is employed. A ratio of one to six is not so bad in the context of comparing crack use to slavery. The comparable ratio in the slavery example is six times worse: Every person who enters into a slavery agreement becomes enslaved. Smith's consent does not merely create a possibility that Legree will enslave him; it creates a certainty.

Opinions about the legitimacy of the slavery example might change if it were modified to reflect this fact. Suppose that Smith were offered one million dollars in exchange for a 5 percent or 10 percent chance that he would become enslaved. This gamble appears more rational, and less repugnant. I am unclear about whether this modification is persuasive in allowing Legree to enforce his agreement, but surely it is a relevant factor.

A fifth difference is that Smith's agreement subjects him to a *continuous* state of slavery. His status as a slave is uninterrupted. Had Smith negotiated permission from Legree to take several extended vacations, his agreement would seem less objectionable. He might have agreed to become a slave only on weekends or holidays, otherwise leading a relatively normal life. Again, I am unclear about how much of a difference this modification makes to the judgment about whether Smith's agreement should be enforceable, but I am confident that it has importance.

Addiction, by way of contrast, is seldom continuous. Heroin addicts commonly undergo periods of semivoluntary abstinence. Less than one-half of the addicts on the street for a year will have used an opiate daily throughout that period.[101] Sometimes addicts interrupt their heroin use to lower their tolerance, so that they can eventually resume consumption at a lower, cheaper, and more euphoric level.[102] This behavior has no analogue in the case of slavery.

A sixth and final difference between these two examples contrasts the plight of the slave with that of the addict. Slavery is a dreadful state. We are loathe to allow Legree to enslave Smith because we imagine that slavery may include torture, humiliation, and working conditions that no person should be made to endure. After all, Smith has given Legree carte blanche to subject him to every kind of indignity. If we could be assured that Legree's treatment of Smith would be humane, involving working conditions no more terrible than those in typical factories, we would become more willing to enforce their agreement.

Comparisons between addiction and enslavement to a sadistic Legree become apt only when the horrors of addiction are grossly exaggerated. The zombielike image of the addict has been perpetuated by our government. Time and time again, the judiciary has presented a parody of the drug addict.[103] Perhaps the most extreme example is the caricature described by Justice Douglas in 1962:

To be a confirmed drug addict is to be one of the walking dead.... The teeth have rotted out; the appetite is lost and the stomach and intestines don't function properly.... Good traits of character disappear and bad ones emerge. Sex organs become affected. Veins collapse and livid purplish scars remain. Boils and abscesses plague the skin; gnawing pain racks the body. Nerves snap; vicious twitching develops. Imaginary and fantastic fears blight the mind and sometimes complete insanity results. Often times, too, death comes – much too early in life. . . . Such is the torment of being a drug addict; such is the plague of being one of the walking dead.[104]

Small wonder that the Court concluded that punishment for such a condition was tantamount to punishment for a disease and thus was unconstitutional according to the Eighth Amendment's prohibition of cruel and unusual punishment. If typical cases of drug addiction conformed to this pathetic description, sympathies for paternalistic restrictions on drug use would be overwhelming.

Media portrayals of heavy drug users reinforce this dreadful stereotype. Television and movie depictions of recreational drug use follow a predictable script. Users initially believe that drugs are "cool," are confident that they can quit anytime, become helplessly addicted, squander their fortunes, turn to crime, abandon their loved ones, and either die a miserable death or are miraculously saved by heroic efforts. These case histories exist. But no effort is made to inform the public that these scenarios are atypical. No media exposure is afforded to moderate, successful, long-term drug users.[105] This media bias is not inadvertent. Lorne Michaels, the producer of the irreverent "Saturday Night Live," admits that "the policy of NBC now is that the only references to drugs must be negative."[106]

Even so, the public has ample reason to abandon this exaggerated stereotype of drug addiction. Many professional athletes have been exposed as drug addicts, and few remind anyone of a zombie. No one can know whether George Rogers was realizing his full potential during the football season in which his staggering cocaine habit came to the attention of the press. But his opponents did not confuse him with one of the walking dead while Rogers led the National Football League in rushing that year.[107]

Empirical research simply does not support this terrible stereotype of drug addiction. Most drug addicts lead relatively normal lives. According to the U.S. Department of Labor, 77 percent of "serious cocaine users" are regularly employed.[108] Bennett has cited this statistic to urge business leaders to join the "front" in the "fight" against drugs.[109] But this statistic can also be used to undermine the dreadful portrayal of drug addiction. It is hard to imagine how the caricature of the drug addict described by Justice Douglas could be gainfully employed.

Despite these six important differences between drug use and slavery, one remaining dissimilarity between Jones's use of an addictive drug and Smith's attempt to enslave himself seems to provide a better reason to oppose the former than the latter. Smith, it will be recalled, gains one million dollars if he is allowed to act according to his preference. Everyone should understand why he is at least tempted by Legree's offer. But what has Jones gained of comparable value? A new pleasurable experience? Is this trivial gain sufficient to run the risk of addiction?

These questions illustrate the importance of the earlier distinction between formal and substantive conceptions of autonomy. Much of the point of opposing paternalism is to prevent the state, through the coercive apparatus of the criminal law, from deciding what persons should value. Jones, like Smith, would prefer to be free to decide for himself whether the prospective gains of his choice outweigh its disadvantages. Suppose that the original slavery example is altered so that Smith's family is not rewarded in exchange for Smith's agreement to become enslaved. Instead, Smith attempts to enslave himself to express his unbounded loyalty to Legree. To what extent is this modification significant? Once it is clear that Smith is sane and his agreement is voluntary, I doubt that the details of his motive should matter much in deciding whether the state should allow him to be bound by his agreement.

If the examples of Smith and Jones are really as dissimilar as I have indicated, why has drug addiction been misleadingly portrayed as an immediate, irrevocable, certain, continuous, and awful state? No single answer is satisfactory. The entire field of drug research has frequently subordinated scientific objectivity to political agendas in the effort to prove preconceived biases and justify punitive responses.[110] In addition, the nonusing public, health care professionals, and law enforcement officials gain most of their experience with drug use by dealing with worst-case scenarios. Addicts who do not conform to this extreme stereotype are less likely to come to the attention of health practitioners or police, and they are rarely identified as heavy drug users by ordinary citizens. Studies of drug addicts have tended to focus on persons with the greatest problems. Because of the tremendous stigma associated with drug use, addicts who depart from this worst-case scenario are inhibited from discussing how their experience with drugs may have been favorable.

The contrasts between the addiction and slavery examples indicate the several respects in which decisions about the justifiability of LAD require sensitivity to the delicate process of drawing lines. Several questions are unresolved. How quickly must withdrawal symptoms become severe before a given drug should be prohibited? What percentage of addicts must be unable to overcome their addictions before a drug should be banned? How many users of an addictive substance must become addicts before criminal penalties are justifiable? To what extent must addiction to a drug be continuous before its use is outlawed? How terrible must addiction be before it is so bad that persons should be protected from it? I have no precise answers. These questions identify what pharmacological and sociological evidence about drugs and drug users is relevant to issues about moral rights.

No drug prohibitionist has indicated, to my knowledge, that any of these issues is important to the case in favor of LAD. It would be too charitable to conclude that the prohibitionists' thinking about LAD fails to take moral rights seriously. More accurately, their thinking about LAD fails to take account of moral rights at all.

I have argued that any support for LAD drawn from comparisons between addiction and slavery depends on controversial empirical assumptions that are seldom articulated and generalizes from worst-case scenarios that fail to conform to the reality of typical drug use. Even if the autonomy principle does not protect an adult's "freedom to be unfree," the attempt to exempt drug use from the scope of the principle of autonomy by regarding it as a form of slavery is a gross distortion. The genuine struggles of real slaves throughout history are demeaned by this comparison.

"SOFT" PATERNALISM AND DRUG USE

Under what conditions should a nonconsequentialist who countenances a principle of autonomy that applies to and protects recreational drug use allow interference on paternalistic grounds? One reasonable answer, given by Feinberg, is that "the state has the right to prevent self-regarding harmful conduct *when but only when* that conduct is substantially nonvoluntary."[111] He labels this position "soft" paternalism. Feinberg contends that an agent's apparent choice is not truly *his* if it is nonvoluntary, so interference with it would not violate his autonomy.

Again, two variations of this basic idea are possible. Perhaps (a) autonomy does not protect nonvoluntary choices at all, or (b) autonomy protects nonvoluntary choices to some extent, but whatever protection it affords is subject to being overridden by competing moral considerations. But specifying the precise relationship between nonvoluntariness and autonomy is less important than recognizing that paternalistic interference is more easily justifiable when conduct harmful to oneself is nonvoluntary.

When is conduct voluntary? Feinberg recognizes that any number of existing models of voluntariness are unhelpful and unrealistic, creating an "impossibly difficult ideal standard, one that would hardly ever be satisfied" in the real world.[112] He contends that a choice is *fully* voluntary "only when [it is made by] a competent and unimpaired adult who has not been threatened, misled, or lied to about relevant facts, nor manipulated by subtle forms of conditioning."[113] But few decisions are the product of such dispassionate, fully informed, rational calculation; they do not conform to this conception of "perfect voluntariness." However, they are not completely nonvoluntary. Feinberg's model of voluntariness is responsive to this fact. He construes voluntariness as a " 'variable concept,' determined by higher and lower cut-off points depending on the nature of the circumstances, the interests at stake, and the moral or legal purpose to be served."[114] Feinberg provides his most detailed discussion of recreational drug use in applying these insights about the "variability" of the concept of voluntariness.

Feinberg describes three scenarios in which Mr. Roe discusses with Dr. Doe his decision to use a dangerous recreational drug called x. In the first example, Roe mistakenly believes that x does not cause him harm. Feinberg concludes that Roe's decision to use x is substantially nonvoluntary, because he does not intend to ingest a substance that will in fact harm him. In the second example, Roe is aware that x is harmful but indicates that he actually intends to harm himself. Feinberg concludes that Roe's odd decision may be nonvoluntary; perhaps Roe has lost the full use of his faculties. However, if further examination does not reveal independent evidence of incapacitation, Roe should be allowed to proceed. In the third and final example, Roe understands the risks of x, has no desire to harm himself, but states: "I don't care if it causes me physical harm. I'll get a lot of pleasure first, so much pleasure in fact, that it is well worth the risk."[115] Feinberg concludes that this case is "easy,"[116] and he is right. There is no reason to believe Roe's decision is nonvoluntary; an interference with his choice would involve "hard" paternalism. If hard paternalism is unjustified, the state should not interfere with Roe's decision.

Feinberg's imaginary conversations between Mr. Roe and Dr. Doe provide valuable insights into the permissibility of paternalism in personal relationships. However, how can they advance our understanding of when legislation is warranted? Statutes cannot be individualized. A defense of paternalism in personal relationships is not easily translated into a defense of paternalistic legislation. Dr. Doe can inquire about *why* Roe decides to engage in risky behavior, and he can assess whether Roe's answer betrays evidence of nonvoluntariness. But the state can hardly engage in a private dialogue with each of its citizens. Feinberg acknowledges that the law must be couched in general terms,[117] but he fails to explain how this concession makes it feasible to apply his hypothetical conversations to arguments for or against LAD.

How might this bridge be crossed? It is tempting to believe that the law, necessarily expressed in general terms, should be responsive to the most common, typical reason why persons assume risks. If so, it is crucial to notice that the overwhelming majority of recreational drug use among adults corresponds most closely to Feinberg's third example. Rarely do persons take drugs for the purpose of harming themselves, so Feinberg's second scenario has little application to LAD. But how about his first scenario? How informed are persons about the hazards of drug use?

This question cannot be answered without identifying the kinds of misconceptions that defeat voluntariness and allow interference. At one extreme, Roe might believe that a substance is something other than what it is. Clearly, interference is permissible if it is the only means to prevent someone from consuming cocaine that is mistakenly believed to be sugar. Decriminalization will minimize this kind of possibility. In today's black market, consumers are unlikely to receive accurate information about the content of their purchases. Legalization would increase the probability that given instances of recreational drug use would resemble Feinberg's third scenario more closely than his first.

What about less extreme kinds of mistakes? Suppose that users know what substance they are consuming but are unaware that it poses a health risk. Fortunately, such cases are relatively rare. Most adults know that drug use may be harmful. Why else would they think that illegal drugs are prohibited? And they are not especially inclined to think that legal drugs would be criminalized unless they were relatively safe. In a recent poll, only 24 percent of heavy smokers claimed to be unaware, or not to believe, that smoking is hazardous to health.[118]

Even those few adult drug users who act *in* ignorance seldom act *from* ignorance. In other words, more accurate information is unlikely to change their behavior. Studies testing the effectiveness of educational programs for adolescents support this conclusion. Efforts to present factual information about the risks of specific substances

> do not reduce or prevent substance use. . . . Increased knowledge has virtually no impact on substance use or on intentions to engage in tobacco, alcohol, or drug use in the near future. There is even some evidence that this approach may lead to increased usage, possibly because it may serve to stimulate adolescents' curiosity.[119]

Drug prohibitionists agree that lack of information is not at the heart of the problem. As Bennett has stated: "If ignorance is the problem, knowledge is the cure. I don't believe that for a large number of kids out there who use drugs, that ignorance is the problem."[120] What is likely to be true of "kids" is even more likely to be true of adults.

To be sure, adult users of both legal and illegal drugs are unable to be very precise about the kinds of risks they confront. Few smokers are aware that their use of nicotine increases the incidence of Buerger's disease, which can require the amputation of limbs.[121] To what extent does this lack of specific, detailed information make their decisions nonvoluntary? Probably very little. Adults who would like to engage in a recreational activity need not be able to identify the exact nature of its risks before they should be allowed to proceed. Such a strong requirement would prohibit a great many risky activities that are not candidates for paternalistic interference. No one would conclude that football is substantially nonvoluntary because players are unable to accu-

rately estimate the likelihood of injuries to the head, as contrasted with those to the knee. Why should more specific
information be required about the dangers of recreational
drugs, as long as users are generally aware that they are
harmful?

Perhaps adults who use drugs recreationally need not be
able to specify the *kinds* of risks they confront. But if they
were woefully misinformed about the *magnitude* of these
risks, their decisions might be sufficiently nonvoluntary to
justify paternalistic intervention. Someone who believes that
smoking only slightly increases the probability of lung cancer
might not be said to assume this risk voluntarily. However,
this basis for deeming conduct nonvoluntary and eligible for
paternalistic interference is not promising for supporters of
LAD. Studies show that the less people know about the
effects of recreational drugs, the more dangerous they consider them to be.[122] Drug prohibitionists have even used these
studies as an argument against introducing drug education
in schools.[123]

Mere knowledge of a risk may not suffice to show that
persons assume it voluntarily. Agents who are able to recite
with tolerable accuracy the facts about the dangers of drugs
might resort to any number of psychological ploys to conclude that their own use of drugs is safe. An individual may
succumb to "wishful thinking," or to the notorious "it can't
happen to me" syndrome. Or the user may be too inclined
to generalize from personal experience: "Drugs haven't
harmed me yet, so they must be safe." Or the individual
may employ "time discounting," supposing that distant dangers are less worrisome than immediate hazards. Goodin
concludes that these "relatively weak forms of irrationality"
justify intervention with decisions that are "far-reaching, potentially life-threatening, and irreversible."[124] Yet this rationale for interference would open a far wider door to
paternalism than almost anyone should accept. Many dangerous recreational activities expose persons to "far-
reaching," "life-threatening," and "irreversible" risks. Persons who climb mountains or hang glide do not believe that

134

they will become fatalities. "Relatively weak" irrationality is a very dubious basis for prohibiting adults from acting for their own good.

A majority of adult Americans who consume drugs probably do so "substantially voluntarily." They are sufficiently aware of the nature and magnitude of the dangers they confront that soft paternalists should be reluctant to intervene. They are no more susceptible to various forms of "weak irrationality" than persons who take other risks. Many use drugs for the same reason that they eat ice cream or ride motorcycles. They believe that the likelihood of immediate pleasure outweighs the risk of eventual harm. In other words, their recreational drug use conforms to Feinberg's third scenario.

Still, a minority of adult users are uniformed about the risks of drugs. A subset of these persons act from ignorance and would desist if they knew the relevant facts. Their use of recreational drugs fails to satisfy whatever criteria of voluntariness are required. If these adults cannot be made to believe the truth about the hazards of drug use, their moral autonomy might not be violated by interfering with their liberty. A friend or relative, aware of their ignorance, might be in an ideal position to intervene.

How should legal policy respond to the fact that a few drug users are in this predicament? Everyone agrees that better education is desirable, but what should be done in the meantime? As I have indicated, decriminalization theorists believe that the repeal of LAD is the best solution. Warnings stronger than those currently appearing on tobacco products could be required on packages containing legalized drugs.[125] These warnings may or may not deter use, but at least consumers would be better informed.

The important point is that the extent of ignorance among users provides a flimsy rationale for prohibiting recreational drug use altogether. It seems preposterous to proscribe drugs for the majority because a minority are unaware of, or cannot be made to appreciate, the risks. To base legal policy on this minority is to generalize yet again from a "worst-case scenario." If I am correct that the overwhelming majority of recreational drug use corresponds most closely to Feinberg's third example, which represents an "easy" case, there is little reason to believe that drug consumption is nonvoluntary, so that interference can be justified by a soft paternalist rationale.

A consistent nonconsequentialist should not, however, base legal policy on the most frequent, typical reason that individuals run given risks. It is crucial to realize that generalizations from any particular scenario, worst case or otherwise, are incompatible with a commitment to preserve the moral autonomy of persons. Consequentialists encounter well-known difficulties in protecting individual rights, since they allow increases in the welfare of some to compensate for losses in the welfare of others. But these sorts of trade-offs are all but alien to a nonconsequentialist moral perspective that takes seriously a commitment to personal autonomy. The fear that some, or even most, adults will use a drug nonvoluntarily is simply not a persuasive reason to withhold it from others whose use is voluntarily. For this reason, utilitarians should be more likely than nonconsequentialists to favor LAD. Arguments in support of LAD are much more compelling in a utilitarian framework that downplays the significance of moral rights and allows the good of some to be enhanced by sacrificing the moral autonomy of others.

Yet almost certainly there is some point at which a recreational drug should be made unavailable to one adult because another will consume it nonvoluntarily. It is here that personal autonomy should be compromised for the sake of utilitarian objectives. In order to keep this problem in its proper perspective, it should be noticed that the difficulty of locating a similar kind of threshold is common to any number of debates about both paternalistic and nonpaternalistic legislation. For example, some theorists have argued that the state should ban pornography altogether, because a given percentage of individuals will be more inclined to commit sex crimes after being exposed to it. How high must this percentage be in order to justify a complete prohibition of pornography? No general answer seems possible. Liberal and conservative legal philosophies differ radically in locating the point at which individual liberties should yield to the general interest. This point will become more distant to the extent that personal autonomy and moral rights are valued.

I suggested in Chapter 1 that issues surrounding the recreational use of drugs may be different from those involving the medical use of drugs. One such difference is that soft paternalists will generally have less reason to prohibit recreational drugs than medical drugs of dubious efficacy. Consider the debate about whether cancer patients should have access to laetrile, despite FDA findings that laetrile is unhelpful and perhaps harmful. Here the desperate patient is simply wrong about the factual characteristics of the drug. The medical profession possesses genuine expertise about such matters. The patient's case corresponds most closely to the first of Feinberg's three conversations between Roe and Dr. Doe. The consumer is misinformed about whether the drug has the causal properties that motivate him to use it. According to Tal Scriven, "The patient's appeal to the principle of autonomy in . . . cases of ineffective drug usage seems to amount to nothing but an appeal to the right to be wrong which is no right at all."[126] Since cancer patients who seek access to laetrile are mistaken about its causal properties, prohibitions do not violate their autonomy.

But adult recreational drug users are much less likely to make this kind of factual mistake. They are almost certain to be reasonably aware that taking the drug includes some risk of harm, but they are prepared to undertake this risk for the sake of the short-term pleasure they are relatively confident will result. Surely the medical profession has little expertise about whether the recreational drug user will derive immediate gratification from the experience. The disagreement between recreational drug users and supporters of LAD is not about facts, but about priorities. Opponents of paternalism have frequently sounded the alarm about exactly this rationale for interference.

"HARD" PATERNALISM AND DRUG USE

Not all philosophers agree that only "soft" paternalism can be justified. Some embrace a wider scope of paternalism and permit interference with voluntary choices. It is important to determine whether their willingness to allow "hard" paternalism is defensible in general, and, if so, whether it warrants the state in enacting LAD.

The most thoughtful defense of "hard" paternalism has been proposed by John Kleinig.[127] He notes, quite correctly, that "our lives do not always display the cohesion and maturity of purpose that exemplifies the liberal ideal of individuality, but instead manifest a carelessness, unreflectiveness, shortsightedness, or foolishness that . . . represents a departure from some of our own more permanent and central commitments and dispositions."[128] In light of this phenomenon, Kleinig cautiously endorses what he calls "the Argument from Personal Integrity":

> Where our conduct or choices place our more permanent, stable, and central projects in jeopardy, and where what comes to expression in this conduct or these choices manifests aspects of our personality that do not rank highly in our constellation of desires, dispositions, etc., benevolent interference will constitute no violation of integrity. Indeed, if anything, it helps to preserve it.[129]

Thus paternalistic interferences with the purely voluntary choices of adults are sometimes permissible.

Kleinig's "Argument from Personal Integrity" improves upon the earlier attempt to justify paternalism by reference to the psychological dependence of addicts. According to the version of this argument that I have discredited, the evidence that users are in need of intervention is that they care more about drugs than the paternalist believes is good for them. Thus paternalists substitute their own priorities for those of the drug user. Kleinig's limited defense of hard paternalism is more sophisticated than this crude account. He would authorize interference only when drug use is incompatible with the "more permanent, stable, and central projects" as acknowledged by the users themselves. Kleinig would restrain only those users who lament their inability to pursue projects *they* deem more important. Only then would interference be justified.

Although Kleinig himself does not relate his concern for personal integrity to the principles of autonomy or freedom, it is easy to do so. Dworkin and Frankfurt emphasize the importance of maintaining a congruity between first- and second-order preferences and desires. If an adult wants to use drugs, but also wants not to want to use drugs, his consumption of drugs might be said to be nonautonomous and unfree. His drug use might be nonautonomous and unfree not because others believe it is bad for him, but because it conflicts with his own second-order preferences.

Despite its appeal, this narrow defense of paternalism is highly controversial. Those who resist hard paternalism would object that it threatens to undermine personal integrity, the very value it is designed to protect. It is exceedingly difficult, even in personal relationships, to correctly distinguish "more permanent, stable, and central projects" from those that are less significant to the agent overall. Any procedure to allow interference under this rationale would be susceptible to extraordinary abuse and mistake. Despite these difficulties, I will tentatively accept Kleinig's strategy as sound and attempt to assess its implications for LAD.

Several familiar problems resurface in attempts to identify these implications. First, consider why the user does not simply remove the discrepancy between his first- and second-order desires by discontinuing his use of recreational drugs. Presumably he fails to quit because he is unable to bring his first-order desires into conformity with his more permanent, stable, and central projects. But why is he unable rather than merely unwilling to do so? His rational faculty must be intact, or he would not have noticed the discrepancy in the first place. The best reason for believing he is unable to quit is that the pain of withdrawal is too severe. But this answer resurrects an earlier argument, and the current version of it fares no better than its predecessor. The pain of withdrawal from existing recreational drugs is not so severe that adults cannot be expected to endure it. Unless some other reason explains why the drug user does not bring his behavior into conformity with his second-order desires, this argument fails to justify paternalistic intervention.

In addition, no general law can be warranted under this limited concession to hard paternalism. It is telling that Kleinig does not provide a single example of legislation that he believes his principle would justify. Should the legislator generalize from the "standard" case? The projects deemed worthy, the importance attached to them, and the extent to which drug use interferes with their pursuit vary so radically from individual to individual that no generalization seems possible. Only a subset of users will acknowledge that recreational drugs interfere with their more significant goals and plans. The promising lives of some people are ruined by drugs; the lives of others are not hampered in any apparent way; the lives of still others are enriched. The same can be said about virtually any other recreational activity. Most of these pursuits do not promote an adult's more important interests. They are, after all, recreational. But few of these activities interfere with an adult's more significant interests, except in the trivial sense that they allow less time and money for central projects.

Moreover, the supposition that the use of recreational drugs interferes with the projects of many individuals, perhaps even a majority, is not a good reason to withhold them from adults whose projects are not hampered by drug use. A legal philosophy that respects rights and autonomy will be reluctant to allow gains for some to justify prohibitions for others whose good is not enhanced. Only utilitarians who allow such trade-offs can be comfortable about translating their concern for personal integrity into an argument for LAD.

Finally, the interest in preserving personal integrity does not support the heavy hand of criminal legislation. By hypothesis, the objective of the paternalist who strives to protect integrity is to help persons who are aware that their preoccupation with drugs interferes with their more important projects. What response to these persons is most likely to achieve this goal? It is hard to see how punishment could be more effective than treatment. Punishment cannot be commended to drug users as a device that will not disrupt their projects. Treatment is less disruptive, and is more likely to be effective, for those users who genuinely want to quit. A concern for personal integrity provides an excellent reason to make treatment rather than punishment available to persons who acknowledge their desire to stop using recreational drugs.

I conclude that Kleinig's limited concession to hard paternalism offers little support for LAD. Of course, other hard paternalist strategies might succeed where Kleinig's has failed. I cannot anticipate and respond to every argument that might be offered on behalf of LAD. Nevertheless, I hope it is clear just how strong and open-ended a hard paternalist rationale would have to be in order to justify LAD. Any such rationale, I suspect, would prove far too much and would justify a wider range of paternalistic interferences over individual liberty than should be tolerated by anyone who is concerned to respect rights and to protect autonomy. Unless some other plausible basis for interfering with voluntary choices can be defended, the prospects for constructing a hard paternalist rationale for criminal laws against recreational drug use appear bleak.

CONCLUSION

I have described the formidable difficulties with attempts to provide a paternalistic justification for laws prohibiting adults from using recreational drugs. Here I will summarize what I take to be the greatest weaknesses of my position. Since so much of my argument depends on empirical claims, I will conclude by briefly describing what possible facts about drugs and drug users would support LAD.

One reason to deny that adults have a moral right to use recreational drugs is that the principle of autonomy does not apply to or protect any recreational activity. According to this school of thought, no one has a right to play baseball, ski, or participate in any nonprofessional sport. Persons are morally permitted to engage in recreational pursuits only as long as consequentialist considerations allow them to do so. But as soon as a net balance of disutility is caused by a given recreational activity, the state would have the authority to prohibit it without infringing moral rights.

Needless to say, this option will strike many philosophers as counterintuitive. A more promising strategy is to attempt to differentiate between recreational activities that are and are not protected by the principle of autonomy. A second variation of this strategy is to endeavor to explain whether and under what circumstances any protection the principle of autonomy affords to recreational pursuits is overridden by a more weighty moral consideration. I have described four reasons to suspect that recreational drug use in particular might turn out to be undeserving of protection.

The first reason is that many drugs are addictive. When addicts lose their power to quit, their continued use of drugs might become nonautonomous. I have tried to describe what addiction would have to be like before addicts could be said to be powerless to stop using drugs. The pain of withdrawal would have to be very severe. Unless withdrawal symptoms were unbearable, I see little reason to believe that addicts are powerless to stop using drugs. I doubt that any existing recreational drug gives rise to sufficiently severe withdrawal symptoms to render continued use nonautonomous, but perhaps I am wrong about this (mostly) empirical question.

A second reason to believe that drug use is nonautonomous is that it leads to a condition comparable to slavery.

Perhaps the principle of autonomy does not protect decisions that result in a total forfeiture of autonomy. The comparison between addiction and slavery would be compelling only if addiction were an immediate, irrevocable, certain, continuous, and terrible state. This horrendous description is not satisfied by addiction to any existing drug. Again, I might be mistaken about this (mostly) empirical question.

A third reason to believe that recreational drug use is nonautonomous is that persons tend to be uninformed about the harmful properties of the drugs they consume. If they lack sufficient information about what they are doing, they cannot be said to be acting fully voluntarily, and their behavior is subject to interference according to a rationale of "soft" paternalism. Reasonable minds might differ about how much knowledge is required before the choices of adults are sufficiently voluntary to preclude interference on paternalistic grounds. Still, there is little evidence that adults are ignorant of the nature or magnitude of the risks they confront by using drugs recreationally. Further empirical research might indicate yet again that I am mistaken about the extent of information possessed by drug users.

Finally, recreational drug use may be undeserving of protection according to a plausible version of "hard" paternalism. Perhaps many heavy users recognize that drugs interfere with their more important projects. These adults may be unable to conform their first-order desires to their second-order preferences. Among other difficulties, this argument provides a better reason to treat than to punish those persons who appreciate that they have assigned recreational drug use too high a priority in their lives.

If the principle of autonomy does not apply to and protect recreational drug use, or if its protection is ultimately outweighed, adults lack a moral right to use recreational drugs. It does not follow, of course, that LAD is justified. Utilitarian considerations justify criminal prohibitions for that sphere of conduct unprotected by a moral right. However, the utilitarian case in favor of LAD must be defended rather than merely assumed. Decriminalization theorists have presented powerful challenges to this assumption, which I will explore more fully in Chapter 3.

I conclude that a paternalistic defense of LAD is unimpressive. Perhaps greater support for LAD is forthcoming from the need to protect nonusers from the harm that recreational drug use causes to them.

Chapter 3

Drugs and harm to others

I have described several difficulties that plague attempts to justify criminal laws against the recreational use of drugs (LAD) on paternalistic grounds, that is, because drugs are harmful to adults who use them. Some philosophers will have become impatient with this extended discussion. They may regard paternalistic arguments on behalf of LAD as quite beside the point. They may have little sympathy for paternalism in general, especially when it is "strong." Even if they tolerate a limited extent of paternalism, I hope to have shown that a paternalistic defense of LAD is not compelling. Many philosophers believe that a more plausible justification for LAD is that the recreational use of drugs is harmful to others, that is, to nonusers. They will insist that the main defect with my attempt to draw analogies between drug use and other dangerous recreational pursuits such as skiing and mountain climbing is that these latter activities pose insignificant risks of harm to nonparticipants. In this chapter, I will explore this rationale for total prohibition of the recreational use of drugs by adults.

The "harm principle," as it has come to be called, enjoys a privileged status in criminal law theory. Unlike paternalists, defenders of the harm principle need not struggle with the legitimacy of their rationale for legal intervention. No one (except anarchists) doubts that the criminal law should prohibit persons from causing harm to others. Instead, controversy centers on three questions. First, is the harm principle the only basis for justified criminal legislation? Second, is the prevention of harm to others a sufficient condition for criminal liability? Third, how should the harm principle be interpreted and applied to particular cases? I will confine most of my attention in this chapter to the second and third of these questions. I have sought to discredit a paternalistic defense of LAD, and, although I will refer to alternatives from time to time, no other rationale offers any reasonable prospects for success.

It is surprisingly difficult to find a single, comprehensive statement of the various harms to others that might justify LAD. No one source has become the authoritative defense of drug prohibitions. William Bennett provides a partial summary of many of the social evils allegedly caused by recreational drug use: "Drug users make inattentive parents, bad neighbors, poor students, and unreliable employees – quite apart from their common involvement in criminal activity."[1] James Q. Wilson offers a similar but more detailed account. He contends that even if we concede that the state

> should only regulate behavior that hurts other people, we would still have to decide what to do about drug-dependent people because such dependency does in fact hurt other people. . . . These users are not likely to be healthy people, productive workers, good parents, reliable neighbors, attentive students, or safe drivers. Moreover, some people are directly harmed by drugs that they have not freely chosen to use. The babies of drug-dependent women suffer because of their mothers' habits. We all pay for drug abuse in lowered productivity, more accidents, higher insurance premiums, bigger welfare costs, and less effective classrooms.[2]

Throughout this chapter, I will add to this litany of evils said to be caused by the use of drugs. One commentator or another has attributed virtually every social problem in America to drug use.

The decriminalization theorists I mentioned in Chapter 1 typically respond to these charges by countering that most of the evils linked to recreational drug use are actually products of drug prohibition. I briefly recounted fifteen of their

objections to the war on drugs, and I will return to some of
their criticisms later. Any reasonable person would find several of their objections to be impressive.

Nonetheless, many of the problems said to be caused by
drug use cannot plausibly be blamed on drug laws. John
Lawn replies: "Legalization theory . . . misses the point.
Drugs themselves, not drug laws, cause the most damage to
society. As I have said many times, drugs are not bad because
they are illegal, they are illegal because they are bad."[3] If
Lawn is correct, and recreational drugs cause even a small
fraction of the evils that have been attributed to them, how
can they be tolerated by a state that cares about the welfare
of its citizens? Surely recreational drug use should be curbed
by invoking the criminal sanction, the most powerful weapon
in the state arsenal.

Despite these allegations, I will conclude that the harm
principle fares no better than its paternalistic predecessor in
justifying LAD in its full generality. In Chapter 4 I will describe circumstances in which the need to prevent harm to
others justifies restrictions on the recreational use of drugs.
But the scope of criminal legislation I will defend falls far
short of the broad, categorical prohibition of illegal drug use
effective throughout America today. In this chapter, I will
show how little support for LAD derives from the need to
protect nonusers from the harm drug users cause to them.

UTILITARIANISM AND DRUG USE

As I have indicated, the overwhelming majority of theorists who have examined proposals to decriminalize the recreational use of drugs have been utilitarians. I presented
several reasons in Chapter 2 to reject consequentialist attempts to defend LAD on the ground that drug prohibition
prevents harm to adult drug users. Real utilitarians, of
course, would not adopt so narrow a focus. They would
assesses the justifiability of LAD by examining its consequences on users and nonusers alike. John Kaplan's approach exemplifies this tendency. He maintains that the case

for or against decriminalization "boils down to a careful weighing of the costs of criminalizing each drug against the public-health costs we would expect if that drug were to become legally available."[4] In this section, I will discuss the prospects for invoking this rationale to support LAD.

I have already suggested that the application of a utilitarian analysis to the issue of decriminalization begs the question against theorists who countenance a moral right to use drugs recreationally. When rights are at stake, ordinary utilitarian arguments are out of court. For example, the case for or against allowing persons to burn the American flag does not depend on predictions about how much disutility would result if flag burners were unpunished. Anyone who is convinced that flag burning is a protected form of expression should not budge from this belief by becoming persuaded that such acts will cause disutility unless they are prohibited. It is a sad testimony to the grip of utilitarian thinking that both scholarly and public opinion about the justifiability of LAD depend almost entirely on predictions about the social consequences of its repeal.

In this respect, the debate about drug policy contrasts sharply with many others. Consider the controversy about gun control. Regardless of however many regulations one ultimately believes should be imposed on gun ownership – from a total ban to no restrictions whatever – those persons who refuse to cast this issue in cost-benefit terms cannot be ignored. The controversy is not simply about whether a proposed regulation would promote utility. Arguably, the controversy also involves civil liberties and rights. Responsible gun owners who do not pose an unreasonable risk of harm to themselves or to others, and who intend to use their weapons only for recreation or for justified self-defense, are at least owed a reply by those who would take their guns away in order to prevent others from using their own weapons unlawfully. Perhaps moral rights are not involved in gun ownership at all, or perhaps any rights that are involved are overridden by the utilitarian goals that stringent regulation would achieve. But these conclusions must be defended, not assumed.[5] However, the parallel questions about illegal drug use are almost never raised. No powerful organization comparable to the National Rifle Association ensures that the debate includes a discussion of the moral rights of drug users.

Although I believe this response to be definitive, I will have little more to say about it here. I want to address the utilitarian position directly, rather than to dismiss it as irrelevant. In this section and the next, I will present several reasons to believe that, despite Kaplan's invitation, no "careful weighing" of the costs and benefits of decriminalization is possible. I will conclude that no one should have the slightest idea about how LAD fares according to a utilitarian analysis.

Most defenders of LAD are convinced that the costs of decriminalization are a simple function of the extent to which it would increase the number of drug users and the quantity of drugs they would consume. The single most hotly contested issue between drug prohibitionists and their critics is how the repeal of LAD would affect patterns of drug use. After structuring the debate in utilitarian terms, Kaplan concludes that "it is the height of irresponsibility to advocate risking the future of the nation" by decriminalizing cocaine use, because "we simply cannot guarantee" that decriminalization would not result in "a fifty fold increase in the number of those dependent on cocaine."[6] Sometimes a similar concern about an increase in drug use is confined to a given population. For example, A. M. Rosenthal writes that "the only worthwhile question" in deciding whether or not to continue the war on drugs is "would legalization mean fewer pregnant crack addicts, fewer babies with damaged brains?"[7]

I will return to the special case of pregnant crack users in Chapter 4. At this time, I want to point out that Rosenthal's question cannot be the only one worth asking. By proposing a "careful weighing of the costs" of criminalization against those of decriminalization, Kaplan must be understood to include both costs *and* benefits. As decriminalization theorists keep emphasizing, the repeal of LAD is likely to bring sub-

149

stantial advantages. The billions of dollars in law enforcement that would be saved by decriminalization should be construed as an "opportunity cost" of drug prohibition.[8] The wise use of this money might actually improve the health of drug users and their dependents. Rosenthal might recant if he could be persuaded that the repeal of LAD would free resources for programs to provide medical treatment to minimize the long-term damage suffered by babies of crack-addicted mothers. The repeal of drug prohibitions might actually reduce the net harm suffered by these infants. No one should believe that "the only worthwhile question" in deciding whether to reintroduce the prohibition of alcohol is whether it would result in fewer pregnant alcoholics who give birth to babies suffering from fetal alcohol syndrome. More drug users consuming greater quantities of drugs does not necessarily translate into a decrease in social utility. A more accurate statement of the goal of a utilitarian drug policy is to minimize disutility or evil rather than to reduce the number of drug users and the quantity of drugs they consume. As Arnold Trebach insists, "harm reduction" (or "disutility reduction") should be the unifying theme of utilitarian drug reformers.[9]

Nonetheless, the overwhelming majority of theorists who oppose decriminalization do so because, like Kaplan, they are apprehensive of a dramatic escalation of drug use. Those who endorse LAD typically allege that its repeal would create a drug epidemic of staggering dimensions. Those who oppose LAD are placed on the defensive. They tend to reply that there is no evidence to establish that decriminalization would have a devastating impact on the number of drug users or the quantity of drugs they consume.

One can only be astounded at the confidence with which commentators on both sides of this debate predict the long-term effects of a repeal of LAD on patterns of drug use. Some defenders of prohibition fear that the lure of illegal drugs is so powerful that if these drugs were decriminalized, a majority of Americans of potential drug-using age might succumb to them. Dr. William Pollin, former director of the

National Institute on Drug Abuse, estimates that between 60 and 100 million Americans would use legalized cocaine.[10] On the other hand, critics of LAD cite polls showing that fewer than 1 in 100 Americans who have not already used cocaine would try it if it were made legal.[11] They argue that most illegal drugs are readily available to anyone determined to use them, even while consumption declines. Neither prediction should inspire great assurance. In what follows, I will argue that no conclusion about the long-term effects of decriminalization on patterns of drug consumption can be drawn with sufficient confidence to justify either supporting or rejecting LAD.

The utilitarian case in favor of LAD depends heavily on the effectiveness of drug prohibitions in discouraging use. The enforcement of criminal penalties is alleged to achieve both "general" and "special" deterrence: A significant number of prospective users are deterred from experimentation with drugs, and actual users are given a prudential motive to quit. As with most claims about the deterrent effect of punishment, this contention is almost impossible to test empirically. At least one consideration, however, indicates that any general reservations a theorist may have about the effectiveness of the criminal law as a deterrent have special force when applied to LAD.

The efficacy of punishment as a deterrent is proportional to the perceived likelihood that offenders will be arrested and prosecuted. But only about 750,000 of the 28 million persons who use illegal drugs annually – approximately 2 percent – are arrested. Studies indicate that almost no cocaine user thinks there is any likelihood of being caught.[12] Based on this evidence, a user is rational in believing that "it won't happen to me." In light of the consensual, private nature of illegal drug use, Steven Wisotsky concludes that the "systematic detection of offenders is not possible within politically realistic budgets and the existing constitutional limits upon law enforcement techniques."[13] The conditions required to make LAD a credible deterrent do not and will not obtain. In view of the widespread availability of drugs, some cynics are occasionally heard to complain that America has already implemented a policy of de facto decriminalization.[14]

The self-reports of drug users might provide some insight into the efficacy of the criminal law in discouraging drug use. In one study, 106 persons who had stopped using cocaine were asked to identify the factors that had contributed to their decision. "Psychological problems or stressful states" were cited by 61.3 percent, and 22.6 percent mentioned "financial problems"; only 3.8 percent expressed "fears of arrest or rip-off."[15] Perhaps a repeal of LAD would not have a major impact on whether many current drug users would decide to quit.

Supporters of LAD sometimes maintain that the criminal law discourages drug use not only by deterrence but also by education. According to Rudolph Giuliani: "The most general purpose of the law is to teach. Laws against the use and sale of drugs say firmly that it is wrong to use these things."[16] This claim is hard to assess. Is the mere fact that a lesson is taught more important than whether anyone is convinced by it? If so, the repeal of LAD need not affect education; decriminalization would not undermine efforts to teach the reasons not to use drugs. Of course, the repeal of LAD would remove the threat of punishment for drug use, but threats cannot be what Giuliani has in mind by "education." But perhaps a change in behavior is the goal of drug education. If so, Giuliani offers no evidence that LAD helps to convince potential users not to try illegal substances; as I have indicated, more direct efforts to discourage the recreational use of drugs through education have not been successful.[17] In addition, the claim that prospective users should be "educated" about the immorality of drugs begs the question against those who believe that such use is not always wrongful. If LAD violates moral rights, "education" about the wrongfulness of drug use is a misnomer.

I will quickly summarize what little evidence might bear on how criminal penalties affect recreational drug use. Precedents from our own history provide very limited guidance. America has been described as a "dope fiend's paradise"[18]

throughout most of our history, until shortly before the enactment of the Harrison Act of 1914. David Musto summarizes the historical situation as follows:

> The United States had no practical control over the health
> professions, no representative national health organizations
> to aid the government in drafting regulations, and no controls
> on the labeling, composition, or advertising of compounds
> that might contain opiates or cocaine. The United States not
> only proclaimed a free marketplace, it practiced this philos-
> ophy with regard to narcotics in a manner unrestrained at
> every level of preparation and consumption.[19]

Shortly before World War I, purified cocaine sold for approximately twenty-five cents a gram.[20] Despite the cheap
supply and absence of legal controls, the per capita consumption of drugs prior to 1914 was probably no greater than
it is today.[21] And drugs were not perceived as an especially
serious problem prior to their prohibition.[22] In a search
through the *New York Times Index*, one commentator found
no articles about the negative effects of cocaine use from 1895
to 1904 – the years of peak use and minimum legal controls.[23]
Of course, supporters of LAD will respond that society is
different today, and perhaps they are correct. But this response undermines any attempt to apply empirical studies
from other times and places to shed light on how a repeal
of LAD would affect patterns of drug consumption here and
now. At the very least, these studies show that countries *can*
prosper without criminalizing drug use. Somehow, America
survived the absence of LAD throughout most of our history.

Both friends and foes of LAD find reason to cite America's
experiment with the prohibition of alcohol as support for
their point of view. Critics of LAD argue that the era of
alcohol prohibition was disastrous and that our present policy of proscribing illegal drugs fares no better. According to
James Bakalar and Lester Grinspoon, the parallels between
drug and alcohol prohibition "are ridiculously precise."[24]
Some columnists confidently proclaim, "Prohibition never

works."[25] Supporters of LAD respond by dividing into two camps. Some boldly describe the prohibition of alcohol as "a success."[26] They cite evidence that the consumption of alcohol was cut approximately in half from 1920 to 1933, and they conclude that our "experience with alcohol is the strongest argument against [drug] legalization."[27] Bennett alleges that "when we had laws against alcohol, there was less consumption of alcohol, less alcohol-related disease, fewer drunken brawls, and a lot less public drunkenness."[28] After this glowing endorsement, it is curious that he stops short of recommending a reinstatement of the prohibition of alcohol.

Other supporters of LAD insist that alcohol is different from other drugs. They are unwilling to draw conclusions about the effects of decriminalizing illegal substances from the repeal of alcohol prohibition. Of course, each drug *is* unique in one or more respects. Today, crack is the drug most frequently identified as different. Bennett describes it as "the most dangerous and quickly addictive drug known to man."[29] Empirical studies have only begun to determine whether crack deserves the public hysteria associated with it.[30] Jeffrey Fagan concludes that these studies "provide a sobering view of the realities of crack use, but also offer evidence that refutes many of the myths surrounding it."[31] In any event, warnings that the horrors of a particular drug are unprecedented have been heard almost every time a new substance is introduced into society.

A few additional empirical results have a possible bearing on the consequences of decriminalization, although it would be rash to place much stock in them. In some places where the use of a number of drugs has been effectively legalized, as in the Netherlands, the rate of consumption has decreased and is lower than in the United States.[32] The frequency of marijuana use among Alaskans, however, is somewhat higher than in the coterminous forty-eight states.[33] In general, no increase in consumption occurred in the several states that decriminalized marijuana in the mid-1970s.[34]

Unfortunately, very little is known about why persons use

illegal drugs today; with or without LAD, no one can possibly predict whether or to what extent Americans will be inclined to use them in the future. Unanticipated social change may alter whatever unknown variables make us more or less likely to consume drugs. Patterns of drug use seem to be influenced more by social conditions than by criminal prohibitions, and many of these conditions could remain intact despite decriminalization.[35] Tobacco is becoming less fashionable throughout America without the introduction of general prohibition, and the per capita consumption of alcohol is declining as well. Similar trends indicate that cocaine use is becoming less chic throughout much of society.

Another reason to doubt the accuracy of speculation about the long-term effects of a repeal of LAD is that other important variables might change if the use of some or all illegal drugs were decriminalized. For example, the policies of corporate America could provide a powerful incentive to resist the use of legalized drugs. If employers fail to hire drug users, or if insurance companies refuse to offer them coverage, adults would have more reason to abstain than if society were totally indifferent to drug use. Despite protests about so-called life-style discrimination, more than six thousand companies now refuse to hire smokers of cigarettes.[36] After decriminalization, the number of companies that would refuse to hire users of newly legalized substances would be much higher.

Moreover, pharmaceutical companies would gain an economic incentive to create totally new substances that retain the properties that attract drug users, but eliminate some or all of their undesirable side effects. If these new substances could be perfected, and gained popularity among persons now inclined to use existing drugs, the disutility of drug use might decline significantly. Or it might not. The point is that it is naive to express much assurance about this sort of speculation. The development of new substances with unknown effects reveals the hazards in attempts to predict the long-term consequences of repealing LAD.

The costs and benefits of decriminalization would differ

depending on the details of whatever model is implemented. This point is most easily illustrated by thinking about the price of drugs under alternative decriminalization schemes. One of the benefits promised by opponents of LAD is the elimination of organized crime that thrives under the black market created by drug prohibition. A second anticipated benefit is the accumulation of vast tax revenues. Unfortunately, these potential benefits compete with one another. As taxes on legal drugs are raised, organized criminals and black marketeers will reappear. As taxes on legal drugs are lowered, revenues available for legitimate purposes will decrease. Opponents of LAD cannot deliver on all promises simultaneously. Without a detailed model to evaluate, one cannot have a very clear idea about what advantages or disadvantages will follow from the vague proposal to decriminalize the recreational use of drugs.

To complicate matters still further, the costs of waging war on drugs constantly change. Victory might be just around the corner, when we finally discover the right strategy. A completely new technology to curb production may be on the horizon. For example, suppose that coca-eating moths could be unleashed in the Andes, destroying most of the world's supply of cocaine. How can utilitarian advocates of decriminalization reply to this scheme other than to scoff that it is unrealistic? Those who stress the disutility of current efforts can have little to say against proposals to win the war with more effective weapons than have been utilized thus far.

Many commentators who do not pretend to be clairvoyant maintain that the very uncertainty of the issue is a decisive reason to retain LAD. Recall Kaplan's claim that the decriminalization of cocaine would be "the height of irresponsibility" because "we simply cannot guarantee" that it would not result in an exponential escalation of cocaine use. Rather than rely on a bold prediction, this position rests on a thesis about how the burden of proof should be allocated. According to James Ostrowski, "The notion that we should not legalize drugs because we are not certain what would happen has become the favored argument of many prohibitionists."[37]

The debate would not get off the ground if the case for decriminalization depended on whether anyone could "guarantee" that drug use would not increase. If the repeal of the prohibition of alcohol had been contingent on whether anyone could have promised that consumption would not escalate, America would still have prohibition today. The same could be said about proposals to remove criminal penalties from virtually any activity. This argument for LAD proves too much. The status quo is not defended simply by pointing out that a bad situation could always get worse.

THE EVALUATIVE ASSUMPTIONS
IN UTILITARIANISM

Although it is important to challenge forecasts that decriminalization will result in an explosion of drug use, I am equally concerned to demonstrate that a utilitarian analysis of LAD involves dubious and unsupported value judgments as well as unwarranted empirical suppositions. The true nature of the controversy between supporters of LAD and their critics is distorted by pretending that their disagreement is purely factual rather than moral.

A general problem in preparing a utilitarian analysis of LAD is to decide what should be included among the costs and benefits of decriminalization and how they should be quantified in the process of "carefully weighing" them. This problem can be illustrated without continuing to belabor the most obvious difficulty: Does the protection of rights count at all? If so, what weight are rights assigned? At some point, rights may have to be balanced against utility, but I see no basis for describing this process as "careful." What sometimes masquerades as precise analysis is not so far from prejudice and arbitrary speculation.

Rights are not the only variables that weigh uneasily on the utilitarian scales. The contributions of the tobacco and alcohol industries to our gross national product are enormous, and revenue that would be gained from the sale of legalized drugs would swell this amount still further. But the use of both legal and illegal drugs exacts tremendous health costs. How should economic gains be balanced against medical losses?

And what about the pleasure that many illegal drug users experience? How should their euphoria be balanced against the disutility caused by recreational drug use? In Chapter 2, I rejected two possible strategies for disqualifying the pleasure of drug use. The euphoria of drug users is neither illusory nor pathological. I will now describe complications that result from including this pleasure in a calculus to assess the effects of LAD on both users and nonusers of recreational drugs.

The practical impossibility of making precise interpersonal comparisons of utility gives rise to the most serious obstacle. If Smith gains pleasure by watching football on television, but his viewing causes his wife to feel unhappy and neglected, no principled means is available to decide whether Smith gains more utility than his wife loses. The problem in this simple example is multiplied by attempts to balance the utility of all spectator sports enthusiasts against the disutility of their television widows. And so with recreational drug use. If any recreational drug user gains utility as a result of his experience with drugs, a utilitarian defense of LAD necessarily requires interpersonal comparisons of utility. Most utilitarian supporters of LAD try to evade this complication by excluding from consideration the variable that creates the problem. They pretend that the pleasure of drug use does not belong on the scales in the first place. By neglecting euphoria in their calculations, prohibitionists are able to conclude that the effects of recreational drug use are invariably negative, so they are spared the embarrassment of having to defend judgments involving interpersonal comparisons of utility.

The concession that some drug users might gain utility

from their experience creates an additional difficulty. At least a few adults whose experience with illegal substances would be favorable choose not to experiment with drugs because they are deterred by criminal prohibitions. Their respect for the law, or their fear of apprehension and conviction, dissuades them from drug use. As a result of their decision to abstain, they never sample a pleasure that might add more to their lives than it would subtract. If any persons satisfy this description, no one is entitled to conclude that an expansion in the number of drug users that might follow from a repeal of LAD would automatically be bad. An enlargement in the size of the drug-using population might actually create a net balance of utility.[38] No one knows whether this hypothesis is true, and no one is in a position to hazard more than a wild guess.

These problems are only one dimension of the more general difficulty of how to identify and quantify the advantages and disadvantages of drug prohibitions. Some effects of recreational drug use are not readily assignable to either category. Consider the number of premature deaths – estimated to be as high as 434,175 each year – suffered by users of nicotine.[39] These deaths, usually of adults who are no longer gainfully employed, reduce private pension expenditures and save the Social Security system from bankruptcy. From a purely economic perspective, it may be ideal for the elderly to die immediately after their socially productive years are over. Should the numbers of premature deaths caused by drug use be counted as a social benefit?

Robert Goodin thinks not. He observes that "most people who are already retired would wish to enjoy a long and happy retirement" and that "those preferences, too, must be factored into any proper calculus of social utility." Of course. What is not so obvious is that including these preferences in a "proper calculus of social utility" would support Goodin's conclusion that these premature deaths "are almost certain to turn out to be costs rather than benefits in the broader scale of values."[40] Those theorists who hope to salvage the plausibility of utilitarianism have every reason to hope that Goodin is correct. But his conclusion is more an expression of faith than it is the product of a careful analysis.

I conclude that a utilitarian approach does not offer much solace either to friends or to foes of LAD. If I am correct, one might wonder why cost-benefit analyses have played such a prominent role in debates about decriminalization. I will mention only one of many possible explanations. A number of commentators suffer from what might be called "moral arguphobia." They are suitably impressed by the difficulties of constructing a moral argument, and they are painfully aware of their inability to persuade their opponents when they attempt to do so. Some subscribe to moral skepticism: I have my moral opinion, you have yours, and there is no rational basis for choosing between them. Thus they gravitate toward analyses that seemingly avoid moral judgments. They are more at home in the world of statistics.

Kaplan, for example, defends his preference for a utilitarian analysis after acknowledging that "many people speak of the individual's right to do what he wishes with his own body, his right to harm himself, or his right to eat, drink, or otherwise ingest what he pleases."[41] But he quickly dismisses attempts to pursue a nonconsequentialist approach to recreational drug use. He claims that "the problem with such 'rights' is that they are all assertions. They do not carry any argument with them."[42] Apparently, Kaplan cannot fathom why anyone would care about rights unless they promote utility. He continues, "Perhaps . . . we would have a better and more moral society if we recognized [such 'rights'] as absolutes – but perhaps not."[43]

To cite a second example, Mark Moore contrasts two "levels of analysis" on which "the legalization debate proceeds."[44] The first, which he mentions only in passing, is "an exercise in political philosophy"; the second, which he develops at length, is "more empirical and consequentialist."[45] I have no doubt that a rights-based, principled analysis of LAD can and should be differentiated from a utilitarian approach and that this is the distinction Moore intends to draw. However, I have two objections to Moore's description of the former as an "exercise in political philosophy" and his characterization of the latter as "empirical."

First, no one should believe that political philosophers can identify our moral rights in the absence of empirical data. In Chapter 2, I attempted to show that the issue of whether adults have a moral right to use a drug recreationally, despite its harmful effects on them, is partly a function of the empirical properties of the particular drug. The connections between empirical analyses and judgments about moral rights will become even more evident later in this chapter. My second objection is more fundamental. Like it or not, political philosophy is necessarily implicated in *any* attempt to assess the justifiability of LAD. The relevance of empirical data can be explained only within the framework of a political philosophy.

Despite suggestions to the contrary, utilitarianism, which provides the foundation of a cost-benefit analysis, *is* a moral and political philosophy. I have tried to show how implementation of a utilitarian theory depends on controversial questions of value that go far beyond empirical uncertainties and the difficulties of foretelling the future. Answers to questions about what to count as a cost or a benefit, and how costs and benefits should be quantified and balanced, presuppose commitments to positions that are unmistakably moral. The difference between my approach, which emphasizes the importance of moral rights, and a utilitarian approach, which does not, cannot be that my inquiry contains controversial moral judgments avoided by utilitarians. Both strategies involve equally controversial moral judgments. The choice between these approaches depends on which set of controversial moral judgments is preferable. The skeptic who professes to be at a loss about how to decide whether to prefer one moral judgment to another is best advised to abandon the project of trying to determine whether LAD is justified.

Those theorists who are enthusiastic about applying a utilitarian perspective should not be disappointed to learn that they, no less than nonconsequentialists, are deeply engaged in moral and political philosophy. This conclusion helps to explain the otherwise puzzling phenomenon of why controversy about LAD tends to be so passionate and heated. Cost-benefit analyses, for all their value, are relatively unexciting. The supposition that fundamental rights and principles are at stake in LAD explains the vehemence many protagonists bring to this debate.

HARM AND DISUTILITY

Thus far in Chapters 2 and 3, I have treated "harm" and "disutility" as though they were synonymous. They are not. Demonstrating that LAD promotes disutility is not equivalent to showing that drug use is eligible for prohibition within a system of criminal justice that includes the harm principle. The issue of whether drug use is harmful to others is not identical to the issue of whether drug use causes a net balance of disutility to others; the former question is much more narrow than the latter. Perhaps the tendency to confuse these distinct issues is due to the fact that John Stuart Mill championed both utilitarianism and the harm principle. But whatever the source of this confusion, I will argue in this section that much of the disutility said to be created by recreational drug use does not amount to harm in the sense capable of justifying criminal prohibitions.

An analysis of the harm principle is required to defend my claim that drug use might cause disutility without causing harm. The most immediate difficulty is to clarify what harm *is*. Anyone who proposes that a given type of conduct should be criminalized because of its unfavorable impact on others will be prepared to describe that impact as harmful. Someone who objects to criminalization will be inclined to deny that the unfavorable impact amounts to harm. How can such a dispute be resolved? Until recently, these debates were often interminable, leading even the best criminal theorists to lament: "The notion of harm appears to be infinitely expandable. At a certain point we have to wonder whether [the harm principle] is still subject to falsification. If we cannot imagine a crime that *would not* threaten harm, the proposition has become vacuous and, in the view of some, meaningless."[46]

Clearly, an analysis of harm is needed so that the harm principle does not become an empty constraint on the content of the criminal law. Recently, important progress in understanding the nature of harm as a precondition for criminal liability has been achieved by Joel Feinberg, from whose work I will again borrow generously.[47] As a result of Feinberg's efforts, the harm principle can be employed as a substantive, nontrivial requirement that criminal legislation must satisfy. In much of this chapter, I will describe several difficulties in supposing that LAD satisfies the harm principle, when that principle is correctly understood and applied. I will begin by exploring the important and relevant features of the harm principle itself.

Imagine a debate about whether a given instance of conduct should be criminalized between two persons who concede that punishment is unjustified in the absence of harm to others. These persons might disagree about any number of issues. First, they might disagree about whether the conduct in question has any impact on others at all. They might disagree, for example, about whether subliminal advertising produces any detectable effects on persons who are subjected to it. This debate is empirical. Second, they might agree that conduct has an impact on others, but disagree about whether that impact is favorable or unfavorable. This second disagreement can take two forms. These persons might agree, for example, that adolescents are affected by playing video games, but disagree about whether this effect is good or bad. Or they might agree that an effect is negative, but disagree about whether it is outweighed by another effect that is positive. These debates, of course, are not empirical.

Although each of these kinds of disagreements is likely to take place in the context of controversy about LAD, I want to focus on yet a different kind of dispute here. Imagine that these persons agree that conduct has a net impact on others that is bad, but disagree about whether that impact amounts to a *harm* that is eligible for prohibition within a system of criminal justice that includes the harm principle. How can a bad effect be anything but a harm? To be sure, some theorists seemingly use the expressions "bad effect," "evil," "dis-utility," and "harm" interchangeably. But distinctions must be drawn if the purpose of attaching these labels is to defend or challenge the imposition of criminal liability.

The most obvious reason to deny that a bad effect qualifies as a harm is that the agent who caused it acted within her rights. One person may be devastated by the conduct of another and yet not be harmed, because the agent who caused the suffering acted permissibly. One example of this phenomenon involves the impact of economic decisions. A small grocer might lose her livelihood if a large supermarket opens across the street. As a result, she may suffer more severe hardships than if someone had stolen her car or broken her leg. Yet few would conclude that the small grocer has been harmed. A second example involves the impact of personal, private decisions. A woman may decide to marry one suitor rather than another, who is driven to deep despair because of her choice. Again, few would conclude that the rejected suitor has been harmed. Why not?

Feinberg would answer that the bankrupt grocer and bro-kenhearted suitor are in a harmed state or condition but that they have not been harmed in the sense required by the criminal law.[48] Criminal liability does not merely require that a victim be in a harmed state or condition but that an agent has harmed him. According to Feinberg, these unfortunates have not been harmed, in the relevant sense, because

> harm . . . must bear a normative sense . . . in any plausible for-mulation of the harm principle. To say that A has harmed B in this sense is to say much the same thing as that A has wronged B, or treated him unjustly. One person *wrongs* an-other when his indefensible conduct violates the other's right. . . . Only setbacks of interests that are wrongs, and wrongs that are setbacks to interest, are to count as harms in the appropriate sense.[49]

What is missing from these two examples that blocks the conclusion that the bankrupt grocer or rejected suitor has been harmed is *wrongful action* by the agents who set back their interests. Persons are not harmed by whatever conduct impacts upon them unfavorably (or places them in a harmed state or condition) unless that conduct is morally wrong. The bankrupt grocer has not been harmed because the owner of the supermarket is permitted to compete with her. The rejected suitor has not been harmed because people are permitted to choose their mates.

If this analysis of harm is correct, the issue of whether recreational drug use is harmful to others cannot be resolved without determining whether and under what circumstances persons are morally permitted to use drugs. If adults have a moral right to use drugs recreationally, someone can demonstrate ad nauseam that their conduct has deleterious consequences upon others, without showing that these consequences count as harms that can support criminal liability. In the absence of an independent reason to believe that an action is morally impermissible, its adverse effects on others are not a sufficient basis to conclude that it is harmful and thus eligible for criminal prohibitions.

This point pertains to all candidates for criminal liability. No one should be persuaded that "since bank robbery harms others, bank robbery is wrong" in the absence of an independent reason to believe that bank robbery is morally impermissible. The harmed condition in which bank robbers place others is not conclusive evidence of wrongdoing; the immorality of bank robbery must be located elsewhere. In this case, as with all paradigm examples of criminality, such conclusive evidence is easy to find. I assume without argument the existence of property rights that are violated by acts of bank robbery. The wrongfulness of bank robbery consists in the violation of these rights.

Supporters of LAD are unlikely to balk at this conclusion. They do not hesitate to condemn recreational drug use as wrong. However, independent support for this moral judgment is by no means easy to provide. As I have suggested in Chapter 1, the most familiar defenses of this judgment depend on conceptions of virtue that are said to be undermined by recreational drug use. These defenses, however, can succeed only in showing that recreational drug use does not promote human excellence. By their own terms, they fail to establish that drug use is impermissible.

Feinberg's remarks indicate a convenient test that must be satisfied before conduct becomes eligible for prohibition under the harm principle. According to Feinberg, conduct that places another in a harmed condition is a wrong to her when it indefensibly violates her moral rights.[50] The person whose rights are violated can be described as a victim. Acts of bank robbery clearly violate the rights of others who are victimized by this crime. But whose rights – and what rights – are violated by acts of recreational drug use? Unless this question can be answered, LAD is incompatible with the harm principle. Every genuinely harmful act must also be a violation of rights. If no one has a moral right that adults refrain from recreational drug use – or if such a right obtains only in limited circumstances that do not warrant the full generality of drug prohibition – LAD will turn out to be an unjustified exercise of state power over individual liberty. Those who disagree with this conclusion either reject the conceptual connection between harm and rights or accept a broader function for the criminal law than is authorized by the harm principle.

In this light, reconsider some of the specific respects in which recreational drug use is said to cause social disutility. Bennett alleges that drugs make users "inattentive parents, bad neighbors, poor students, and unreliable employees."[51] Although supporting data are rarely presented, I will tentatively suppose that the empirical evidence in favor of these allegations is compelling. If so, one should not take Bennett's charges lightly. Yet the consequences he describes, however undesirable, do not amount to harms capable of justifying criminal legislation under the harm principle in the absence of a victim whose moral rights have been violated. In other words, the consequences cited by Bennett are not harms unless someone has a moral right that the drug user be an attentive parent, a good neighbor, a proficient student, or a reliable employee. If no such moral rights exist, actions that cause these consequences are not harmful, and they are in-eligible for prohibition within a system of criminal justice that includes the harm principle.

Several of the consequences Bennett describes promote disutility, but harm no one; they do not violate anyone's moral rights, and should not be subjected to criminal liability. Bad neighbors decrease the amount of utility in a community, but they do not harm anyone simply by being bad neighbors. Undoubtedly I could create more utility by turning off my television and dedicating myself to community service, but I do not harm anyone by persisting in my slothful behavior. One of the standard difficulties with utilitarianism is that it must strain to provide room for a private sphere of conduct in which I am morally permitted to do as I please. The theory seemingly requires me to constantly strive to maximize social utility.[52] Perhaps recreational activities generally, including the use of drugs, fall squarely within this private sphere.

Of course, a drug prohibitionist might reply that persons *do* have a moral right that their neighbors be good, that their employees be reliable, that their students be proficient, and that their parents be attentive. At its deepest level, this reply cannot be evaluated without an entire theory of moral rights. Unfortunately, I have no such theory to offer. However, even without such a theory, evidence against the existence of these supposed rights is easy to provide. Almost no one would countenance these rights as a reason to prohibit behavior in contexts not involving recreational drug use. If these rights exist, they would be violated by a wide range of conduct unlikely to be condemned as wrongful. Again, consider the adult who deliberately decides to be an unreliable employee because she prefers to watch television. Her decision should not be applauded. It might cause enormous disutility. How-ever, no one is likely to believe that it violates rights and that it is eligible for criminal punishment. Employers should be permitted to fire unreliable employees, but the state should not be allowed to put them in prison. Few persons really believe that such behavior creates victims whose moral rights are violated.

I conclude that much of the disutility that recreational drug use is alleged to cause is not a harm capable of justifying criminal liability under the harm principle. No one has a right that adults refrain from causing many of the undesirable effects said to follow from recreational drug use. This conclusion applies to the possible consequence that opponents of decriminalization fear most – an expansion in the number of recreational drug users brought about by the repeal of LAD. I will argue that decriminalization might lead to an increase in drug use, and a corresponding decrease in utility, without leading to an increase in harm. If I am correct, the fear that decriminalization will multiply the number of drug users and create disutility is not itself relevant to the question of whether LAD can be supported under the harm principle.

Suppose decriminalization leads to an increase in recreational drug use and that this result promotes social disutility. It does not follow that a moral right has been violated, or that anyone has been harmed, by this consequence of repealing LAD. The following example supports this conclusion. Suppose that the use of cocaine is prohibited. Smith breaks the law and uses cocaine; Jones yearns to try cocaine but refrains because of his respect for the law and his fear of punishment; Black has no desire to use cocaine and abstains. Does Jones or Black have a right that is violated by Smith's illegal act? What right could they possibly have that Smith has violated? Surely no one has a right that others do not break the law.[53]

Now suppose that the prohibition of cocaine use is repealed. Smith continues his consumption, albeit legally; Jones happily joins him; Black continues to abstain. Neither Jones nor Black has a moral right that is violated by this new state of affairs. Surely Jones has no right that the state continue to prevent him from doing what he yearned to do all along. Any such right could only serve to protect Jones from his own inclinations. Nor is Black's right violated by this change. If his right was not violated when Smith used cocaine illegally, it is hard to see how his right is violated when Smith and Jones use cocaine legally.

If neither Jones nor Black has a moral right that is violated in this second hypothetical, I conclude that they are not harmed by the repeal of LAD, even though decriminalization results in a 100 percent increase in drug use. If I am correct, a dramatic rise in drug use does not itself harm anyone. If criminal liability is unjustified in the absence of harm to others, LAD cannot be supported by the specter of escalating drug use that is raised whenever decriminalization is proposed. Predictions about the epidemic of drug use that would follow from decriminalization are irrelevant under the harm principle. Their relevance depends on yet a second set of controversial predictions about how the growing numbers of drug users would behave.

This argument does not prove too much. Consider any example of a crime that clearly violates moral rights. Criminal assault, for example, violates the moral rights of its victims. If the repeal of this offense resulted in greater numbers of assaults, the additional victims could complain that the change had harmed them and violated their rights. But most of the antisocial behavior associated with recreational drug use is not comparable. Suppose that the repeal of LAD leads more adults to become less productive, ignore their neighbors, neglect their studies, and become less healthy. Although these changes have repercussions throughout society, and undoubtedly decrease utility, no one is *harmed* by them.

But what if the repeal of LAD increases not only the number of recreational drug users but also the incidence of antisocial conduct that violates moral rights? Suppose, for example, that White is the deformed baby of Jones, his cocaine-abusing mother. Or suppose that Jones, who was previously deterred by LAD but who now uses legalized cocaine, commits a crime that he would not have committed but for his newly acquired drug habit. I will address these important suppositions later. At this time, I have attempted to support two propositions. First, an increase in the number of recreational drug users that might follow from de-criminalization is not itself a harm that justifies retaining LAD. The case in favor of criminal liability depends on further claims about the harmful ways that this growing army of drug users would behave. Second, not all of the disutility these users might cause constitutes harm. In order to qualify as harm, the disutility caused by the wrongful acts of drug users must create victims whose moral rights are violated.

THE NATURE OF CRIMINAL HARM

The existence of a victim whose moral rights are violated by the wrongful acts of recreational drug users would still be insufficient to identify a harm that is eligible for punishment within a system of criminal justice that includes the harm principle. Not every harm is a *criminal* harm. The criminal law does not provide the appropriate legal response to every harmful activity. When members of the public demand that "there ought to be a law" against some harmful behavior, they almost always have the criminal law in mind. But persons might agree that conduct is harmful and violates the moral rights of a victim, while still disagreeing about whether that conduct should be punished. Some harms should be redressed by imposing civil rather than criminal liability.

Examples are plentiful. Suppose that a person ruins another's business by breaching a contract. Or suppose that a person damages another's reputation by slander or libel. These harms are treated within the civil rather than the criminal law, typically by awarding money damages to victims (called "plaintiffs" in civil law). Conceivably, some or all of the harms to others caused by recreational drug use could be treated in the same way. If so, the prevention of these harms would not require criminal laws against the recreational use of drugs.

Surprisingly, no satisfactory basis has been found to distinguish criminal from civil harms. Standard textbooks in criminal law typically evade this difficult issue entirely. Although the viability of this distinction is almost universally accepted, no one pretends to thoroughly understand its deeper rationale.[54] In what follows, I will describe two possible bases for distinguishing criminal from civil harms and discuss their implications for the justifiability of LAD and the issue of whether adults have a moral right to use drugs recreationally.

The first approach to this problem might be called *pragmatic*. According to a pragmatic approach, criminal harms are not different in kind from noncriminal harms. The difference between criminal and civil law has nothing to do with the nature of the respective harms that the laws are designed to prevent. According to Feinberg, the choice between criminal or noncriminal legal intervention is "determined by such practical matters as the use of available resources, court facilities, police time, enforcement costs, effects on individual expectations, and the like."[55] The dichotomy between criminal and civil law "has more to do with administrative convenience than with philosophical principle."[56]

Pragmatists have good reason to be skeptical that the putative harms of recreational drug use should be treated as criminal. Surely the decriminalization theorists whose arguments were summarized in Chapter 1 have made an impressive case to establish the unprecedented "administrative inconvenience" of LAD. It is hard to imagine a single example of criminal legislation that has created more headaches for administrators. Feinberg almost seems to have had LAD in mind in listing the considerations on which he believes the choice between criminal and noncriminal intervention should depend.

Although the administrative inconvenience of LAD should discourage pragmatists, many would support drug prohibitions if the criminal sanction could be shown to be more effective than noncriminal alternatives in achieving the legitimate objectives of drug policy. The foremost difficulty in assessing the relative advantages of criminal and noncriminal alternatives is to decide what these objectives should be. If drug prohibitionists are determined to eliminate the scourge of drug use altogether, they will stop at nothing short of severe criminal punishments. In what follows I will posit two less ambitious goals that I hope are beyond serious controversy. A sensible drug policy should strive to minimize the harms that result from drug use and should devise means to compensate victims when such harms occur.

A number of commentators have attempted to evaluate whether various alternatives to the criminal law might accomplish these two objectives more efficiently. Since my primary aim is to protect moral rights rather than to solve America's drug problem as a matter of public policy, I will sketch only a few of their insights here. The following remarks barely scratch the surface of a deep and difficult problem.

Chester Mitchell proposes that the creative use of tort liability would be preferable to the criminal law in achieving the objectives of a rational drug policy.[57] He concedes that "arguing for private law regulation of drug activities is challenging because the system is difficult to visualize."[58] Still, the potential for tort law to compensate victims and to minimize the harm that results from drug use is indicated by the wide range of possible civil suits that would help to achieve these goals. Mitchell invites us to imagine

> tobacco producers sued by millions of customers for negligent failure to warn of risks; employers and restaurants sued for permitting employees or customers to be harmed by sidestream smoke; taverns sued for damage caused by or suffered by inebriated patrons; insurance firms suing alcohol and diazepam producers for the $30 billion cost of drug-related automobile claims in 1990; municipal governments suing opiate producers for drug-related crime; and parent groups suing distillers for not providing alcohol in childproof containers. This list of possible law suits should indicate that for some drug-related activities private law can have a major impact.[59]

Mitchell's enthusiasm for tort liability is tempered, despite the obvious potential of these civil suits to minimize the harms that result from drug use and to compensate victims when these harms occur. He notes that most of the harms caused by particular acts of drug use are too small to motivate anyone to sue, even though the total social costs of recreational drug use are large. One inconsiderate smoker in a restaurant who exposes patrons to side-stream smoke does not cause them much harm. For this reason, Mitchell concludes that the "largest gap in private law control is in protection from low-level, diffuse social harm caused by drug users."[60]

One intriguing proposal to help meet this difficulty is to impose a "harmfulness tax" on the lawful sale of recreational drugs. Bakalar and Grinspoon would establish a commission to calculate the "medical and social costs of drug abuse," and they would include this amount in the purchase price of each drug. They regard such a tax as "a way of making people buy insurance for the risks to themselves and others in their use of drugs," since "society would pay for the costs of drug abuse by extracting them from the drug users in proportion to the amount they contribute to the problem."[61] If this tax were sufficiently high, and if the demand for recreational drugs were reasonably elastic, Bakalar and Grinspoon's proposal might keep the incidence of drug use within tolerable bounds.[62]

I am confident that noncriminal alternatives will assume a higher and higher profile as the war on drugs evolves. But this trend will not be due to disenchantment with a punitive approach. Instead, it will derive from the tendency of drug prohibitionists to regard the procedural safeguards afforded to criminal defendants as a hinderance to winning the war on drugs. The presumption of innocence and the requirement of proof beyond a reasonable doubt have frustrated punitive objectives, and the creative use of civil liability offers a promising means to circumvent these procedural safeguards. This trend is only distantly related to the pragmatic approach I am describing here.

The pragmatic school poses a serious challenge to LAD. But whatever its merits, this approach is not congenial to those who countenance a moral right to use drugs recreationally. Nonconsequentialists may applaud the conclusion, but not the rationale. Pragmatists would not decriminalize drug use because punishment violates the moral rights of drug users, but because they believe that noncriminal alternatives are a better bargain in achieving the objectives of a rational drug policy. If they turn out to be mistaken, LAD might have to be reintroduced, and drug users could not complain that their rights had been violated.

The second approach to differentiate criminal from noncriminal harms might be called *principled*. According to a principled approach, the nature of criminal harm is conceptually distinct from the nature of noncriminal harm. The former possesses one or more characteristics not shared by the latter. Identifying this characteristic has proved elusive. All theorists in the principled school seem to agree that criminal harms are "public" or "social" in a way that noncriminal harms are not. But these descriptions rephrase rather than solve the problem. What makes some but not all harms "public" or "social"?

Several answers have been given. According to a version of this approach defended by Lawrence Becker, harm is criminal when it is "socially volatile,"[63] that is, when it is a "destructive disturbance of fundamental social structures."[64] Robert Nozick's version of the "distinction between private wrongs and wrongs having a public component" emphasizes "fear."[65] If the state allows Smith to break Jones's arm, requiring only that Smith pay compensation, fear would be created, not only in Jones but also in others. John Kleinig's version focuses on the importance of "social trust." "Criminal harms," he writes, "are destructive of the trust that people must be able to put in each other and in the institutions on which their welfare depends if they are to have the means for making or keeping for themselves satisfactory lives."[66]

It is hard to decide whether any or all of the putative harms of recreational drug use qualify as criminal according to any of these principled accounts, since the allegedly distinctive nature of criminal harm is so vague and imprecise. But even if each of these bad results is accurately described as a *harm* – which I have disputed – many do not seem to qualify as *criminal* harms. Consider yet another set of allegations by theorists who favor the retention of LAD. James Inciardi and Duane McBride emphasize the "escapism" of drug use: Drugs allow persons "to tolerate problems rather than to face them and make changes that might increase the quality of their social functioning and satisfaction with life."[67] They also protest that drug use tends to extend adolescence: "Frequent drug use prevented the acquisition of coping mechanisms that are part of maturing," contributing to "rapid family break-ups, job instability, serious crime, and ineffective personal relationships."[68]

No data are presented to indicate what percentage of drug users are guilty of escaping from reality or of extending adolescence. But I will not challenge these allegations on empirical grounds. Instead, I want to emphasize that few of these results, however unfortunate, seem to create social volatility, evoke fear, or erode public trust. They do not satisfy any of the foregoing criteria of criminal harms. Except for the allegation about "serious crime," the kinds of evils described by Inciardi and McBride play little role in a respectable argument that the harm of drug use should be criminalized.

Still, I have little doubt that recreational drug use *is* feared by many citizens, although not in the same way they fear clear criminal harms like robbery and rape. The explanation of why drug use creates apprehension may reveal a possible defect in principled accounts. As Barbara Levenbook has pointed out, almost any conduct has the capacity to be "socially volatile," or to evoke "fear," or to "erode public trust," given the "right mix of mass psychology, mass beliefs (rational or irrational), demagoguery, and attendant circumstances (like economic or political problems and the lack of civil remedies)."[69] Reactions to proposals to decriminalize some or all illegal drugs are a function of what the public has been led to expect, and the public's expectations may be erroneous. Perhaps the public anxiety about drugs and drug use is unwarranted. Do principled accounts justify criminal sanctions for conduct that citizens fear, even if their fear is irrational? Or do these accounts justify criminal sanctions only for conduct that citizens ought to fear?

Suppose that this question can be answered, salvaging a principled account of the distinction between criminal and noncriminal harms. If such an account properly categorizes recreational drug use as noncriminal, the conclusion that adults should be permitted to use drugs recreationally becomes somewhat easier to defend. The crucial premise in the argument for this conclusion is that persons are conditionally permitted to cause noncriminal harms. Initially, this premise might appear implausible. To be sure, no one is permitted to breach a contract or to commit a tort *simpliciter*, just as no one has a moral right to commit arson or larceny. But unlike a crime, which is categorically proscribed, persons may be permitted to breach a contract or to commit a tort *if* they compensate their plaintiffs. When the action is accompanied by adequate compensation, the state might tolerate, or perhaps even encourage, the commission of a tort or the breach of an agreement when it is efficient. The payment of compensation might justify the wrongdoing that would otherwise attach to acts that cause noncriminal harms.[70]

Are persons permitted to cause noncriminal harms if they compensate their victims? Some disciples of the economic analysis of law would answer this question affirmatively. Suppose that Smith promises to provide a given quantity of fish for $2.00 each to Jones, who sells them to his customers for $3.00 (Jones's customers would switch to chicken if he charged them more than this amount). Initially, Smith incurs costs of $1.00 in delivering each fish. Subsequently, however, an oil spill reduces the availability of fish so that they now cost Smith $5.00 to catch. Is Smith permitted to breach his contract with Jones? If he compensates Jones fully, considerations of efficiency suggest that his breach is permissible. If Smith pays Jones $3.00 for each fish he promised to deliver, Jones cannot complain about losing his supply. Under these circumstances, Smith is justified in defaulting on his contractual commitment.

Any number of devices might enable adult users of recreational drugs to compensate victims for many of the harms they cause. Some combination of Bakalar and Grinspoon's "harmfulness tax" and Mitchell's imaginative expansion of tort liability would go a long way toward accomplishing this objective. If users of recreational drugs compensate their victims, many of the harms they cause seem comparable to the harm Smith causes by breaching his agreement with Jones. For example, consider the "harm" of reduced productivity. Presumably others suffer economic losses if drug use leads Green to be less productive. For example, smaller amounts of income tax will be collected from a less productive Green. It might seem outrageous to suppose that Green owes anyone compensation for becoming less productive. But suppose that others do have a right that Green be productive, so that his failure can be said to cause a harm. Yet how can anyone complain about Green's nonproductivity if the purchase price of his drugs includes an amount that compensates them for nonpayment of his income tax? His payment of this sales tax would seem to discharge any duty he would otherwise have had to pay a higher income tax.

Admittedly, not all of the harms alleged to be caused by drug use are relevantly similar to the economic loss suffered by Jones. No person has a right to drive under the influence of drugs and subject others to substantial and unjustifiable risks of physical injury. Criminal punishment will still be required for acts of drug use that cause harms for which compensation is inappropriate or inadequate.[71] In Chapter 4 I will suggest that the circumstances under which acts of drug use cause such harms constitute the exception rather than the rule. At this point, I hope only to have raised doubts about the justifiability of criminalizing recreational drug use altogether, even though it may cause harm to others. Drug prohibitionists must also argue that the kinds of harms they seek to prevent should be subjected to criminal rather than to noncriminal sanctions.

My more speculative conclusion is that a principled approach to distinguish criminal from noncriminal harms is compatible with supposing that adults are conditionally permitted to use drugs recreationally. The full argument in support of this conclusion is as follows:

1. Some characteristic(s) (call it x) is present in criminal harms to differentiate them from noncriminal harms.
2. Some of the harms of drug use (call them h) lack characteristic x. Therefore,
3. h is a noncriminal rather than a criminal harm.
4. Adults are permitted to cause h if they compensate their victim(s).
5. Mechanisms to ensure that adults will compensate their victim(s) for h can be implemented. Therefore,
6. Adults are permitted to cause some of the harms of recreational drug use.

A more complete defense of each of these premises would be an ambitious undertaking. Even this brief sketch indicates that the claim that recreational drug use should be criminalized simply because it causes harm to others accepts uncritically a number of highly controversial assumptions about the boundaries between criminal and noncriminal liability. Some acts that are harmful to others might be conditionally permissible, and many instances of recreational drug use may be among them.

ANTICIPATORY OFFENSES

I have argued that recreational drug use itself is not the criminal harm that can justify LAD. Drugs may injure persons who use them, but paternalistic defenses of LAD are not compelling. If drugs harm others, it must be because users are more likely than nonusers to violate rights. Drug use per se is almost never harmful to others in the absence of further acts the drug user performs or fails to perform. This simple point seems to have escaped even the most

astute commentators. Kaplan writes that "the two most relevant social variables" that must be considered before the
use of any given drug is decriminalized are "how many people would use the drug in various use patterns, and how
harmful would their use be for them and society?"[72] I fail to
understand why Kaplan thinks he has identified two distinct
issues rather than one. What is the significance to the criminal
law of whether more persons will consume a drug, apart
from a concern that they will cause greater harm to themselves or to others?

Only three strategies are capable of avoiding this result,
and two have already been discredited. The first is legal
moralism. If recreational drug use were wrong per se, apart
from any harm it causes, and the wrongfulness of conduct
were a sufficient ground for criminalization, LAD could be
upheld without reference to the harm that drug use might
cause either to oneself or to others. The second is legalism.
If recreational drug use were analogous to treason or insurrection, the mere act of consuming illicit substances would
be objectionable and subject to punishment, regardless of
any subsequent consequences it might cause. But neither of
these two strategies is plausible, and I will discuss them no
further.

A third strategy, heretofore unmentioned, is to hold recreational drug users jointly responsible for the crimes and
atrocities committed in the illegal drug trade. Sometimes the
rhetoric of drug prohibitionists adopts this position. Bennett
claims that "anyone who uses [drugs] is involved in an in-
tentional criminal enterprise that is killing thousands of
Americans each year."[73] Nancy Reagan is more blunt: "If
you're a casual drug user, you are an accomplice to murder."[74] In Anglo-American criminal law, accomplices are
jointly responsible for the crimes committed by perpetrators.
If recreational drug users were jointly responsible for the
criminal violence in the illegal drug trade, they would violate
the rights of others simply by using drugs.

This rhetoric represents a gross exaggeration and misunderstanding of Anglo-American law. The sense in which typ-

179

ical drug users are "involved" in a "criminal enterprise" would not begin to support liability under widely accepted principles. No student of criminal law theory ever believed that recreational cocaine users, for example, were accurately described as accomplices to the murders perpetrated by the kingpins of the Colombian drug cartels. Most courts hold that a person is not an accomplice unless she acts with the *purpose* that another commit a crime.[75] Almost no drug user consumes a drug *in order* to facilitate an offense; the purpose in using drugs is not to assist criminal activity. Similarly, manufacturers of handguns are not accomplices to the murders they know will be committed by the use of their weapons. For this reason, recreational drug users cannot plausibly be held jointly responsible for the crimes of drug traffickers.

Seldom is recreational drug use per se harmful to others in the same respects as most other serious crimes. There are two crucial differences. First, mens rea, or criminal intent, is generally lacking in the case of drug users. Adults rarely use drugs with the intention of harming anyone. Occasionally persons consume alcohol or illegal substances in order to muster the courage to commit a crime, but this use of drugs is surely the exception rather than the rule. At most, the drug user who harms another acts recklessly or negligently. Most serious crimes involve a higher degree of culpability; the harm to others is typically caused purposely or knowingly.

In addition, the adult drug user creates only a *risk* of harm to others. Each user does not harm anyone in the same sense that each burglar or rapist harms a victim. These criminals do not merely create a risk of harm; their actions are harmful per se. One possible way to describe this distinction is to say that drug use is *indirectly* harmful to others, whereas these other crimes are *directly* harmful to others. These labels draw the following distinction. Every act of burglary or rape is harmful to others; each invariably violates the rights of identifiable victims. By contrast, not every act of drug use is harmful to others; each does not invariably violate the rights of identifiable victims. Consider any of the several evils that recreational drug use has been alleged to cause throughout this chapter. Many, if not most, recreational drug users will not cause the particular evil under consideration. Many, if not most, recreational drug users are attentive parents, good neighbors, fine students, and reliable employees. Most will not resort to (further) crime. How, then, can their recreational use of drugs be condemned on the ground that it is harmful to others? The answer must be that their recreational use of drugs impermissibly increases the risk or the likelihood of a harm to others. Since the harm that is risked by acts of drug use does not materialize on each and every occasion, recreational drug use might be said to harm others indirectly.

I do not describe recreational drug use as indirectly harmful to others in order to make LAD impossible to defend. It would be a serious mistake to suppose that the criminal law should prohibit only conduct that is directly harmful to others. Many examples of conduct indirectly harmful to others in the sense just described are and ought to be prohibited by the criminal law. These offenses are called *anticipatory* (or *inchoate*) offenses. They prohibit some conduct x because it impermissibly increases the likelihood of harm y. Conduct x does not invariably harm anyone, but it impermissibly increases the likelihood that a harm y (called a *consummate harm*) will occur.

Conduct x might impermissibly increase the likelihood of harm y in at least two ways. Sometimes the probability of y is raised because the agent who performs x is more likely to commit a subsequent harmful act. For example, persons who use illegal drugs might be more likely to commit robberies. On other occasions, the probability of y is raised because of something that happens to the agent who performs x. For example, persons who use illegal drugs might be more likely to get sick and miss work (although I have contested whether this result should be described as a harm).

I assume that persons lack a moral right to commit an anticipatory offense that can be justified. No one has a moral right to indirectly harm others by performing an act (or omission) that impermissibly increases the likelihood of harm to others. Adults lack the moral right to use drugs recreationally if LAD is defensible as an anticipatory offense.

Textbooks generally list attempt, solicitation, and conspiracy as the most familiar examples of anticipatory offenses. I assume that persons lack a moral right to conspire, solicit, or attempt to commit a criminal offense. But these offenses do not begin to exhaust the anticipatory offenses known to the criminal law. Almost all crimes of possession, including drug possession, are anticipatory offenses as well. Unfortunately, it is hard to be confident about additional examples.[76] Since legislators need not explicitly identify the consummate evil a statute is designed to prevent, it may be impossible to determine whether a particular offense is anticipatory or consummate.[77] For example, the dissemination of pornography might be regarded as objectionable per se, or it might be condemned because of further evils to which it is thought to lead.

Why is recreational drug use almost never included on a list of anticipatory offenses? It is difficult to believe that anyone would think that each and every act of recreational drug use harms others. Perhaps the omission of recreational drug use from a list of anticipatory offenses is explained by the fact that LAD might be construed as paternalistic. But anticipatory paternalistic offenses can and do exist, and recreational drug use might be among them. Clearly the failure to wear a seat belt does not always result in injury to the driver. Recreational drug use seems comparable; a single experiment with illegal drugs need not harm the user. In any event, in what follows I propose to assess LAD by whatever standards are used to determine the justifiability of anticipatory offenses.

A free society governed by the rule of law should place clear limits on the authority of the state to create anticipatory offenses. The wide use of anticipatory offenses results in an enormous expansion of police power. The state should not be given unbridled authority to reach far into someone's life and punish her for conduct that might eventually lead to harm, even though it is not harmful per se. The parameters of the law of attempt, solicitation, and conspiracy continue to be hotly contested among theorists of the criminal law.

Curiously, the scope of state authority to create anticipatory offenses has not been carefully delimited. No commentator on the criminal law has proposed an adequate theory of the general boundaries of anticipatory legislation. Feinberg's four-volume treatise on the moral limits of the criminal law barely mentions this issue. George Fletcher indicates that "the threat of harm," and not harm itself, is the better candidate for a requirement of criminal liability.[78] Perhaps so. But this modification of the harm principle enlarges its content exponentially, and Fletcher does not endeavor to narrow it. If "threat" is construed broadly, a wide range of conduct otherwise disqualified from prohibition under the harm principle becomes eligible for punishment. For example, the decision of an adolescent to drop out of school increases the threat of subsequent harm, since persons without high school degrees are more likely than graduates to engage in criminal activity. I assume that no one would be enthusiastic about using the criminal law to punish high school dropouts. But what principled considerations, if any, prevent the state from prohibiting such conduct as an anticipatory offense?

In what follows, I will take a small step towards remedying this general deficiency in criminal law theory by identifying four principles that play an important role in justifying anticipatory offenses. Although these principles are somewhat vague and imprecise, they are crucial in helping to establish the boundary between state authority and individual freedom. They are not mere guides to the efficient use of law, but valuable aids in identifying the moral rights of adults against our government. The application of these principles should clarify why some but not all behavior that increases the likelihood of a subsequent harm to others is justifiably prohibited by anticipatory legislation. The use of the criminal law to prevent dropping out of school turns out to violate several of these principles. By contrast, consider an example of an anticipatory offense that is almost never challenged as unjustified. Drunk driving is a somewhat serious offense not because the act of driving while intoxicated causes harm on each and every occasion, but because it impermissibly increases the likelihood that harm will result. The application of my principles should help to explain why drunk driving is relatively unproblematic as an anticipatory offense, whereas punishment for dropping out of school would be an unacceptable use of the criminal sanction.

Of course, my purpose in developing these principles is not to produce a comprehensive theory of anticipatory liability, but to assess whether LAD is defensible as an anticipatory offense, that is, on the ground that recreational drug use impermissibly increases the likelihood that others will be harmed. There may be special cases in which these four principles are satisfied. For example, in Chapter 4 I will concede that driving under the influence of drugs should be prohibited. Here I continue to assess LAD in its full generality, as proscribing the recreational use of drugs altogether. I will conclude that the application of these principles reveals serious defects in attempts to justify an anticipatory offense of recreational drug use.

I will refer to the first requirement of justified anticipatory legislation as the *inchoate principle:* Conduct *x* should not be criminalized on the ground that it increases the likelihood of harm *y* unless conduct that directly and deliberately causes *y* should also be prohibited. The criminal sanction is the ultimate weapon in the state arsenal. It is disingenuous to employ the last resort to prohibit conduct because it might lead to a subsequent harm unless conduct that deliberately causes that subsequent harm should also be prohibited. It cannot be worse to create a risk that some evil will occur than to directly cause that very evil.

No criminal law theorist has explicitly formulated the inchoate principle as a requirement of justified anticipatory legislation, but not because it is controversial. The inchoate principle has escaped notice because the very nature of anticipatory liability virtually guarantees that it will be satisfied. There is no crime of attempt (or conspiracy or solicitation) per se; a criminal attempt is always an attempt to do x. The variable x must be instantiated by a crime if liability is to be imposed. Perhaps "legal impossibility" is the only context in which there is any temptation to prosecute a defendant for an attempt to do something that would not be an offense were she to succeed. For example, suppose a defendant "smuggles" goods into the country under the mistaken belief that the goods are illegal to import. The principle of legality – no punishment without a crime – renders this attempt "legally impossible," precluding the imposition of liability.

Even though the inchoate principle seems obvious, its application creates immediate difficulties for many of the most familiar arguments in favor of criminalizing recreational drug use. As I have indicated, one such argument cites the alleged effects of drug use on the productivity of workers. As George Bush laments: "Drug use is job abuse. It's time to say: we've had enough."[79] Rather than trust the private sector to discipline workers with productivity problems, the Drug-Free Workplace Amendment to the 1988 Omnibus Drug Bill requires businesses above a given size to devise a clear prohibitory drug policy by establishing educational programs, by requiring that they be notified of any drug-related convictions of their employees, and by maintaining a good faith effort to create a drug-free workplace.

Kaplan has endorsed this rationale for LAD. Although he raises "both practical and moral questions" in "advocating the prohibition of [drugs] on the grounds that we must preserve the social productivity of the citizenry," and admits that "we do not usually think that the government should require us to be productive," he detects "no logical inconsistency between saying that a government should not punish laziness and saying that it may use its law to prevent access to things that make people lazy – or even aid in their being lazy."[80] Kaplan is correct that these statements betray no contradiction. The inchoate principle is not a requirement of logic. Still, the fact that the inchoate principle *can* be denied is no reason to do so. If applied consistently rather than selectively – to contexts not involving recreational drug use

– the suggestion that the state may punish persons for using devices to facilitate their laziness would be too fantastic to warrant refutation. If laziness itself should not be criminalized, persons should be permitted to use devices that increase the likelihood that they will become lazy.

Many other undesirable consequences alleged to be risked by recreational drug use cannot be invoked to support LAD without contravening the inchoate principle. Consider the claim that recreational drug users are more likely to neglect their spouses. Drug use should not be criminalized on the ground that it increases the likelihood of neglect unless the state is prepared to criminalize neglect itself. Why should acts that merely risk neglect be punished, when the decision to deliberately neglect one's spouse is not even a tort?

Of course, it does not follow that laziness or neglect (or dropping out of school, ignoring neighbors, and the like) are beyond moral reproach. The exercise of a right may fall short of a moral ideal. The principles advanced here are designed only to limit the authority of the state to enact anticipatory offenses. Conduct that fails to satisfy these principles need not be morally innocent. The application of these principles helps to establish the general point of most of this chapter: Conduct that creates a social problem, either directly or indirectly, does not automatically become eligible for criminal liability.

I will call the second requirement of justified anticipatory legislation the *triviality principle:* Conduct x should not be criminalized on the ground that it increases the likelihood of harm y unless y is a substantial harm. The commission of an anticipatory offense can be no more serious than directly causing the consummate harm it anticipates. Unless this consummate harm is substantial, there is little reason to create an anticipatory offense to prevent it. Commentators agree that a system of criminal justice should include the rule *de minimis non curat lex* (the law ought not to proscribe trivial harms). They disagree, however, about the rationale for this rule. Should it be construed as a matter of principle, so that defendants have a moral right not to be held criminally liable for causing trivial harms? Or should the rule be construed as a matter of efficiency, to prevent the waste that results when the "cure" of law enforcement is worse than the "disease" of criminal behavior?[81]

Neither alternative should be dismissed out of hand. Initially, the latter may seem to be more plausible. It may be unwise and impractical to annihilate a mosquito with a howitzer, but the offending insect has no cause to complain because it was not crushed by an ordinary swatter. On the other hand, criminal defendants are often indignant when they are punished for trivial harms. A person charged with littering for disposing of a used match is likely to feel maltreated.[82] Such a reaction cannot be explained by supposing that punishment for a trivial offense is merely inefficient. Arguably, persons have a moral right not to be subjected to criminal liability for conduct that causes an insignificant harm. Perhaps minimal harms should not be counted as harms at all; a trivial violation of a right may not leave the victim in what Feinberg describes as a harmed condition.[83]

Whatever the rationale of the *de minimis* defense, it might seem implausible to suppose that its application would pose any difficulties for the justifiability of LAD. Drug prohibitionists have attributed a staggering volume of harm to the illegal use of substances. Lawn writes, "All told, illicit drugs cost the United States more than $60 billion a year in lost employment, prison and other criminal justice costs and treatment programs."[84] Decriminalization theorists typically counter that this statistic confuses the harm caused by drugs with the harm caused by drug prohibitions. Surely the cost of imprisoning drug offenders should not be included in the total cost of illicit drug use.

Nonetheless, suppose it is true that a sensible and realistic calculation of the aggregate cost of recreational drug use is very high. It does not follow that typical, standard instances of drug use are especially harmful. These aggregate figures say nothing about the amount of harm caused by individual acts of drug use. Although the aggregate social cost may be great, the contributions of given drug users to this total may be small. The attribution of aggregate figures to particular agents commits what might be called the ecological fallacy.[85]

For two reasons, the typical drug user may create almost no harm, even though the aggregate social cost of drug use is enormous. First, the aggregate figure may be high because there are many drug users, each of whom is responsible for only a small amount of harm. Even the grossly exaggerated figure of $60 billion seems less worrisome when apportioned among 28 million persons who use illegal drugs annually. By simple division, the contribution of the average drug user is about $2,150 annually, hardly an amount that warrants treating drug use as a significantly more serious social problem than, say, income tax evasion. This figure might again be divided by the numerous occasions – literally billions, according to Ethan Nadelmann – on which users consume drugs.[86] The harm caused per incidence of drug use is minute.

Mitchell concludes that the small amount of harm per incidence of both legal and illegal drug use explains why the imposition of tort liability would not discourage consumption altogether. According to Mitchell,

> Tort law did not produce criminal-type prohibitions of specific drugs [because] the ordinary, individual user of alcohol, tobacco, heroin or cocaine is not worth suing. Their drug use does not cause much harm, nor is it antisocial enough to warrant significant punitive damages.[87]

He estimates that the average dose of alcohol, for example, "causes no more than 50 cents in public harm."[88] If Mitchell is correct that the amount of social harm caused by the average drug user is so small that the user "is not worth suing," it seems fair to ask whether this amount is too trivial to qualify for criminal liability as well.

Second, the typical, standard drug user may create almost no harm because a subgroup of users creates virtually all of the harm. Precise figures about how the aggregate social harm of illegal drug use is apportioned among users are difficult to obtain. More reliable data can be drawn from the consumption of alcohol, which may conform to a pattern similar to many other drugs. About 13% of all drinkers consume 66 percent of the alcohol used in America, leaving only 34 percent of the total for the remaining 87 percent of more moderate drinkers.[89] If the distribution of other drugs is roughly similar, and the likelihood of causing harm to others is, ceteris paribus, a function of the amount a person consumes,[90] the typical drug user may not cause much harm.

It would be crucial to establish that the average, typical drug user does not create substantial amounts of harm, since criminal liability should be based on standard cases.[91] Generalizations from exceptional cases would be unfair. Each user of a legal or illegal drug should not be treated as though she were a member of the relatively small class of persons who cause large amounts of social harm. Persons should be held liable only for the harm they cause; vicarious liability for the acts of others (except perhaps in the most unusual and carefully defined circumstances) is unjust. I have repeatedly emphasized how drug policy tends to be driven by unwarranted generalizations from worst-case scenarios that diverge from the reality of typical recreational drug use. Sensitivity to the ecological fallacy helps to avoid this tendency.

I will call the third requirement of justified anticipatory legislation the *remoteness principle:* Conduct x should not be criminalized on the ground that it increases the likelihood of harm y unless x and y are sufficiently proximate. The concept "proximate" makes this principle vague and imprecise. The general idea is that an anticipatory offense should not be created if the conduct to be criminalized is too remote or far removed from the consummate harm. Examples may help to clarify this elusive principle. The probability of a traffic accident that is reduced by prohibiting drunken driving could be reduced still further by prohibiting conduct that is more remote from the consummate harm. For example, the state could create an anticipatory offense of drinking at a bar without a designated sober driver. Criminalizing such conduct would contribute to the goal of preventing traffic accidents.

Yet this proposal is objectionable because it would criminalize conduct that is not sufficiently proximate to the consummate harm.

Any number of factors contribute to the complex determination of whether conduct x is sufficiently proximate to a consummate harm y. Among the most important of these factors is whether the victim had the opportunity to avoid the harm by taking reasonable precautions. Suppose some inexpensive and convenient device could somehow insulate motorists from the risks created by intoxicated drivers. Under this (barely imaginable) condition, the act of drunken driving would become less proximate to the injuries suffered by motorists who failed to adopt these reasonable precautions.

The remoteness principle has two distinct but related rationales, each of which supports the judgment that adults are more likely to have a moral right to engage in conduct the further it is removed from a consummate harm. The first rationale is simply a function of probabilities. The greater the distance between x and y, the less the likelihood that persons who commit the anticipatory offense will cause the consummate harm. Few persons who drink in bars without a designated sober driver will cause a traffic accident. As conduct becomes less likely to culminate in a consummate harm, the more persuasive is the judgment that persons have a moral right to engage in it.

The second rationale invokes a conception of a responsible human agent. Persons who perform the anticipatory conduct might take any number of intermediate steps to minimize the risk that the consummate harm will occur. For example, many persons who drink in bars without a designated sober driver choose not to become intoxicated, or they elect to use public transportation to take them home. Because of the availability of these intermediate steps, the creation of an anticipatory offense of drinking at a bar without a designated sober driver would sweep too broadly. Any such offense would punish persons who would have taken steps to prevent the occurrence of the consummate harm. To punish persons without first determining whether they would choose to take these steps would treat them as less than responsible human agents.[92]

Although criminal theorists have not explicitly identified the remoteness principle as a general requirement of justified anticipatory legislation, it plays a prominent role in arguments about how existing anticipatory offenses should be interpreted. For example, commentators have long struggled to identify the point at which a defendant commits the acts that constitute a criminal attempt. Does a person commit an attempted rape by lying in wait for a possible victim? Reasonable minds have disagreed. As a general matter, if liability attaches too early, many defendants who would have changed their minds and abandoned their plans will be convicted unfairly.[93] The rule requiring that a defendant is not guilty unless he takes a "substantial step" toward the commission of a crime applies the remoteness principle to interpret the law of criminal attempt.[94]

The remoteness principle also plays a significant role in debates about proposals to create new criminal offenses. Most states recently raised the minimum drinking age from eighteen to twenty-one. One of the rationales in favor of this change was that intoxicated drivers between eighteen and twenty-one are more likely than intoxicated drivers who are older to cause traffic accidents. This rationale construes the new crime of drinking between the ages of eighteen and twenty-one as an anticipatory offense designed to reduce the risk of highway mayhem. Of course, driving while intoxicated is already an anticipatory offense in every state. This new offense is more remote from the consummate harm to be prevented, and thus it is subject to great controversy.[95]

The remoteness principle creates difficulties for justifying an anticipatory offense of recreational drug use. Much of the rhetoric in favor of LAD construes the crime of recreational drug use as doubly, triply, quadruply, or n-tuply anticipatory: Jones's use of marijuana should be prohibited because it might induce him to try cocaine, which might cause him to become addicted, which might lead him to become poor, which might make him more inclined to commit a crime.

Each additional link in this causal chain decreases the chance that the consummate harm will occur and increases the probability that the initial act is protected by a moral right. Moreover, the fact that drug users might choose to take any number of intermediate steps to reduce the likelihood that the consummate harm will occur is ignored or forgotten when this rhetoric is used to support LAD. Many drug users adopt elaborate precautions to minimize the risk that their consumption will result in harm.[96] It is unfair to punish the prudent because others are imprudent.

In this light, consider Bennett's putative justification for targeting casual users in the war on drugs. He contends that the "non-addicted casual" drug user "remains a grave issue of national concern," even though such a person "is likely to have a still-intact family, social and work life" and "to 'enjoy' his drug for the pleasure it offers."[97] Nonetheless, Bennett argues, the casual drug user should be punished severely, because he is "much more willing and able to proselytize his drug use – by action or example – among his remaining non-user peers, friends, and acquaintances. A non-addict's drug use, in other words, is *highly* contagious."[98]

Bennett's rationale adds even more distance between the anticipatory offense and the consummate harm to be prevented. Smith's problem-free and casual use of a recreational drug should be prohibited because it might lead Jones to experiment with a drug that might make his behavior more likely to conform to the (already lengthy) causal scenario just described. In perhaps no other context is this theory of "imitative harms" accepted as an adequate justification for criminal liability. It seems preposterous to punish Smith's harmless behavior on the ground that Jones might imitate it. And if Smith's life has not been adversely affected by his use of drugs, why worry that Jones might mimic it? The imitation, like the original, may not be harmful either to Jones or to others.

I will refer to the fourth and most important requirement of justified anticipatory legislation as the *empirical principle:*

Conduct x should not be criminalized on the ground that it increases the likelihood of harm y unless there is an established causal connection between x and y in a reasonably high percentage of cases. The empirical principle is perhaps the most obvious, and yet the most difficult to apply of the four requirements of justified anticipatory legislation. This principle again employs a vague and imprecise standard, in this case the criterion of reasonableness. Exactly how often must x cause y before x is justifiably prohibited? Persons will answer this question differently in the context of particular examples.

But the foremost difficulty in applying the empirical principle is to establish whether a correlation between x and y constitutes a genuine causal connection. As any social scientist knows, this determination is extremely problematic. Decades of careful scientific study were required to confirm that cigarettes cause cancer, even though researchers were long aware of the correlation between the two.

Any sensible application of the empirical principle must be mediated by several ancillary principles.[99] I will mention only two. First, the causal connection between x and y must be more firmly established if conduct x has a significant value in its own right. The state should be reluctant to prohibit an important activity, even though it frequently leads to a serious consummate harm. The application of this first ancillary principle to the case for LAD is bound to generate controversy, since the value of recreational activities in general, and drug use in particular, is so unclear. Second, the causal connection between x and y need be less firmly established as y becomes more harmful. If the consummate harm y is sufficiently great, conduct x may be criminalized, even if it leads to y only occasionally. Difficulties in applying this second ancillary principle to the case for LAD will soon become apparent.

Thus far I have assumed that the several accusations of drug prohibitionists were true. For example, I have not challenged whether drug users make inattentive parents, because I was anxious to show how the imposition of criminal liability could be contested even if such a charge were accurate. Now it is time to critically examine whether recreational drug use really causes the evils cited by prohibitionists.

Of course, drug use might occasionally lead to just about any given evil. Drug prohibitionists frequently offer anecdotes about how users of an illegal substance commit some terrible atrocity. According to the second ancillary principle that was just mentioned, such atrocities would not have to occur very often in order to justify LAD. Still, these stories cannot be used to support the imposition of criminal liability if they are rare and exceptional.[100] As they stand, these anecdotes provide no indication of the likelihood that given drug users will behave similarly. In the absence of supporting evidence, they fail to satisfy the minimal requirements of the empirical principle.

Some of the difficulties in establishing a causal connection between recreational drug use and many of its purported effects are due to the lack of clarity in describing these effects. Since it is hard to know what makes someone a "bad neighbor," no one should have any clear idea about whether drug use causes this consequence. Somewhat more research has investigated whether recreational drug users are "poor employees." Little of this research has explored the connection between drug use and actual job performance. However, research has assessed whether drug users tend to exhibit characteristics that make them less attractive to employers. In one study, applicants hired by the post office whose preemployment tests indicated cocaine use showed "a pattern of increased risks of accidents, injuries, and discipline relative to those with negative urine samples," although only the risk for injuries was statistically significant.[101]

Do data of this kind establish a causal connection between recreational drug use and poor job performance and thus satisfy the empirical principle? Some of the difficulties in answering this question will be pursued in the following section. I will discuss these problems in the broader context of examining what may be the most important defense of

LAD: Recreational drugs should be prohibited because they increase the likelihood that users will commit crimes.

DRUGS AND CRIME

The correlation between drug use and crime, particularly in inner cities, is frightening. A majority of males arrested in each of the largest American cities test positive for one or more illegal drugs.[102] Cocaine, especially in the form of crack, is particularly worrisome. In New York City, 77 percent of all males arrested tested positive for cocaine use.[103] These statistics surprised even hardened law-enforcement agents, for whom the association between drug use and crime was old hat. This correlation between drugs and crime fuels the argument that LAD is justified as an anticipatory offense to reduce the incidence of consummate crime.

Some theorists have cautioned against uncritically supposing that the prevalence of drug use among arrestees is shared by the general population of criminal offenders. According to Jan and Marcia Chaiken, "High-rate criminals who do not use drugs, or use them only sporadically, are far less likely to be arrested than their counterparts who use drugs frequently."[104] Nonetheless, by all accounts, the incidence of drug use among offenders is remarkably high. Can this fact be used to justify LAD?

Conservatives who do not waiver in their support for LAD are divided in their answers. Bennett and Wilson, who claim in nearly identical language that LAD is needed to prevent drug users from harming others, disagree about whether drugs cause crime. Although Bennett endorses this argument,[105] Wilson has recently repudiated it. He concludes: "It is not clear that enforcing the laws against drug use would reduce crime. On the contrary, crime may be caused by such enforcement."[106]

Despite mixed reviews from drug prohibitionists, a critical evaluation of this argument for LAD is crucial. Unlike most of the reasoning previously discussed in this chapter, the claim that LAD is justified as an anticipatory offense to reduce further criminality has the structure of an impressive defense. The objective that LAD is designed to prevent is genuine harm, not mere disutility that does not violate anyone's moral rights. Nor is this harm arguably noncriminal in nature. Here the rationale of anticipatory legislation is clear and beyond reproach: Prevent conduct that increases the likelihood of a consummate crime, and the incidence of consummate crime will be reduced.

Each of the four requirements of justified anticipatory legislation must be satisfied before data about arrestees warrant prohibiting recreational drug use in order to reduce the likelihood of subsequent criminality. The first two conditions are easily met. The inchoate principle creates no obstacle, since the consummate harm alleged to be caused by recreational drug use is already justifiably criminal. The triviality principle is satisfied as well, since the consummate harm is sufficiently serious. Those who support LAD because of the connection between drugs and crime are not likely to be bothered by shoplifting or other petty offenses, but by crimes that employ or threaten violence, including robbery, burglary, and murder.

However, I will argue that both the remoteness and the empirical principles create major difficulties for this defense of LAD. The following discussion briefly summarizes the current state of knowledge among social scientists about the connection between drugs and crime. This survey is necessarily incomplete and oversimplified; entire volumes have been written supporting one hypothesis or another. I conclude that LAD probably cannot be justified as an anticipatory offense designed to reduce the incidence of further criminality. Some drugs may cause some users, under some circumstances, to commit crimes. But empirical research suggests that this pattern constitutes the rare exception rather than the general rule. The evidence does not indicate that LAD is needed to reduce crime.

Still, it is hard to be sure. According to Michael Tonry:

> Drug and crime research is a minor scholarly activity and is
> poorly funded. The literature is scant, much of it is fugitive,
> the research community is fragmented, and too much of the
> research is poor in quality and weak in design. One striking
> feature of research on drug policy is its scantiness.[107]

Only tentative conclusions can be drawn about whether LAD
can be justified as an anticipatory offense. A more definitive
answer awaits further empirical research on the connection
between drugs and crime.

A defense of LAD based on data about arrestees may have
some troubling implications for existing law. Arrestees are
more likely to test positive for the use of alcohol than for any
illegal drug. Nearly half of all prisoners were actually "under
the influence" of alcohol when committing their crimes, and
the percentage is even higher for violent crimes.[108] If the basis
for preventing drug use is to reduce the risk of subsequent
criminality, there is better reason to prohibit alcohol than to
prohibit illegal substances. Perhaps there are excellent
grounds not to reintroduce the prohibition of alcohol, but
evidence about the prevalence of alcohol use among arrestees
is not among them.

Do drugs cause crime? Data about arrestees are not very
helpful in answering this question. Theorists who answer
affirmatively after noting the remarkably high percentage of
criminals who test positive for both legal and illegal drugs
have focused on the wrong population. The ultimate issue
is whether, ceteris paribus, persons who use drugs are significantly more likely to commit crimes than persons who do
not use drugs. No insight into this issue is gained by establishing that persons who commit crimes are significantly
more likely to use drugs than persons who do not commit
crimes.

Theorists who believe that drugs cause crime must explain
why relatively few users of recreational drugs become criminals. Although the majority of criminals may be drug users,
the majority of drug users are not (otherwise) criminals. Con-

tinued criminality is more predictive of drug use than continued drug use is predictive of criminality.[109] Approximately 14.5 million people use an illicit drug each month.[110] Only a tiny fraction are arrested for crimes, although no one knows how many commit offenses that are undetected. The fact that only a small minority of drug users resort to criminality raises a serious difficulty for those who conclude that LAD satisfies the conditions for justified anticipatory legislation. Reasonable minds will differ about what percentage of drug users would have to become criminals before an anticipatory offense should be enacted. But few would defend the creation of an anticipatory offense of conspiracy, for example, if a comparable minority of those who conspired to commit an offense ultimately succeeded in doing so. The empirical standards used to justify an anticipatory offense of recreational drug use should be no lower.

What can be said for or against the hypothesis that drugs cause crime, even if data about arrestees are largely immaterial in supporting it? Perhaps progress can be made in assessing this hypothesis by investigating the causal mechanisms that might motivate drug users to commit offenses. At least three models have been proposed.[111] First, the *psychopharmacological* effects of drug use might lead to crime. Drugs might cause users to become violent, excitable, or irrational. Even drugs with sedative properties that initially suppress aggressive tendencies might later give rise to violence, since some users become irritable during withdrawal. Second, the *economic* effects of drug use might lead to crime. Drug users might commit robberies and burglaries to support their costly drug habits. What begins as a property offense might end in death or injury, either to the perpetrator or the victim. Third, the *systemic* effects of drug use might lead to crime. This category includes offenses within dealing hierarchies to enforce normative codes, retaliate for real or imagined crimes of competitors or informers, resolve disputes involving territory or possession of drugs, punish customers who fail to pay debts, and so on. I will briefly discuss each of these three models in reverse order.

Drugs and crime

There is little doubt that drugs lead to systemic crime, although their role may be exaggerated. Some evidence suggests that even the notorious violence of crack dealers is a function of individual predispositions toward violent lifestyles that were manifest long before these persons became involved in selling drugs.[112] In any event, most of the systemic crime is committed by dealers rather than by consumers and thus is less relevant to the issue of whether prohibition of recreational drug use can be justified. Finally and most importantly, the inclusion of this category of offenses creates a methodological problem in exploring the connection between drugs and crime. Since a wide range of conduct involving most drugs is already criminal, any interesting connection between drugs and crime must exclude many systemic offenses from consideration. The controversial issue is not whether drug use causes crime, but whether drug use causes behavior that would persist and remain illegal even if drug use were decriminalized. Theorists who favor decriminalization are most persuasive in promising that the repeal of LAD would drastically reduce the incidence of systemic crime. Recall the confidence of Ostrowski: "The day after legalization goes into effect, the streets of America will be safer. The drug dealers will be gone. The shootouts between drug dealers will end. Innocent bystanders will not be murdered anymore."[113] Although this prediction may be overly optimistic, I assume that systemic offenses would be much less frequent under most models of decriminalization. For these reasons, I will not further discuss systemic crimes.

Excluding systemic crimes from consideration goes a long way toward eroding the hypothesis that drugs cause crime. According to some studies, the majority of drug-related homicides, perhaps as many as 74 percent, are systemic.[114] The correlation between drug use and crime would be far less alarming if systemic crimes were not included in empirical studies.

Decriminalization theorists also argue that the economic motivations for crime among drug users are more a consequence of drug prohibition than of drugs. They point out

that "drug laws increase the price of illegal drugs, often forcing users to steal to get the money to obtain them."[115] The
repeal of LAD could make drugs more affordable. Needless
to say, few drug prohibitionists are persuaded of the wisdom
of this proposal. In order to undercut the economic motivation to steal to purchase drugs, Bennett speculates that
"we would probably have to make [cocaine] legally available
at not much more than $10 a gram. And then an average
dose of cocaine would cost about 50 cents – well within the
lunch-money budget of the average American elementary
school student."[116]

Notice that Bennett's response apparently concedes that
decriminalization has the potential to make drugs more affordable, and thus to reduce or eliminate the incidence of
economic crime. In order to accomplish this objective, however, he believes that drugs would have to become *too* affordable. Thus the dispute between drug prohibitionists and
their critics is not about whether decriminalization would
drastically reduce economic crime. Instead, the dispute is
about whether the availability of inexpensive drugs would
bring about even greater evils than economic crime. But this
issue, however important to makers of social policy, is largely
irrelevant to the claim that LAD is needed as an anticipatory
offense to prevent drug users from committing economic
crimes. Once again, Bennett's response raises the specter of
escalating drug use as a reason to oppose decriminalization.
But whatever the reasons to be apprehensive about this possible escalation, they do not include the fear that more drug
users will inevitably commit more economic crimes.

Both drug prohibitionists and decriminalization theorists
could afford to be more skeptical about economic explanations for the connection between drugs and crime. The supposition that typical drug users are likely to commit predatory
crimes to finance their habits may not withstand empirical
scrutiny. According to Chaiken and Chaiken,

> No single sequential or causal relationship is now believed to
> relate drug use to predatory crime. When the behaviors of

large groups of people are studied in the aggregate, no coherent general patterns emerge associating drug use per se
with participation in predatory crime.[117]

Few drug-using delinquents admit to committing property
crimes in order to raise money to buy drugs. Among youths
who both use drugs and commit predatory crimes, "the connection appears to be due more to a style of everyday life
than to simply committing predatory crimes to get money."[118]
Theft for direct acquisition appears to be a more common
activity than theft for resale among drug users who steal.[119]
These conclusions are confirmed by retrospective studies of
adult offenders. When adult inmates were surveyed about
their main reasons for becoming involved in crime, only 26
percent of those who used illegal drugs cited drug use as
their primary motive, and still fewer (20 percent) cited drug
use as their sole reason for committing crimes.[120] Chaiken
and Chaiken contend that these data "do not give much hope
that even major reductions in the numbers of people who
use illicit drugs could significantly reduce the numbers of
incidents of predatory crime."[121] This conclusion, if correct,
is fatal to the argument that LAD is justified as an anticipatory
offense to reduce the likelihood of economic crime.

Still, the connection between drug use and economic crime
is not entirely illusory. Research indicates that *"high-frequency
drug users are also very likely to be high-rate predators."*[122]
Criminality is highly concentrated among a very small proportion of delinquents who use massive quantities of
drugs.[123] If so, the incidence of economic crime may be reduced by discouraging the consumption of large amounts of
drugs. Prohibitionists will seize on this datum to attempt to
salvage LAD. They can be expected to reason that the most
effective way to prevent persons from consuming large quantities of drugs is to prevent them from consuming small quantities of drugs. Thus the prohibitionists will endorse a policy
of "zero tolerance." This gambit also provides some justification for banning the use of recreational drugs that do not
lead to economic crime. No one suggests that prohibition of

LSD is warranted because users are inclined to steal to acquire the two or three dollars needed to buy it. But prohibiting the use of so-called gateway drugs may be part of the best strategy to prevent the use of other drugs that are alleged to cause economic crime.

This defense of LAD can be challenged on empirical grounds. Perhaps the most effective way to discourage the consumption of large amounts of drugs is to punish the consumption of large amounts of drugs directly, and not to implement a policy of "zero tolerance."[124]

In any event, this rationale for LAD begins to compromise the remoteness principle. It adds yet another layer between the anticipatory offense and the consummate harm to be prevented: All illegal recreational drugs should continue to be prohibited, because some users of any drug will become consumers of large amounts of those drugs that make them more likely to commit property crimes. The likelihood that a given person who commits the anticipatory offense would ever cause the consummate harm is relatively low. Moreover, a person who commits the anticipatory offense can take precautions to reduce the probability of consuming large amounts of drugs and thereby become at risk of causing the consummate harm. Many researchers have described means by which persons manage to keep their drug intake within responsible limits.[125] Whether LAD should be supported because of the connection between drug use and economic crime may depend on how great a barrier the remoteness principle raises to the creation of justified anticipatory legislation.

Some drug prohibitionists defend psychopharmacological explanations of the connection between drugs and crime. In the course of describing "a teen-aged addict in Manhattan that was smoking crack when he sexually abused and caused permanent internal injuries to his one-month old daughter," Bennett asks:

> Does any rational person believe that a cut-rate price for drugs at a government outlet will stop such psychopathic behavior?

The fact is that under the influence of drugs, normal people do not act normally, and abnormal people behave in chilling and horrible ways.[126]

Bennett concludes this anecdote by comparing drug decriminalization to a surrender by Churchill to Hitler.

Once again, this defense of LAD might infringe the remoteness principle, since drug users can take any number of intermediate steps to reduce the likelihood of the consummate harm. Because many drug users adopt precautions to minimize the possibility of violence or antisocial conduct, it seems unfair to prohibit their drug consumption in order to prevent aggression by the minority of drug users who might not behave similarly.

Moreover, researchers are far more ambivalent than Bennett about this explanation for why drug use might cause crime. Helene White concludes that "the psychopharmacological explanation for the drugs-cause-crime model has been largely refuted in the literature with regard to heroin and marijuana, but has received strong support in the alcohol literature and occasionally with other drugs."[127] The issue of whether and under what circumstances some or all drugs have properties that lead persons to lose control and engage in criminal activities they would not otherwise have committed is difficult to resolve. But psychopharmacological explanations for crime are given little credence in the self-reports of adolescent offenders who were under the influence of drugs at the time of their offenses. None attributed their criminal behavior to "consuming large amounts of alcohol or drugs and subsequently losing control of their behavior and doing crimes they would not otherwise commit."[128] Instead, these subjects typically regulated their drug intake in order to avoid detection, to ensure their safety, or to execute their crimes more skillfully.[129] Some consumed sizeable amounts of drugs to muster the courage to commit a crime,[130] but this use of drugs enhances rather than undermines self-control.

Fagan has conducted the most thorough study of the possible mechanisms by which intoxication might lead to aggression.[131] He examines four possible models that have gained some currency in explaining any increased levels of aggression that have been detected among intoxicated persons: biological and physiological, psychopharmacological, psychological and psychiatric, and sociological and cultural. He judges each of these perspectives to be "deficient," since "no single framework can be expected to explain what obviously is an extremely complex relation between substance use and aggression."[132] Indeed, "how aggressive behavior is influenced by the ingestion of various substances is not well understood."[133]

Evidence is sketchy, because it is so hard to separate the effects of drugs from the effects of other variables. But Fagan concludes that "there is little explanatory power to the intoxication – aggression association when the partial correlations of culture and social interaction are removed."[134] Sociocultural factors appear to channel the arousal effects of various substances into behaviors that may or may not involve aggression.[135] Other researchers concur in this assessment,[136] although the jury is still out on the precise connection between the use of various drugs and the loss of control that can result in criminal behavior.

The empirical principle creates difficulties for this defense of LAD, since "intoxication does not consistently lead to aggressive behavior."[137] The likelihood that given users of any drug will become aggressive is relatively small. In one study, 83 percent of cocaine users answered "never" when asked whether they felt aggressive or violent while under the influence of cocaine; none answered "most times" or "always."[138]

Apart from the strengths and weaknesses of these various models, three conditions must be satisfied to confirm the hypothesis that x causes y, that is, that drug use causes crime.[139] First, a statistical correlation must be established in the relevant population. Since I have already discussed how most data about the correlation between drugs and crime generalize from the wrong population, I will focus on the last two conditions. Next, the cause must precede its effect.

If criminal activity occurs prior to drug use among persons involved in both, the hypothesis that crime causes drug use is more plausible than the hypothesis that drug use causes crime.[140] Finally, the relationship between drugs and crime must not be spurious. If drug use and crime are elements in a cluster of other problem behaviors, or if both drug use and crime can be explained by a common cause, the hypothesis that drug use causes crime is refuted.

Neglect of these last two requirements is pervasive among drug prohibitionists. Rarely do the prohibitionists ensure that the alleged cause precedes its consequence. Even less often do they control for variables other than drug use that might explain the supposed effect. For example, the study among postal workers mentioned in the preceding section might provide valuable information to prospective employers,[141] but hardly establishes a causal connection between drug use and poor job performance. The researchers did not inquire whether the drug users were poor employees before they began using drugs. Nor did they ascertain whether the association between cocaine use and employment outcome could be explained by alcohol abuse, which tends to be correlated with the use of cocaine.[142] Nor did they exclude the possibility that some common cause might explain both drug use and poor job performance. In short, this study provides little reason to believe that the very applicants who test positive for cocaine would have been better employees if only they had abstained from drug use. Yet such studies are frequently cited by drug prohibitionists as empirical evidence that drugs cause harm to others. Over twenty years ago, Andrew Weil cautioned against the tendency to make illegal drugs the cause of what we associate with them.[143] His warning has not been heeded.

The requirement that a cause must precede its effect also undermines the hypothesis that drug use causes crime. Studies consistently show that criminal activity developmentally precedes the use of drugs among adolescents who both use drugs and commit crimes.[144] Few studies have concluded that aggression did not precede substance use.[145]

Generally, onset of drug use is not even associated with an increase in delinquency among youths.[146] Drug use may lengthen the time required for adolescents to "mature out" of criminality, although it does not appear to increase the probability that they will become criminals in the first place.[147] Perhaps drug use serves to reinforce the life-styles of those persons already involved in aggression or criminal activity.

According to White, the empirical evidence suggests that drug use and crime are spuriously related, at least among adolescents, who have been studied more extensively than adults.[148] Many researchers have attempted to identify one or more common causes to explain both criminality and drug use. The plausible candidates include early antisocial behavior in elementary school, inconsistent parenting, lack of communication with parents, school adjustment problems, association with deviant peers, low degree of social bonding to prosocial individuals, positive attitudes toward drug use and delinquency, low self-esteem, high sensation seeking, low attachments to school and family, alcoholic parents, poor school performance, low IQ, and inadequate moral development.[149] Franklin Zimring and Gordon Hawkins speculate that the correlation between drugs and crime might be explained by a willingness to take risks.[150]

The conclusion that drug use and crime are spuriously related is bound to be dismissed by many commentators. They look at the inner cities and see massive amounts of both drugs and crime; who could deny that the epidemic of crime is caused at least in part by the use of drugs? However, there are two things these commentators do *not* see. First, they do not see how much drug-related crime is systemic and a consequence of drug prohibitions rather than of drug use itself. Second, they do not see how much crime would occur in the inner cities if someone could wave a magic wand and make drugs disappear. In light of the best available empirical evidence, the causal inference these commentators make between drug use and crime seems to be fallacious.

Those who subscribe to the "politically convenient"

belief[151] that drugs cause significant amounts of crime may be guilty of wishful thinking. If drugs do not cause crime, what does? The drug problem may be intractable. But alternative explanations for America's crime problem place the solution even further beyond our control. Social scientists probably have better ideas about how to reduce drug use than about how to combat whatever socioeconomic and psychological factors contribute to crime. For this reason, no one concerned about America's crime problem should be especially happy to conclude that drug use and crime are spuriously related. But those who endeavor to find genuine solutions to America's crime problem should not be persuaded that the war on drugs is a large part of the answer.

CONCLUSION

The claim that criminal legislation against the recreational use of drugs is justified to prevent persons from causing harm to others has encountered several difficulties. Much of the social disutility that prohibitionists allege to be caused by drugs does not amount to a harm capable of supporting liability within a system of criminal justice that includes the harm principle. Not all disutility is harm; many of the bad consequences said to be caused by drug use do not violate anyone's moral rights. In particular, it is doubtful that anyone has a right that the number of drug users does not increase. In addition, many of the harms to others that *are* caused by recreational drug use might be noncriminal rather than criminal in nature.

The most promising strategy is to defend LAD as an anticipatory offense. In other words, recreational drug use might be construed as indirectly harmful, in that it impermissibly increases various risks of harm to others. LAD might be justified in order to prevent adults from exposing others to these risks. I identified four principles that any justified anticipatory offense must satisfy and attempted to show why the application of these principles creates problems for a defense of LAD.

I will not summarize these problems here. Instead, I will briefly describe a recreational drug that adults would lack a moral right to use, and that the state could justifiably prohibit, on the basis of these four principles. First, this drug must increase the likelihood that users will cause a consummate harm that should be considered a criminal offense if caused directly and deliberately. Second, the harm caused by users of this drug must be substantial. Third, the use of this drug must be sufficiently proximate to the consummate harm. There must be little that a person can realistically do to decrease the probability that his use of this drug will lead him to bring about the consummate harm. Fourth, this drug must actually cause a significant percentage of users to commit the consummate offense. The connection between the use of this drug and harm to others must not be spurious. In other words, research would have to establish that the tendency to violate the rights of others did not predate the consumption of this drug and that no common cause could explain both the propensity to harm others as well as the use of this drug.

No one should have much difficulty imagining a drug that satisfies these criteria. The plots of many science fiction novels involve substances that clearly qualify. The substances used to "brainwash" captured soldiers in stories such as *The Manchurian Candidate* fit this description,[152] although it is hard to fathom why anyone would want to experiment with them for recreational purposes. Much of the public probably believes that crack meets these criteria. Once again, it is best not to be too dogmatic about whether crack or any other actual substance satisfies my conditions for criminalization. Since several of these criteria are vague and imprecise, their application to particular cases is not entirely clear. But empirical research does not inspire overwhelming confidence that such a recreational drug actually exists.

Chapter 4

Restrictions on drug use

Thus far I have provided reasons to doubt that criminal laws against the use of recreational drugs (LAD) are justified in their full generality, that is, that recreational drug use should be totally prohibited. My conclusion is incompatible with the way drugs are treated under federal law today. Except for a handful of exemptions, most notably for alcohol and tobacco, the Controlled Substances Act punishes the recreational use of drugs altogether. State law is only slightly more permissive. Eleven states have decriminalized the use and possession of small amounts of marijuana, although they continue to treat it as a noncriminal violation resembling a parking or speeding ticket. Alaska has recently ended its more radical experiment with the removal of all penalties for the private use of marijuana. Apart from these few exceptions, the recreational use of drugs is a criminal offense. Recreational drug use is not permitted under some circumstances, in some places, at some times, by some persons.

In this chapter, I will assume that my arguments from Chapters 2 and 3 are sound and that harm either to drug users or to others does not justify LAD in its full generality. The arguments in favor of a moral right to use drugs recreationally are more persuasive than the arguments against such a right. Respect for moral rights requires that recreational drug use should be *decriminalized*. This word means different things to different people. The core meaning is that punishment should not be imposed for recreational drug use. LAD should be repealed or, at the very least, unenforced.

Many decriminalization theorists would be satisfied if all recreational drugs were treated like marijuana in the eleven states just mentioned. Drug users could not lose their liberty but might still be fined for a noncriminal offense. This position is frequently endorsed as a compromise between total surrender and continuation of the ineffective and counterproductive war on drugs. This compromise might have important utilitarian advantages over our present policy. However, it has less to recommend it from the standpoint of moral rights. If my arguments are persuasive, the use of drugs is not analogous to driving in excess of the speed limit or parking overtime, wrongful but not very serious activities that merit little punishment. No one has a moral right to speed or to park overtime. But if adults have a moral right to use drugs, as I have argued, drug users should no more be fined than imprisoned. Some commentators might prefer to describe my position as *legalization*, although little is gained by attaching a label that lacks a standard definition and is likely to be misunderstood.[1] In the minds of some commentators, legalization suggests that no regulatory regime should be imposed on recreational drugs. As I see no reason to believe that a reasonable scheme of regulation must violate moral rights, I prefer the label "decriminalization."

As so construed, decriminalization is the most important conclusion I reach, but it does not put an end to my inquiry. Persons do not have an unqualified moral right to use any drug whenever and wherever they please. The criminal law will always have an important role to play in the regulation of recreational drug use; the outstanding problem is to specify what that role should be.[2] Beyond the core of agreement that drug use should generally not be punished, decriminalization theorists may differ radically about this matter.

I will suppose that utilitarianism is an adequate theory to govern that sphere of behavior unprotected by a moral right. In other words, the pursuit of social utility provides a perfectly good reason to limit those aspects of drug use that fall outside the scope of a moral right. The difficulty, then, is to identify the boundaries of the moral right to use recreational drugs, so that the parameters of utilitarianism are not exceeded.

These boundaries are difficult to locate. When the state seeks to promote social utility by regulating conduct that may or may not be protected by a moral right, there is no obvious way to decide whether that regulation falls outside the scope of the behavior protected by the right or affects the right itself. If the latter, it is always possible to argue that the right is overridden. This argument becomes plausible if the stakes are sufficiently high. Moral and political philosophers continue to debate the boundaries of familiar rights such as speech and religious expression, and there is every reason to believe that the boundaries of the moral right to use recreational drugs will prove equally controversial.

One complication is that the moral right to use recreational drugs does not protect the use of any conceivable drug that might someday be created. I have already described hypothetical drugs that adults would lack the right to use, and I will provide additional such descriptions in this chapter. Perhaps I am mistaken to suppose that the use of all existing recreational drugs is protected by a moral right.[3] Just as social utility may be maximized by different regulatory schemes for different drugs, so may different rights apply to different drugs. Various rights are and ought to be subject to different kinds of regulations, making analogies suspect and generalizations all but impossible.

Despite these formidable difficulties, in this chapter I will examine a number of the restrictions that might be placed on drug use in order to assess whether they violate the moral right of adults to use drugs recreationally. Even my sketchy and inconclusive remarks demonstrate that the state need not choose between the Charybdis of drug prohibition and the Scylla of an unregulated market. An intermediate position can protect the interests of society while respecting personal rights.

LOCAL CONTROLS AND THE IMPORTANCE
OF COMMUNITY

I have examined questions about recreational drug use from an individual rather than from a social perspective. I trust that philosophers will appreciate the importance of adopting this perspective and that they are likely to agree that it has been neglected in most contemporary discussions of drug policy. This emphasis should help to balance the excessively utilitarian flavor of the current debate.

Almost everyone believes that moral rights should be taken seriously. Still, some philosophers will protest that my focus on moral rights is too narrow. Persons are not isolated entities, but live in societies. So far, I have been unwilling to consider how the exercise of rights can undermine the quality of life for others. I have dismissed the negative effects of drug use on communities by arguing that these effects do not amount to genuine harms. No one has a moral right that these negative effects not occur; they form an inadequate basis for criminal liability. I have allowed only a near catastrophe or a conflict with other rights to override the moral right to use drugs recreationally. Arguably, these features of my approach take moral rights too seriously.

Philosophers who are skeptical of my approach might express their reservations in a variety of ways. One familiar response is to insist that societies, no less than persons, have moral rights. If so, these rights might conflict with and override those of adult users of recreational drugs. Perhaps societies, like persons, can be harmed. If so, the harm suffered by a society may not always be reducible to the harms suffered by persons in that society. According to this school of thought, recreational drug use should be prohibited because it is harmful to others after all, when "others" is construed to include society itself.

Other philosophers will convey their uneasiness somewhat differently. They will be reluctant to suppose that societies have rights or are capable of being harmed. Instead, their belief that I pay insufficient attention to the social consequences of recreational drug use will lead them to abandon the harm principle as I have interpreted it. Barbara Levenbook writes that it would be "a mistake to confine all criminal prohibitions to harmful conduct, at least when the harm is restricted to identifiable individuals."[4] Dan Beauchamp argues that regulations of alcohol are not designed "to prevent harm to others or to the self," but "rest on a common interest of all, or what is sometimes called the common good."[5]

I hope to avoid commitment about whether these reservations are better expressed as a reason to reject the harm principle or to refine it. Ultimately, it may be unimportant to decide whether persons believe that an activity should be criminalized because it harms society, or because it has bad effects on society that should not be countenanced as harms. What is important is that philosophers who seek to identify the moral limits of the criminal law should defend a principled position about how the state is entitled to respond to conduct that is detrimental to society but that does not violate the rights of particular individuals.

Social and political philosophers often raise these issues in the context of a general debate between liberals and communitarians. This complex debate cannot be summarized without oversimplification and distortion, and I will not attempt to do so here.[6] Suffice it to say that the liberal emphasis on individual rights has recently been challenged by theorists who contend that it pays insufficient attention to the importance of community values. Many communitarians argue that the state has the legitimate authority to uphold and enforce its own distinctive mores, norms, and standards, in order to preserve its unique identity and way of life.[7]

Few communitarians assess arguments about whether a given activity is right or wrong, or collect data to determine whether it increases or decreases the level of social utility. Instead, they evaluate conduct by reference to the mores and traditions of the society in which it occurs. In other words, the "way of life" of the community should be protected not because it is morally preferable to alternatives, but simply because it *is* the way of life of the community.

This debate is important in the context of recreational drug use. It should be clear that my defense of the moral right to use drugs recreationally is more congenial in a liberal framework. I have agreed with Joel Feinberg that the competent and reasonably well-informed adult named Mr. Roe should be permitted to use a drug when he explains to Dr. Doe: "I don't care if it causes me physical harm. I'll get a lot of pleasure first, so much pleasure in fact, that it is well worth the risk."[8] In agreeing with Feinberg that this case is "easy," I have not paused to consider how Mr. Roe's decision coheres with the mores and traditions of his community. Thus my defense may be unpersuasive to communitarians. If a society disapproves of recreational drug use, and the state has the authority to enforce its mores and traditions by criminal legislation, the supposed moral right to use drugs recreationally is jeopardized.

The communitarian challenge to my defense of a moral right to use drugs recreationally may become stronger as societies become smaller and more homogeneous. If LAD is rejected in its full generality, the intolerance many communities can be expected to exhibit toward recreational drug users will resurface at the local level. May states or municipalities create "drug-free" zones throughout their jurisdictions, forcing adults to exercise their supposed rights elsewhere? Is a community allowed to prohibit drug use altogether, even in private, within its boundaries? Should local governments be encouraged to compete with one another for the most sensible drug policy?[9] These are only a few of the issues that may be at stake in disagreements between liberals and communitarians about recreational drug use.

Decriminalization theorists tend to regard greater local control over recreational drug use as a small (or even as a large) victory. Arnold Trebach argues that

> we should experiment with various forms of decriminalization or legalization of currently outlawed recreational drugs during the remainder of this century. This could include experiments that involve state laws providing for full legalization of vir-

214

tually all illegal drugs for adults. If the experiments work well, we can move on to more widespread legalization; if not, we should again invoke the full weight of the criminal law.[10]

In effect, Trebach is calling for a return to the model that existed throughout America prior to the Harrison Act of 1914, when drugs were subjected to a bewildering patchwork of state regulations.[11] Needless to say, drug prohibitionists are not enthusiastic about conducting these experiments. Drug czar William Bennett traveled to Alaska to support an initiative against the private consumption of marijuana. Our federal government is not prepared to tolerate a return to greater local control over drug regulation.

Trebach's proposal may appear plausible, but greater local control would probably not yield accurate experimental data. Suppose that one or two states repealed all laws against recreational drug use on a temporary basis. Drug users from throughout the country would probably congregate in these states, skewing the results of the experiment. An estimated 30 percent of the drug addicts so conspicuous in Amsterdam are foreigners.[12] For this reason, no one should extrapolate from the Dutch experience to imagine what drug decriminalization would be like if implemented on a global scale.

In any event, my objective is to respect moral rights, not to suggest experiments that might lead to a more sensible drug policy. From this vantage point, an increase in local control makes little sense. I suppose it is preferable that moral rights are protected somewhere rather than nowhere. Still, respect for moral rights should not vary from place to place. If my arguments are sound, voters in Kansas have no more authority than voters in Georgia to prohibit adults from consuming recreational drugs. The whole point of moral rights is to protect persons from interference supported by a majority.

David Richards shares my unwillingness to disregard moral rights in order to preserve community values. He notes that recreational drug use has been attacked as subversive of social institutions throughout American history. The drugs in disfavor at any given period are generally associated with immigrants, aliens, and others who have been alleged to threaten our "way of life."[13] Richards flatly denies that communities have the authority to enforce their traditions and mores against nonconformists. According to him, "It is difficult to see anything in these claims but familiar sociological manifestations of cultural hegemony."[14] Richards concludes that communitarians "assume what should be in dispute, the moral legitimacy of existing institutions."[15]

Although I suspect that Richards's retort is sound, I will pursue a different response to the communitarian challenge in the remainder of this section. The debate between communitarians and liberals need not be joined at its most general level in order to decide whether some jurisdictions should be allowed to proscribe recreational drug use by adults. In what follows, I will attempt to undermine support for drug prohibitions even if liberals make far-reaching concessions to communitarians.

This strategy has affinities with some of my earlier arguments. In Chapter 2 I did not respond to a paternalistic defense of LAD by following those liberals who categorically deny that states have the authority to prohibit adults from harming themselves.[16] Instead, I sought to expose the particular weaknesses in the case for LAD, even if some degree of paternalism is tolerated. I argued that plausible paternalistic principles are capable of justifying prohibition of existing drugs only if these drugs possessed properties they do not appear to have. In light of the best empirical data about drugs and drug use, an unacceptably "hard" form of paternalism would be needed to support LAD. Analogously, I will not respond to the communitarian challenge by upholding the superiority of liberalism. I will argue that plausible communitarian principles are capable of justifying prohibition of existing drugs only if drug use were more discrepant with community values than it appears to be. In light of the best empirical data about drugs and drug use, an unacceptably strong form of communitarianism would be needed to support local prohibitions in any but a few places.

Of course, the strongest versions of communitarianism are hostile to all illegal drug use. According to one such version, majorities have the authority to enforce whatever values they happen to hold. A solid majority of Americans oppose the use of illegal recreational drugs.[17] But this form of communitarianism is indefensible; even the right of religious expression would not survive the implementation of so strong a version of communitarianism. Surely individual rights protect persons from at least some restrictions the state might impose. The majority should not be granted the sweeping authority to annihilate individual rights altogether.[18]

What constraints would a more moderate version of communitarianism place on the authority of majorities to enforce community values? Some decisions, to be sure, must be made in an all-or-nothing, winner-take-all fashion. For example, either the state commits significant resources to the Strategic Defense Initiative, or it does not.[19] The majority has an especially strong claim to make decisions of this sort. But the personal choice to use recreational drugs is not comparable. There is no more need to make this choice collectively than to make religious choices collectively.

What personal choices should majorities control, given that they need not, and should not, be allowed to control them all? Communitarians provide very different replies to this question, and I do not pretend to speak for them all. Perhaps the most plausible answer is that majorities have the authority to protect whatever is most distinctive and valuable in their communities.

Although I would expect broad agreement about this general answer, it is not very helpful when applied to particular moral controversies. Does the dissemination of pornography undermine what is most important to a community? Does homosexuality threaten mores essential to a society? Communitarians who would use the criminal law to punish pornographers and homosexuals are likely to exaggerate the dangers these persons pose to our traditions.[20] What criteria should be used to decide whether these activities really subvert what is precious about a way of life? Many communitarians would answer by reciting the alleged evils of pornography and homosexuality. Yet this recitation provides only half of a satisfactory reply. In addition, communitarians must identify what is distinctive and valuable about the way of life of the society they seek to protect. George Bush alleges that our "nation risks losing its very soul to drug abuse."[21] Can this concern be made more precise?

An obvious problem is to specify what should be included in our "way of life." Considered as a whole, our country is diverse and pluralistic. America contains such a multitude of ways of life that none can claim, without distortion or special pleading, to represent "our" conventional morality.[22] Once the referent of "community" is expanded to encompass the scope of moral opinions and beliefs among the full panoply of Americans, the claim that our social morality contains a distinctive substantive component – a particular list of "do's" and "don'ts" – rings hollow. But if such a list were to be generated, it would not include bans on the recreational use of drugs. For better or worse, the widespread use of illegal drugs for recreational purposes has long been a staple of American society. Of 203 million Americans over twelve years of age, 79 million (39 percent) have used illegal drugs, and 19 million did so in the last month of 1991.[23] More Americans used drugs a decade ago, and the per capita rate of drug use among Americans was perhaps even higher a century ago.[24] No one can pretend that recreational drug use is alien to mainstream American society.

What is true of the whole is true of almost all of its parts. Illegal recreational drugs are prevalent in virtually every American community. There may have been a time when illegal drugs were confined to hippie communities on the East and West coasts. But that time is a distant memory. Although local differences persist,[25] throughout each demographic region of America – Northeast, North Central, South, and West – at least 33.3 percent (South) and as many as 44.9 percent (West) of all persons aged twelve and above have tried illegal drugs at some time in their lives, and more than 11.5 percent (South) used illegal drugs in 1991.[26] These figures are not distorted because drug use tends to be congregated in densely populated urban areas. Even in rural locals in each region, at least 31 percent of Americans aged twelve and older have tried illegal drugs at some time in their lives, and more than 11.6 percent used illegal drugs in 1990.[27]

Attitudes about illegal drugs cohere with the actual behavior of Americans. Barely three-quarters of high school seniors express disapproval of persons who "smoke marijuana occasionally"; almost exactly the same percentage disapprove of persons who "take one or two drinks nearly every day."[28] Less than three-quarters believe that taking heroin in private should be criminalized.[29] And the disapproval of these respondents does not seem to be especially vehement.[30] This degree of tolerance is remarkable, since virtually every public pronouncement about drugs and drug use has been excessively negative. A more accurate, balanced presentation of the evidence would be likely to increase the tolerance of Americans still further. Although communitarians are seldom specific about the degree or depth of social consensus that is needed to justify a criminal prohibition, these statistics probably fall far short of whatever standard is required. No other serious crime gives rise to such ambivalence and indifference.

Two features seem central to the traditions of American communities, insofar as it is possible to generalize about them. First, Americans usually are willing to subject moral opinions and convictions to critical scrutiny. Only rarely does one adult say to another, as a parent might say to a child: "Well, that's just the way we do things around here." Jeremy Waldron observes, "By asking what is really right and really wrong, the liberal is closer to participating in the spirit of our traditions than the communitarian who says that what matters to us is nothing more than that *these* happen to be *our* traditions."[31] Second, Americans generally are tolerant of a wide range of beliefs and practices that differ from our own, and we are not especially insistent that persons with nontraditional life-styles be assimilated to our "way of life." Waldron claims, "Not only do different moral outlooks co-exist and succeed one another, but it is distinctive of our society that we recognize this and that we evolve and develop various second-level standards and practices for coping with it."[32]

These two features characterize what Feinberg calls "the idea of a liberal community."[33] This ideal represents a vision of how persons should live together, pursuing their own interests as they see fit while respecting the rights of others to do the same. This vision is only a small but a very important part of a complete moral code – it describes a principled limitation on the authority of the state to enforce a moral code. If these features accurately characterize the conventional morality of most American communities, those who countenance a moral right to use drugs recreationally need not be reluctant to make limited concessions to communitarians.

The intolerance of drug prohibitionists represents the more radical departure from our way of life. Those who advocate "zero tolerance" toward drug users self-consciously hope to alter the moral climate, not to enforce moral norms that already exist. When consumption in most categories peaked in 1979, drug use was somewhat more evenly distributed throughout all demographic groups in the country. Some commentators predicted that drugs would actually "bring the country together."[34] But "get-tough" attitudes, especially when targeted at casual users, tend to drive drugs into lower socioeconomic classes, where users have less to lose from arrest. As a result, the policies of drug prohibitionists may do more to divide communities than to unify them.

To suppose that community values are subverted by the illegal use of recreational drugs would be more plausible if standard instances conformed to worst-case scenarios. In previous chapters, I have tried to describe a more accurate profile of the typical drug user. Most Americans who experiment with even the most dangerous illegal drugs at a particular stage of their lives eventually stop using them.[35] The prevalence of drug use is strongly correlated with late adolescence and early adulthood.[36] Those who persist in using drugs usually do so in a controlled fashion.[37] Based on the empirical evidence about patterns of drug consumption, the claim that recreational drug use poses a fundamental threat to the fabric of American society seems unlikely.

But this conclusion cannot be generalized to all imaginary drugs or to all conceivable societies. Someday, a drug might be created that would undermine what is valuable about American traditions. Such hypothetical substances are favorite topics of science fiction writers. But no one could pretend that any existing drug remotely resembles the soma in *Brave New World*[38] without grossly misrepresenting the empirical evidence.

Foreign countries might have cultures and traditions more intolerant of recreational drug use. Perhaps the "way of life" of fundamentalist Muslim countries, far less solicitous of moral diversity, would be threatened by the widespread use of recreational drugs.[39] A few American communities might fit this description as well. The "way of life" of Amish societies might be devastated by drug use. Theorists with communitarian sympathies should not extend my defense of the moral right to use drugs to all times and places. Only a more general defense of liberalism can succeed in showing why no community should be allowed to prohibit the use of existing recreational drugs.

For this reason, legal philosophers who make substantial concessions to communitarians must be prepared to allow significant restriction, and perhaps a total prohibition, of recreational drug use within some local jurisdictions. No society has the authority to exclude drug use on the simple ground that the majority disapproves of it. Before local bans are defensible, something valuable and important in the way of life of a particular community must be jeopardized by recreational drug use. However, this concession applies to only a small number of American communities.

REASONABLE REGULATION OF DRUG USE

Those who dissent from the war on drugs but are fearful of the chaos that might ensue if LAD were repealed and replaced by a totally free market have proposed various schemes for regulating drugs. I will comment on a few such proposals here. Almost all of these schemes have been designed to minimize the disutility that decriminalization would be expected to cause. However, I will not assess these proposals from a utilitarian perspective. Instead, I will briefly discuss whether and to what extent they are compatible with the moral rights of adult users of recreational drugs.

My emphasis on moral rights helps me to avoid an objection frequently leveled by drug prohibitionists against their critics. The decriminalization theorists whose views I summarized in Chapter 1 have argued that the war on drugs is both ineffective and counterproductive. Drug prohibitionists have challenged these theorists to devise a concrete alternative that is preferable. In the absence of such a plan, "legalization proposals are not proposals at all."[40] According to Daniel Koshland, "What should no longer be tolerated, whether in erudite publications or in the bombast of political debate, is the advocacy of 'get tough' or 'legalize' without the development of specific, significant plans of action to make the proposed program successful."[41]

Although a few decriminalization theorists have taken important steps toward producing such a plan,[42] others have protested that this criticism is unfair.[43] James Ostrowski goes so far as to say that "*any* system of legalization would be better than the current drug war or any escalation of that war."[44] A war can be opposed even without a detailed peace plan. Still, drug prohibitionists have scored an important point. A policy should not be abandoned because it is ineffective and counterproductive unless an alternative is preferable according to this same criterion. It is not enough for utilitarians to show that a punitive approach "does not work"; they must also provide a reason to believe that some other approach will "work better."

Since I reject the utilitarian context in which this debate is usually placed, I hope not to be criticized for my failure to improve on LAD as social policy. I would like to believe that some specific decriminalization model will promote more utility than the present war on drugs. However, my primary objective is not to describe a set of regulations that "works better," but to assess whether and to what extent some proposed regulations exhibit respect for the moral right of adults to use drugs recreationally.

An example may help to illustrate this point. Suppose we lived in a society that violated what all Americans take for granted as a moral right. Imagine that this society established a state church and punished persons who exercised religious beliefs that differed from those of the majority. A few bold reformers would object to these laws. Their complaints might take either of two forms. They might object that these laws "don't work," that is, that these laws are both ineffective and counterproductive. Deviant religions cannot be suppressed, and actually flourish, as a result of state persecution. Or these reformers might object that these laws violate the moral right of freedom of religion. Critics who rest their case on the first objection should expect to be pressed by defenders of the status quo to produce an alternative that will "work better." These reformers will not be persuasive if every competing approach would be likely to create more problems than the current policy. But reformers who rest their case on the moral right of freedom of religion need not suppose that some alternative will create more social utility.

States do not disrespect moral rights because they are governed by sadists. Unfortunately, respect for moral rights does not always maximize social utility. Conservatives appreciate that a respect for moral rights can be an obstacle in a war on crime. Cruel and unusual punishments, as well as vicarious and collective punishments, are not prohibited because experience has shown them to be ineffective. They are prohibited because they are unjust; they violate moral rights.

I reach the same conclusion about the war on drugs. To demand that reformers who countenance a moral right to use recreational drugs present an alternative that will "work better" is to misunderstand the nature of their complaint about the status quo. A legal system should respect moral rights, even if disrespect turns out to be the more effective social policy.

What restrictions on drug use violate moral rights? A few proposed reforms can be quickly dismissed from this perspective, whatever else their virtues may be. For example, some theorists are impressed by the merits of the so-called British system and recommend a "public-health model" to entrust control over the distribution of some or all Schedule I substances to the medical profession.[45] Doctors or pharmacists would be given the authority to dispense drugs that currently are said to lack an accepted medical use. Would this proposal create more utility than our present policy? Reasonable minds disagree. Of course, my question is different: Would this proposal respect or violate the moral rights of adult users of recreational drugs?

When assessed in this light, a "public-health" alternative to criminal punishment would represent a marginal improvement at best. Drug users would have to persuade a health practitioner that they suffered from a condition that requires treatment before they could gain access to drugs. Chester Mitchell believes that many drug users could succeed in couching their motives for taking drugs in therapeutic terms, "given that 'medicalese' is a fluid language."[46] As I indicated in Chapter 1, the contrast between recreational and medical use is elusive. Still, drugs used explicitly for recreational purposes would continue to be prohibited. Adults who experience the fewest problems with drugs would have the greatest difficulty obtaining them. Some theorists speculate that this model might give nonaddicts an incentive to increase their dosages in order to gain access to their drug of choice.[47] To assign control of drugs to the medical profession is to lose sight of the fact that many adults use drugs for pleasure, not to treat a condition over which physicians have a special expertise. No one should believe that the moral right to use drugs recreationally would be protected by such a scheme.

A few other proposals are easy to assess as well. For example, most decriminalization theorists readily concede that recreational drugs should not be advertised. The point of this restriction, of course, is to prevent the increase in consumption that advertising might create. There is ample room for doubt about whether legalized advertising would really stimulate drug use. According to Mitchell, "The simple thesis that more advertising leads to higher per-capita drug use or more drug use is not supported by the available data."[48] Nonetheless, nearly all decriminalization theorists are quick to allow a ban on advertising in order to persuade skeptics that they are serious about not wanting to see an explosion in drug use throughout society.

The theorist who seeks to protect the moral right to use recreational drugs should be prepared to allow restrictions on advertising too, but for a different reason. If any rights are violated by restrictions on advertising, they are the rights of persons who produce or distribute a product. The right to advertise, if it exists at all, has long been regulated for the public good. Perhaps there is some force to the principle "if it's legal to sell a product, then it should be legal to advertise it,"[49] even though, as Robert Goodin points out, "How, exactly, that logical entailment is meant to work remains something of a mystery."[50] In any event, the rights of consumers are not violated by prohibitions of advertising. Although consumers are entitled to accurate information, this interest does not justify allowing others to promote drugs. Smokers themselves had no cause for complaint when greater restrictions were imposed on the advertising of tobacco.

The several modes of regulation I will mention in the remainder of this section are much more difficult to evaluate from the perspective of moral rights. When does a regulation merely inconvenience a consumer, and when does it violate a moral right? These waters are muddy, and I can do little to clarify them. A system of regulation that is overly burdensome will simply replace one form of tyranny with another,[51] but precise criteria for when a regulation becomes so onerous that it violates a moral right are impossible to formulate. I have no definitive answers to the questions I will raise.

The difficulty of resolving this issue in the abstract leads commentators to search for analogies. When pressed, almost all decriminalization theorists cite alcohol as an acceptable model of regulation.[52] Theorists probably favor the adoption of an alcohol model for illegal drugs because they believe that this model works tolerably well. Of course, I am interested in the alcohol model for a wholly different reason. Perhaps the alcohol model shows sufficient respect for the moral rights of drinkers.

Unfortunately, the so-called alcohol model is less readily adaptable to illegal drugs than is ordinarily supposed. The main difficulty is that no single alcohol model exists. Regulation of alcohol varies greatly throughout the country.[53] What specific mode of alcohol regulation maximizes utility while respecting moral rights? Is even the least permissive model worth emulating? At one extreme, from 1920 to 1933, the sale and distribution of alcohol was a criminal offense, and only private use was permitted. Ironically, this scheme of regulation, aptly named "prohibition" in the context of alcohol, is usually called "decriminalization" in the context of other drugs. Yet I cannot believe that any decriminalization theorist has such a system in mind when proposing that illegal substances should be regulated according to the alcohol model. Few of the utilitarian benefits promised by these theorists could be achieved if punishment for distribution were retained.

Nor is it plausible to suppose that this scheme would protect the moral right to use recreational drugs, even though use per se would no longer be a crime. Those who believe that adults have a moral right to drink alcohol did not think that this right was respected during the era of prohibition. According to David Richards, the right to use a substance includes the right to buy it, which must extend to the right to sell it.[54] To be sure, states have rejected this inference in a number of contexts, such as prostitution. Richards insists that these contexts are "morally questionable, reflecting un-

226

just, indeed immoral, assumptions that have no proper place in the enforcement of law."[55] A moral right to use heroin, but not to obtain it through commercial channels, would not be worth very much. Adults might as well be told that their moral right to use recreational drugs is respected because the criminal law of most states prohibits possession but not use per se.

If the sale of recreational drugs should not be totally prohibited, regulations on vendors might take the form of those imposed on alcohol today. But where? Some jurisdictions allow alcohol to be sold in supermarkets; others confine sale to a state monopoly. Restrictions on time and place of sale vary among jurisdictions as well. The choice between these various alternatives might have profound policy implications, affecting levels of consumption,[56] but does not seem especially significant from the perspective of the moral rights of the user. Why should it matter who is allowed to sell drugs, or when they are allowed to be sold, as long as regulations do not become so burdensome that drugs become practically unavailable?

Other proposals are equally hard to evaluate. For example, consider the issue of how the sale of legalized drugs should be taxed. Once again, utilitarianism dominates contemporary discussions of this issue; theorists struggle to identify the precise point at which taxes are sufficiently high to generate substantial revenue, yet sufficiently low to destroy the black market. Locating this point may be a difficult exercise for economists, but a concern for moral rights raises an entirely new set of issues. Users of a given recreational drug have no cause for complaint if the purchase price includes a tax to pay for the disutility caused by their consumption, although the tax may not always be paid by the right people. Some theorists contend that even though alcohol abusers pay more in taxes than moderate drinkers, the extra amount is insufficient to cover the additional disutility the abusers create.[57] Others argue that the amount of tax paid by each drinker is roughly proportionate to the social costs he brings about.[58]

The more difficult question is whether and to what extent taxation may exceed this amount in order to discourage use. The levy of a sumptuary tax to inhibit consumption is acceptable to many decriminalization theorists who do not want to be accused of being too soft on drugs. Higher retail prices are probably more effective than is education or the prohibition of advertising in bringing about a decrease in consumption,[59] and higher prices have the added benefit of increasing revenue. Still, the legitimacy of sumptuary taxes is open to dispute. John Stuart Mill believed that "to tax stimulants for the sole purpose of making them more difficult to be obtained is a measure differing only in degree from their entire prohibition; and would be justifiable only if that were justifiable."[60] Yet surely this belief is not shared by most Americans. Those who countenance a moral right to drink alcohol, and believe that this right was violated during prohibition, do not think that sumptuary taxes violate this right as well, albeit to a lesser degree. At some point taxes would become so high that many Americans would complain about an infringement of their right to drink, but this point is not automatically reached whenever taxes are used to reduce consumption. The state may discourage what it should not prohibit, as it may encourage what it should not require.

Limitations on the potency of various drugs represent yet another gray area. According to Michael Aldrich, "Diluting the strength of a drug for social use has been the most frequent means of harm reduction in world history."[61] Consumers who are given the option frequently prefer drugs with less potency. Sales of liquor are lower and falling faster than sales of beer and wine. Still, should very pure drugs be available to adults who want them?

The most intriguing possibility to minimize the social harm of drug use while showing respect for moral rights is to license users. Although decriminalization theorists routinely propose schemes to license distribution,[62] few attempts to license users have been taken seriously, probably because of the enormous administrative problems.[63] Even if a fair system to license users could be implemented, enforcement would be nearly impossible. Countries that once licensed drinkers, like Sweden from 1917 to 1955 and Finland from 1946 to 1970, eventually abandoned their systems as "cumbersome, irritating, and ineffective."[64] Persons with the greatest drug problems, who would be the first to lose their licenses, would be the most likely to consume drugs after their licenses had been revoked. Despite these formidable practical obstacles, it is not apparent that a system to license users would disregard moral rights.

Two basic models of licensure are available, each containing countless variations.[65] The first restricts licenses to a small minority, who must pass a rigorous qualifying examination. Access to most professions is controlled by this form of licensure. The second model grants licenses to a large majority, who must satisfy minimal conditions of eligibility. Automobile drivers are licensed in this way. Either model might be combined with some form of drug rationing, allowing adults to purchase limited quantities of a drug over a given period of time. Mitchell makes an impressive case in favor of permitting nonusers to sell their rations. He claims, "By compensating non-users, the sale of rations would duplicate the effects of a collective class-action suit against all drug users."[66] The total amount of a given drug consumed throughout society could be controlled by increasing or decreasing the ration available to each licensee.

Whether any of these models to license drug users exhibits sufficient respect for moral rights is uncertain. Each construes recreational drug use as a privilege rather than as an irrevocable right. These models have the virtue of acknowledging that many adults are capable of consuming legal and illegal drugs without causing serious social problems. The rights of the majority are not sacrificed because a minority of adults use drugs irresponsibly. The role of the criminal law is preserved in ensuring that buyers and sellers conform to whatever requirements are enacted by the licensing authority. The (enormous) obstacles to implementing any of these models are more practical than principled.

This discussion barely scratches the surface of a difficult

issue that will not become the focus of attention until commentators are persuaded that decriminalization is defensible in principle. Some problems are almost impossible to anticipate in advance; there will be no substitute for experience in developing a specific model of decriminalization. A few of these questions might not require solutions. If the repeal of LAD would not result in the explosion of use feared by drug prohibitionists, assessing modes of regulation designed primarily to inhibit consumption will become a purely academic exercise.

SPECIAL CASES: PREGNANT DRUG USERS

In Chapter 3, I argued that LAD could not be justified in its full generality as an anticipatory offense. However, it does not follow that recreational drug use should not be prohibited in special circumstances in which it impermissibly increases the likelihood of harm to others. In a number of carefully defined situations, prohibiting adults from using given recreational drugs appears to satisfy my four requirements of justified anticipatory legislation. In this section, I will describe three special circumstances in which the case for criminal prohibition is strong.

Perhaps the clearest example of a justified anticipatory offense is driving while under the influence of a drug that impairs performance. The vast majority of prosecutions for driving while intoxicated involve alcohol, largely because other recreational drugs are more difficult to detect. Urine tests can show that a driver has used various other drugs in the past, but are not especially helpful to determine whether she is under the influence at the time she is stopped. The creation of a reliable and inexpensive test for nonalcoholic substances that impair performance would extend the campaign against drunk driving to these other recreational drugs.

The most serious difficulty with the justifiability of this anticipatory offense is that conviction under existing law does not require that the driving skills of the defendant were actually diminished. Instead, liability is predicated on the assumption that drivers who have consumed a specified amount of a given drug are impaired and thus are more likely to be involved in an accident than drivers who have abstained. In the case of alcohol, a driver whose blood alcohol content exceeds a given threshold is conclusively presumed to be under the influence. However, persons vary tremendously in their abilities to function after having consumed identical quantities of alcohol or other drugs. Only some drivers whose blood alcohol content exceeds this threshold are actually impaired to a significant degree. A criminal law based on the culpability of particular defendants would make actual debilitation an element of this offense.[67] In principle, if not in practice, existing statutes could be revised to overcome this difficulty. Persons should be prohibited from driving while under the influence of whatever quantity of drugs significantly impairs their performance.

If a simple test could detect diminished driving skills, a criminal offense against impaired driving need not retain drug use as an element. Drug use is only one of many possible explanations of why individuals may be unable to operate their vehicles to the best of their ability. Sleepy and fatigued drivers also impermissibly increase the likelihood that they will cause harm to others. Intoxication should be singled out from other avoidable causes of impairment only if, in the words of James Jacobs, "intoxicated driving is more dangerous, by an order of magnitude, than other forms of impaired driving."[68]

The example of driving while under the influence of drugs is a specific instance of a more general prohibition. Recreational drug use should be proscribed whenever a person has a special opportunity to harm others, and the impairment of judgment or reflexes impermissibly increases the likelihood that an accident will occur. For this reason, no one should be permitted to fly a plane, perform surgery, or use firearms while under the influence of mind-altering drugs. Undoubtedly other examples could be added to this list. To minimize controversy, a statute should explicitly describe the several circumstances in which drug use is prohibited because of "a special opportunity to harm others."

"Passive smoking" is a second special circumstance in which drug use seems to create an impermissible risk of harm to others. Public smoking in confined areas subjects bystanders to side-stream smoke. This is a rare case in which drug use itself risks harm to others; the smoker herself need not do or fail to do anything further for harm to result. Still, since no one is harmed on each and every occasion, the justifiability of a criminal prohibition must be assessed by the standards that govern anticipatory offenses.

Any controversy that would surround the creation of an offense of subjecting persons to side-stream tobacco smoke is no longer likely to involve the empirical principle. The question is not whether passive smoking causes cancer, but how much cancer it causes.[69] Goodin states that exposure to side-stream smoke increases the nonsmoker's risk of lung cancer by approximately 34 percent.[70] The inchoate principle is satisfied as well. The act of directly and deliberately giving someone cancer (if it were possible to do so) would clearly be a serious crime.

But satisfying the remaining two principles is more problematic. The triviality principle creates difficulties. The number of fatalities caused by passive smoking is considerable; a recent draft report sponsored by the Environmental Protection Agency put the toll at an astonishing 53,000 nonsmokers per year, mostly from heart disease.[71] This figure is far higher than for many other activities that are regulated in the interests of public health. Nonetheless, each incidence of public smoking may make only a minuscule contribution to this total. Since so many adults discharge side-stream smoke in public, the quantity of harm attributable to individual agents may be too trivial to justify the creation of a criminal offense.

The most important dispute, however, involves the remoteness principle. In many environments, nonsmokers cannot do much to insulate themselves from side-stream smoke. In other environments, however, the demand that nonsmokers take precautions to avoid harm is more defensible. Reasonable minds will differ about whether and under what circumstances persons should be expected to confine themselves to No Smoking sections of public places in order to minimize their exposure to side-stream smoke. If it is reasonable to ask nonsmokers to segregate themselves from smokers, the emission of side-stream smoke may be insufficiently proximate to the consummate harm of disease to justify the enactment of anticipatory legislation.

The crucial point about the examples of impaired driving and passive smoking is that they should not be generalized to create total bans of recreational drug use. Conceding that persons should not be allowed to operate heavy machinery while under the influence of a given illegal substance no more justifies the complete prohibition of that substance than conceding that persons should not be allowed to drive while under the influence of alcohol justifies the complete prohibition of alcohol. A higher incidence of drunk driving and traffic fatalities is the price society must pay if the right to drink is to be respected.

There are two reasons why a general prohibition is unwarranted despite the existence of these special circumstances in which the use of a given drug impermissibly increases the likelihood of harm to others. First, these circumstances represent the statistical exception rather than the norm. They do not describe the standard, ordinary use of a given drug, and generalizations from the exception rather than from the rule are unfair. Few drugs are consumed on occasions in which users pose a special risk of harm to others. Most smoking is not in confined, public areas. Second, these circumstances can be clearly defined and easily distinguished from other occasions in which drug use does not create a special risk. It is possible to imagine a debate about whether a particular act of smoking is public, or about whether a person is actually driving, but these debates are exceptional and probably can be resolved without too much difficulty.

Perhaps recreational drug use should be prohibited in

other special circumstances. Rather than attempt to be comprehensive, I will devote the remainder of this section to a more extended discussion of an example in which the call for criminal legislation is highly controversial and emotionally charged. Some states have sought to protect the health of newborn infants by prosecuting mothers for using recreational drugs while pregnant. Since 1987, more than fifty women in nineteen states have been arrested after having given birth to babies who test positive for drugs.[72] The majority of these women have been crack users.[73]

In utero exposure to crack is widely regarded as a serious problem. Estimates vary widely,[74] but each year perhaps as many as 300,000 infants are born to women who smoke crack.[75] Many of these infants are born prematurely and have a mildly decreased birth weight, head circumference, and body length.[76] Their neurobehavioral problems include "mood dysfunction, organizational deficits, poor attention, and impaired human interaction."[77]

Many prosecutions of mothers of infants who have tested positive for drugs have involved novel and creative interpretations of existing statutes. For example, mothers have been charged with the "unlawful delivery of drugs to a minor" by transferring cocaine through an unsevered umbilical cord.[78] Reliance on strained statutory constructions raises serious problems with the principle of legality. Defendants who used drugs throughout their pregnancies could hardly have anticipated that they would be "delivering" drugs to a minor while giving birth. Some courts have dismissed prosecutions under these statutes, denying their authority "to create a crime."[79] Moreover, commentators have argued that the exchange of drugs through the placenta is a nonvoluntary bodily function, not a volitional act on which criminal liability can be predicated.[80] Surely the more straightforward device to protect the health of infants would be to enact a new offense of drug use by a woman who knows she is pregnant. Various bills creating such an offense are now pending before several state legislatures. In what follows, I will examine whether such an offense would be justified.

234

A statute designed to protect infant health by prohibiting recreational drug use during pregnancy would be yet another example of an anticipatory offense. Drug use throughout pregnancy might impermissibly increase the likelihood that a consummate harm will occur. Not all newborns are adversely affected by the drug use of their mothers, but liability for an anticipatory offense does not require that each crime actually results in harm.

There is ample room for doubt about whether a fetus qualifies as an "other" who possesses moral rights and is capable of being harmed. The permissibility of abortion is jeopardized by the supposition that fetuses have rights. Of course, those who oppose abortion will not balk at this result. Nonetheless, doubts that fetuses have moral rights and can be harmed has led to what might be called the "born alive" rule.[81] According to this rule, prosecutions for drug use by pregnant women will not be initiated unless the defendant gives birth to a living infant. The harmed victim whose moral rights are alleged to have been violated by prenatal drug use is not the unborn fetus, but the living infant who tests positive for illegal drugs. A justifiable anticipatory offense to protect infant health should probably incorporate this "born alive" rule.

Contemporary discussions of this proposed legislation are tainted by the unlawful status of most recreational drug use. Curiously, the illegality of many drugs has been cited both as a reason to oppose as well as a reason to favor the punishment of pregnant drug users. Some commentators have argued that these prosecutions are unnecessary precisely because many drugs are already illegal to use.[82] Why not simply prosecute pregnant women for their drug use and avoid the controversies that surround strained interpretations of existing law and the enactment of new anticipatory legislation?

Other commentators point to the fact that many drugs are already illegal as the best reason to create a new offense to punish pregnant drug users. They concede that a wide range of maternal behavior that can injure a newborn does not involve the use of drugs. Poor diet, too much or too little exercise, obesity, or an unwillingness to follow medical advice can pose a risk to infant health as well. When drugs are involved, the primary culprits are alcohol and tobacco. Each year, more than 750,000 infants are exposed to by-products of passive smoke during the prenatal period, and the level of exposure is more than one pack per day in approximately 200,000 of these cases.[83] The health consequences can be serious.[84] About 75 percent of all pregnant women drink alcohol at least twice a month, and several thousand infants suffer from fetal alcohol syndrome annually.[85] Some health practitioners believe that prenatal exposure to alcohol is the major cause of mental retardation in America today.[86] Why single out illegal drug use from the variety of conduct that can cause prenatal harm? The most familiar answer is that illegal drugs are already illegal. John Myers writes:

> The state has already decided that in a contest between autonomy and [illegal] drug use, autonomy loses. . . . If criminalization of maternal drug use is restricted to substances that are prohibited for all adults, it is difficult to see how any morally defensible interest of the woman is implicated. There is no moral right to take illegal drugs.[87]

Thus illegality is cited as a reason to differentiate drug use from other maternal behaviors that can cause harm to newborns.

Among other difficulties, Myers's response does not explain why most of these prosecutions are relatively recent and typically involve the use of crack. Illegal drug use by pregnant women has been commonplace for a long time. Is crack more harmful to a fetus than other drugs? According to Dorothy Roberts, the selection of crack use for punishment is justified neither by the number of users nor by the extent of harm to the fetus.[88] She argues that these prosecutions involve racism, because black communities tend to have the highest concentrations of crack users.[89]

In any event, the illegal status of most recreational drugs

can play no role in my discussion. I propose to assess the justifiability of new anticipatory legislation under an entirely different background assumption – the repeal of LAD. If recreational drug use were decriminalized, commentators could no longer cite the illegality of drugs as a reason either to oppose or to favor the enactment of an offense. I assume that any justifiable statute should prohibit all conduct that impermissibly increases the likelihood that newborn infants will suffer significant harm. The use of alcohol and tobacco would not be exempted, and some conduct not involving drugs might be included as well.

If LAD were repealed, should the state create an anticipatory offense of recreational drug use by pregnant women? Several objections that have been raised against this proposal are strikingly similar to more general difficulties with LAD. Rights that are jeopardized by prosecution of pregnant women are also at stake in a complete prohibition of drug use. Commentators point out how "these prosecutions threaten to open the door to wholesale invasions of women's rights to bodily integrity, self-determination, and privacy."[90] These reasons to oppose the punishment of pregnant drug users are even more persuasive against LAD, since violations of the "rights to bodily integrity, self-determination and privacy" of drug users who are not pregnant cannot be defended on behalf of newborn victims.

As usual, utilitarian objections are voiced most frequently. In particular, a number of commentators have argued that enforcement of this offense would be counterproductive and would do more to hurt infants than to help them. One problem is that incarceration of drug-using mothers immediately after delivery might injure children by preventing early mother–child bonding.[91] A more serious problem is that pregnant drug users who fear prosecution would attempt to avoid detection by refusing to seek medical treatment. According to one report on prenatal care, "It is safer for the baby to be born to a drug-abusing, anemic or diabetic mother who visits the doctor throughout her pregnancy than to be born to a normal woman who does not."[92] Empirical evidence indicates that some drug users may already be deterred from seeking prenatal care.[93]

This objection is probably fatal to the case for creating anticipatory legislation.[94] No state should pursue a policy that will result in more evil than good. However, my focus is not on analyses of costs and benefits. I am more concerned to assess whether moral rights would be violated by punishing pregnant women who use recreational drugs. The fact that this statute would be inefficient and counterproductive does not establish that it violates moral rights. A law may be unwise without being unjust.

Even commentators who oppose this legislation are reluctant to argue directly that the conduct to be prohibited is protected by a moral right. No one seems to believe that women have a moral right to use recreational drugs while pregnant. One article that vehemently denounces this proposed legislation for treating women as "chattel, as inert 'fetal containers' "[95] concedes that "few would argue that a pregnant woman has no moral responsibility to her developing fetus."[96] Yet the authors cite no instances of behavior that would violate this responsibility. What examples of irresponsible conduct by pregnant women could these authors have in mind, and why is recreational drug use not among them?[97] Since few commentators seem to believe that recreational drug use itself is protected by a moral right, even fewer should believe that it is protected in circumstances in which it increases the likelihood of harm to another.

In order to conclude that the conduct to be prohibited is protected by a moral right, some feminist scholars reinterpret the nature of the behavior to be punished.[98] Consider the following argument advanced by Roberts:

> When a drug-addicted woman becomes pregnant, she has only one realistic avenue to escape criminal charges: abortion. Thus, she is penalized for choosing to have the baby rather than having an abortion. In this way, the state's punitive action may coerce women to have abortions rather than risk

being charged with a crime. Thus, it is the *choice of carrying a pregnancy to term* that is being penalized.[99]

This statute would clearly violate a moral and legal right if Roberts's interpretation were correct. The right to decide "whether to bear or beget a child"[100] has long been recognized to be of fundamental importance. Given her interpretation, Roberts has little difficulty concluding that "it is the right to choose to be a mother that is burdened by the criminalization of conduct during pregnancy."[101]

But Roberts's argument suffers from two defects. The first is general. Roberts contends that because a pregnant drug user can avoid prosecution under the "born alive" rule only by procuring an abortion, it follows that she is really being punished for choosing not to terminate her pregnancy. This inference is fallacious. The fact that a defendant can avoid prosecution for x only by doing y does not show that she is really being punished for her failure to do y, rather than for x. For example, a person who is convicted for unlawful possession of drugs can avoid prosecution by consuming the drugs. But it hardly follows that this statute should be reinterpreted to prohibit the failure to consume drugs. Appearances are not deceptive here. Punishment is imposed for unlawful possession.

The second defect in Roberts's argument is specific to the context of drugs. Notice that she supposes the defendant to be a drug addict rather than merely a drug user. But defendants who violate this proposed anticipatory legislation need not be addicts. The crime involves drug use by a woman who knows she is pregnant; whether the defendant is an addict is immaterial. Roberts's characterization of the defendant as an addict is not inadvertent. Without this characterization, her claim that abortion is the "only one realistic avenue to escape criminal charges" becomes totally implausible. The drug user, as opposed to the drug addict, has a second avenue to escape conviction that is eminently realistic: She can stop using drugs.

Suppose that a mother is prosecuted for committing this

proposed anticipatory offense. Of what relevance is the fact that she is a drug addict rather than a drug user? Might addiction be recognized as an excuse? I see no more reason to recognize addiction as an excuse for this crime than for any other crime, including the offense of drug use itself. I argued in Chapter 2 that *U.S. v. Moore* was decided correctly,[102] and I will only summarize this argument here. I invoked the law of duress to argue that drug addiction should be a defense from liability for causing a serious harm only if the pain of withdrawal were sufficiently severe. However, the pain of withdrawal from the prolonged use of crack is not so agonizing as to excuse a criminal offense. I trust that no one will deny that birth defects are a serious harm.

Evidently Roberts assumes that requiring addicts to stop using drugs is not "realistic." Other commentators have reached this conclusion explicitly. According to Lynn Paltrow, "Ending an addiction without help is virtually impossible."[103] From this premise, her argument parallels Roberts's. Paltrow writes that "the only option to avoid prosecution or imprisonment may be an abortion,"[104] so that "these prosecutions penalize a woman for her decision to continue a pregnancy."[105] This conclusion makes it easy to appreciate how liability violates a moral right without having to suppose that pregnant women have a moral right to use recreational drugs.

The claim that addicts cannot realistically stop using drugs does not withstand empirical scrutiny. As I have repeatedly emphasized, most persons who are addicted to any given drug eventually cease their use, and the majority do so without treatment. Many persons stop using drugs because of some important event in their lives. A concern for their children is among the most commonly cited reasons addicts decide to quit using drugs.[106] Several women have stopped using heroin upon learning that they were pregnant.[107]

Roberts and Paltrow emphasize that the state's lack of commitment to the health of newborns is betrayed by its failure to provide treatment for pregnant addicts who need help. As many as 85 percent of all addicts who seek treatment are turned away.[108] The significance of this observation is not totally clear, however. No treatment program has been shown to be especially effective.[109] It cannot be said that we know how to get addicts to discontinue their use of drugs but are unwilling to fund programs to help them succeed. Treatment for pregnant addicts is especially uncertain.[110] Even if treatment were a better means to promote infant health than punishment, the failure to offer treatment would not establish the injustice of punishment. In no other context is the unwillingness of the state to provide adequate treatment for addicts cited as a reason to oppose prosecution of drug users who impermissibly increase the likelihood of a consummate harm. Laws against drunk driving are not unjustified because the state fails to provide adequate treatment for alcoholics. Perhaps fewer highway fatalities would occur if treatment facilities were expanded. In the meantime, the state's failure to pursue the more effective strategy to promote highway safety does not demonstrate the injustice of a punitive response to drunk driving.

The argument that addicts should not be punished unless treatment is readily available proves far more than any of these commentators acknowledge. This argument provides an equally good reason not to punish addicts who are *not* pregnant. A more effective strategy to decrease drug use in general may be to expand the availability of treatment facilities rather than to rely so heavily on the criminal justice system. Nonetheless, the failure of the state to implement the best solution to a problem does not demonstrate the injustice of its present approach.

Of course, the refutation of one objection to the enactment of anticipatory legislation does not show that this law would not violate moral rights. Are the four requirements of justified anticipatory legislation satisfied? The greatest problem involves the empirical principle. The causal connection between the use of various drugs and harm to newborns remains uncertain.

At least four difficulties complicate the application of the empirical principle. First, the causal connection between the use of a particular drug and harm to a newborn is almost impossible to isolate, since a number of independent factors that compound the risk are almost always present.[111] Many crack users suffer from the effects of poverty; they receive little or no prenatal care and often are malnourished. Second, few theorists are prepared to guess at the percentage of infants exposed to crack who are actually harmed.[112] Statistics are almost always presented in the aggregate, with little indication of the likelihood that a particular infant will experience any difficulty. According to one estimate, more than two of every three crack-exposed babies have no apparent problems at birth.[113] Third, the degree to which crack-exposed children are actually prejudiced in their long-term development remains to be seen.[114] According to one report, crack-exposed babies observed for four years "compete quite well and live among their peers in a healthy way. Unlike fetal alcohol babies, they are not born mentally retarded and are as bright as normal children."[115] Fortunately, fetuses exhibit remarkable resilience, and few who are exposed to various hazards suffer serious, long-term adverse health consequences. Fourth, there is evidence that drug use is harmful to a fetus only during a relatively brief period of pregnancy,[116] thereby undermining the case for prohibition throughout the entire term.

In view of these four complications, the best reason to believe that pregnant women might have a moral right to use recreational drugs is that this conduct has not been shown to cause a significant increase in the risk of a serious consummate harm.[117] However, even this best reason may not be good enough to support the conclusion that pregnant women actually do have a moral right to use recreational drugs. Each of the four complications just mentioned has been contested. A few studies report harms to infants that are specifically attributable to cocaine rather than to other compounding factors.[118] Moreover, another researcher found harm "in most of the cocaine-exposed children studied, regardless of whether their mother used the drug only during the first trimester or throughout pregnancy."[119] After reviewing the literature, Myers expresses "little doubt that thousands of children will suffer long-term damage."[120]

I conclude that there seem to be no sound argument of principle against the creation of an anticipatory offense of recreational drug use by pregnant women. I have little doubt that such a law would be counterproductive, but I cannot identify a moral right that it would violate. When pregnant, women probably lack a moral right to use drugs recreationally. Pregnancy may well represent a special circumstance to which the moral right to use recreational drugs should not be applied.

ADOLESCENTS AND ADULTS

I have provided reasons to believe that LAD violates the moral rights of adults. I have tried to be careful not to indicate that these arguments apply to adolescents as well. My willingness to differentiate between the rights of adolescents and adults is not unusual. To my knowledge, no decriminalization theorist has gone so far as to propose that adolescents and adults have equal rights to use drugs recreationally. Many of these theorists go out of their way to underscore their hostility toward drug use by proposing even more severe punishments for the offense of selling drugs to a minor than are imposed today.

This almost universal tendency to differentiate between the rights of adolescents and adults has not been given a satisfactory justification. According to Zimring and Hawkins: "The special status of children and youth in drug policy is not only uncontested in the literature on drug policy; it is also unexamined. Little has been written on the topic by either academics or policy analysts."[121] A basis for distinguishing between the rights of adolescents and adults has not been needed, since the use of most recreational drugs is illegal for persons of all ages. Arguments in favor of unequal treatment have been made almost exclusively in the context of alcohol. Even though forty-four states prohibit selling cigarettes to minors or bar them from possessing tobacco, these laws are rarely enforced.[122] Alcohol is a different story; states vigorously prohibit underage drinking in bars and restaurants, although adolescents are rarely prevented from consuming alcohol at home, under parental supervision. This exemption is typically rationalized as a means to facilitate the transition to responsible drinking among young adults. Needless to say, no such exemption applies to other recreational drugs.

The disparate treatment of adults and adolescents is not easily defended in the utilitarian terms familiar to decriminalization theorists. As I have indicated, these theorists oppose LAD not because of their commitment to moral rights, but because of their frustration with existing policy. But why does their frustration never extend to the point that they question the use of criminal sanctions to protect adolescents? Our criminal justice system has been equally ineffective and counterproductive in its attempts to prevent both adults and minors from using illegal substances. The retention of a wide array of drug offenses to protect adolescents threatens to undermine many of the practical advantages decriminalization theorists hope to achieve. Those theorists who promise that decriminalization will bring about an end to the evils of the black market must be deluding themselves, since a limited war on drugs will still have to be waged on behalf of adolescents.

Two questions must be addressed in order to approach this issue from the perspective of moral rights. First, do adolescents have the same moral rights to use recreational drugs as adults, or do their rights differ? Second, if their rights differ, what are the implications for the justifiability of LAD as enforced against adults? In this section I will comment briefly on each of these questions.

Two basic rationales might support different moral rights for adolescents and adults to use a given recreational drug. First, a drug might be more harmful when it is used by adolescents than when it is used by adults. Second, adolescents might be less competent than adults to voluntarily assume the risks of harm involved in drug use. Of course, these two reasons can be combined to form a powerful argument against allowing adolescent drug use.

Each rationale has countless variations. Consider the effects of drugs on adolescents. There is some evidence that the physical effects of a number of drugs, for example, heroin, are more deleterious when consumed by a youth.[123] However, few commentators attempt to justify unequal treatment by claiming that comparable amounts of a given drug create greater health hazards for adolescents than for adults. More often the disparity is based on behavioral differences between adolescent and adult users. For example, adolescents who drink are disproportionately represented in traffic fatalities; as drivers age, they are somewhat less likely to cause accidents, even if they continue to drink.[124]

Perhaps the most common argument is that recreational drug use interferes with education, placing adolescents at a subsequent disadvantage in a competitive economy. Drug use among high school students has been shown to correlate with worse grades, more absences and cut classes, and lower academic aspirations.[125] It is somewhat unclear whether these effects are caused by drug use, or if they are manifestations of the nonconventional and rebellious behavior that young drug users tend to exhibit.[126] Of course, drug prohibitionists find no ambiguity in these data. According to Lauro Cavazos, former secretary of education, "The biggest threat that now stands in the way of achieving the kind of educational system we know is needed is the widespread use of illegal drugs by our nation's young people."[127]

Yet another variant of this first rationale is defended in the following terms by the authors of a Rand Corporation study:

> If drugs do have ill effects, it is advisable to postpone the onset of drug use as long as possible. Many toxic substances require a long incubation period for the effect to become manifest. Thus the older the point at which use is begun, the less likely are adverse effects. In addition, postponing the age of first use may reduce the likelihood that the individual will become a habitual user, as in the case of cigarette smoking.[128]

245

Perhaps additional reasons could be given to show that the effects of drug use on adolescents are different from and more serious than those on adults.

Commentators are just as likely to emphasize the second rationale – that adolescents are less competent than adults – to justify differentiating between their rights. Several grounds have been cited to show why adolescents are and ought to be subject to a much wider range of paternalistic interference than adults. Many adolescent choices tend to depart more radically from Feinberg's ideal of perfect voluntariness.[129] In particular, juveniles are said to be more likely to be misinformed about the risks of their conduct, less able to defer gratification, and more susceptible to peer pressure. Empirical evidence in favor of these claims is seldom provided.[130] But if any of these claims is true, several of my arguments in Chapter 2 would require serious qualification as applied to adolescents. Still, an unbiased assessment of the evidence might well indicate that adolescents should be permitted to use recreational drugs, including alcohol, before they reach the age of twenty-one.

The justifiability of punishing adolescents for drug use does not follow from accepting either or both of these rationales for differentiating their moral rights from those of adults. If adolescents should not be punished for using recreational drugs, it need not be because their conduct is protected by a moral right, but because juvenile justice is and ought to be more therapeutic than punitive. The same incapacities that prevent adolescents from making fully voluntary choices provide a reason not to punish them for the choices they make. Laws can help to keep drugs out of the hands of adolescents without resorting to punishment for those who manage to obtain them.[131] Almost every state has modified the penalty structure of the Controlled Substances Act to increase the punishment of offenders who distribute illegal drugs to minors.

Although this issue deserves more thorough treatment, I will not further debate the moral rights of adolescents. The matter cannot be resolved without a deeper understanding of the philosophical foundation of moral rights for adults and adolescents alike. In what follows, I will assess whether and to what extent the concession that adolescents lack a moral right to use drugs recreationally undermines my conclusions about the moral rights of adults.

The phenomenon of "leakage" provides the best reason to believe that the desirability of making drugs inaccessible to adolescents justifies LAD in its full generality. Although the percentage has steadily declined throughout the last decade, large numbers of adolescents persist in using illegal drugs today. Adolescent use would probably escalate as a consequence of the greater availability of drugs that would follow from decriminalization for adults. The most effective strategy to deny access to adolescents is to deny access to everyone. This rationale construes the prohibition of some or all recreational drug use by adults as an anticipatory offense designed to reduce the likelihood of whatever consummate harm results from drug use by adolescents.

When applied to some drugs, this rationale violates the remoteness principle of justified anticipatory legislation. Consider the following convoluted chain: Although heroin is used infrequently by adolescents, adults should be prohibited from using all illegal drugs, including marijuana, because if marijuana is permitted, more of it would become available to adolescents, who then will be more inclined to use it, and will be more tempted to graduate to heroin as adults, and thus will be more likely to bring about whatever consummate harms heroin users are alleged to cause.

Even without such difficulties involving the remoteness principle, it might seem preposterous to suppose that any of my arguments on behalf of adults would be jeopardized by the need to prevent drugs from leaking to adolescents. Adults are treated like children when their behavior is restricted for the sake of children. John Kaplan observes that this kind of reasoning "allow[s] the tail to wag the dog."[132] In virtually no other context does anyone suggest that adults should be punished for an activity in order to reduce the tendency of adolescents to engage in it. This argument is not invoked as a reason to reintroduce the prohibition of alcohol, even though more adolescents suffer from the abuse of alcohol than from all illegal drugs combined. About 8 million American junior and senior high school students are weekly users of alcohol, including 454,000 "binge" drinkers who consume an average of fifteen drinks each week.[133]

On the other hand, the powerful political appeal of this argument indicates that it should not be dismissed out of hand. Groups of outraged parents were instrumental in reversing the trend toward greater tolerance of drug use shown throughout the 1970s.[134] An extraordinary amount of the rhetoric of drug prohibitionists continues to emphasize the special need to protect children. No drug prohibitionist will long allow decriminalization theorists to ignore the impact of their proposals on our nation's youth.

Why should the prevention of leakage be accepted as a reason to enact LAD in its full generality, when it is not accepted as a reason to prohibit any other activity that is undesirable for adolescents? Although I am unaware of a drug prohibitionist who has explicitly addressed this issue, I can imagine at least three possible answers that might be given. Each reason hints at the empirical properties a recreational drug would have to possess before it should be banned entirely in order to reduce the probability that adolescents will use it.

First, adolescents might represent such a high percentage of the users of a given drug that an infringement of the rights of the relatively few adult users would be justified in order to curtail its availability among the comparatively many adolescents. This rationale provides a possible basis for rejecting the leakage argument with respect to alcohol while accepting it with respect to some or all illegal drugs. Since so many adults drink, banning alcohol altogether in order to prevent leakage to adolescents would impose an enormous sacrifice. This argument becomes less plausible as adults represent a higher and higher percentage of the consumers of a given drug.

Many complex variables affect how the use of a given drug

is apportioned between adolescents and adults. One obvious factor is price, since adolescents tend to have less money to spend. Another factor is the length of time the drug has been available in a community: The more established the substance is, the higher the percentage of older users. One would expect that application of this first argument would result in the prohibition of new and inexpensive drugs – crack, for example.

However, the application of this argument to any existing drug is unpromising for prohibitionists. The National Household Survey on Drug Abuse distinguishes between users aged 12 to 17, 18 to 25, 26 to 34, and older than 35. Not surprisingly, persons between 18 and 25 represent the highest percentage of users of any given illegal drug included in the survey. No drug is consumed by half as many persons under 18 as by persons between 18 and 25. Over 20 million Americans smoked marijuana in 1990; less than 10 percent of them were between 12 to 17. More than 850,000 of the approximately 1 million Americans who used crack in 1990 were 18 or older.[135] Although 140,000 crack users under 18 may be 140,000 too many, no one can claim that restrictions on adult behavior for the sake of these relatively few young Americans is a trivial sacrifice. It is conceivable that a drug might have a special appeal to juveniles, who outnumber adult users, but no existing recreational drug comes close to satisfying this description.

A second argument is defended by Robert Goodin in his critique of tobacco. Goodin claims, "If people start smoking before they are of the age of consent, and are addicted by the time they reach that age, then they have never had the opportunity to give their informed consent in any morally meaningful way to the risks of smoking."[136] This argument can be generalized to include any given addictive recreational drug that persons tend to first use during adolescence. If this argument were persuasive, there might be good reason to sacrifice the freedom of the minority of persons who began using that drug as adults in order to protect the majority of persons who became addicted as adolescents. Goodin confines the application of this argument to tobacco, where it is most defensible. About 60 percent of current smokers began by the age of 13 or 14,[137] and as many as 95 percent became addicted before reaching maturity.[138]

However, Goodin's argument can apply only to addictive drugs, and not all illegal drugs qualify. The illegal drug usually identified as the most addictive – heroin – is not nearly as popular among the very young as the illegal drug seldom or never said to be addictive – marijuana. One study indicated the median age of first heroin use to be about 19.[139] Although precise lines are hard to draw, I doubt that the consent of persons aged 19 is not "morally meaningful." In addition, Goodin's argument supposes that the drug use of an addict is nonvoluntary and nonautonomous, a supposition I contested in Chapter 2. If the drug use of an addict is sufficiently voluntary and autonomous, the fact that she began using drugs during adolescence and persisted throughout adulthood is not decisive to the case for prohibition.

A third and final argument is that the consequences of a given illegal drug might be so severe for adolescents that adult use should be proscribed in order to prevent them. To cite an extreme example, imagine a substance that induced harmless euphoria in adults but was lethal for adolescents. This hypothetical substance should be prohibited altogether. The moral rights of adults would be overridden to reduce the availability of a drug that kills large numbers of children.

The trouble with this argument is that no such drug exists. Defending this conclusion requires a return to the issue I discussed earlier in this section: How bad are drugs for adolescents? If illegal drugs are indeed worse for adolescents than for adults, exactly how much worse are they? The available evidence does not demonstrate that drug use is *that* harmful for adolescents relative to adults. In the absence of several longitudinal studies, one cannot be certain about the fates of the millions of Americans who used recreational drugs during adolescence. One longitudinal study concluded that adults who had used moderate quantities of drugs while young tend to be psychologically healthier than adults who had abstained.[140] Moreover, the problems many adolescent drug users seem to experience typically predate their use of drugs and thus cannot be said to have been caused by drugs.[141] It is one thing to believe that adolescents would be better off not using drugs, and it is quite another to believe that drugs are so incredibly harmful for adolescents that adults should be willing to sacrifice their liberty in order to reduce the incidence of adolescent drug use.

Perhaps drug prohibitionists can defend some other basis to justify restrictions for adults to prevent leakage to minors. No one can be confident until such an argument is produced and evaluated. I will conclude with a final observation about any such argument. Those who favor LAD on this ground should be apologetic; they would authorize punishment for adults as an unfortunate but unavoidable price to be paid in order to achieve a greater good. Needless to say, drug pro-hibitionists who endorse this argument have not expressed much regret about the sacrifice of liberty that they are pre-pared to require. Their attitude gives rise to the suspicion that they support LAD for entirely different reasons, al-though they identify their concern for youth when they need to cloak their objections to recreational drug use in an aura of respectability. I am skeptical of any rationale for LAD that emphasizes the special status and vulnerability of adoles-cents. Even if adolescents lack the moral right to use drugs recreationally, I see little reason to revise any of my argu-ments in favor of the moral rights of adults.

A MORAL RIGHT TO USE DRUGS: MISINTERPRETATIONS

I have concluded that the arguments in favor of believing that adults have a moral right to use drugs recreationally are more persuasive than the arguments on the other side. This conclusion is easily misinterpreted. In this final section, I will identify two claims that are not entailed by my conclusion. The root of each misinterpretation is the supposition that rights exhaust the universe of moral discourse.

First, the conclusion that adults have a moral right to use drugs recreationally does not amount to advocating drug use. The distinction between encouraging conduct and conceding that adults have a right to engage in it might seem too obvious to belabor, except that many drug prohibitionists have apparently failed to recognize it. This basic distinction is widely appreciated in most other contexts. Adults have the moral right to preach communism or to practice Buddhism. Yet no one who defends this right would be misunderstood to recommend a conversion to communism or Buddhism.

Nonetheless, one of the most widely voiced objections to the proposal to repeal LAD is that it would express the wrong symbolism about drug use, especially among adolescents. John Lawn maintains: "Legalization of drugs would send the wrong message to our nation's youth. At a time when we have urged our young people to 'just say no' to drugs, legalization would suggest that they need only say no until they reach an appropriate age."[142] Drug prohibitionists who emphasize the symbolic significance of LAD seldom offer a detailed account of why they believe it to be sufficiently important to justify a war on drugs. Is sending the right message about drug use intrinsically or instrumentally valuable? Perhaps this argument is just another version of the concern that a repeal of LAD would encourage drug use.

In order to dispel the impression that support for a right to use drugs is tantamount to encouraging drug use, those who reject LAD should be described as endorsing a *pro-choice* position on recreational drug use. This label has been carefully crafted by persons who uphold the right of women to terminate their pregnancies. These persons are not "pro-death," or "anti-life," as their critics would like the public to believe. Perhaps many of them would not elect abortion as their own solution to an unwanted pregnancy. Still, they believe that women have the right to make this choice for themselves. Misunderstanding would be avoided if the debate about the decriminalization of recreational drug use borrowed this terminology. The conclusion that adults have a moral right to use drugs recreationally should be described as the pro-choice position on recreational drug use.

Suppose, however, that this message becomes distorted and that the public has difficulty distinguishing between respecting a right to perform an activity and recommending that the activity be performed. Can LAD be defended in order to prevent persons from becoming confused in this way? Should the rights of adults be infringed in order to ensure that the wrong message is not received by the public (to whom this argument extends very little credit)? The main problem is that this rationale for LAD would not allow the decriminalization of *any* activity that is less than exemplary. At bottom, this argument is simply another utilitarian defense of the status quo. The rights of some adults should not be sacrificed so that others do not misinterpret a message. This injustice is multiplied when the rights of millions of Americans are at stake.

Still, some concessions can be made without abandoning a commitment to the moral rights of recreational drug users. One possibility is to retain criminal prohibitions of recreational drug use, while failing to enforce them. This option is more politically realistic than a repeal of LAD, since it would avoid a bitterly divisive legislative debate. A policy of nonenforcement has been pursued in the Netherlands. Dutch laws against the recreational use of drugs are not significantly different from those in America, yet "the social reality of modern penal law involvement with illegal drugs may be described as *de facto* abolition in regard to small quantities of all illegal substances."[143] This policy retains de jure criminalization while adopting de facto decriminalization. Some commentators have praised this policy in cost-benefit terms, at least as applied to marijuana.[144] Whether it respects the moral rights of adult users of recreational drugs is less obvious. There is reason to be apprehensive about entrusting the protection of moral rights to exercises of discretion by police and prosecutors. Still, de facto respect for moral rights would represent immense progress over the current state of war against drug users.

A second related but distinct misunderstanding of my position is as follows. The conclusion that the adult use of recreational drugs is protected by a moral right does not entail that drug use is beyond moral reproach. The exercise of a moral right may be subject to criticism. Perhaps all recreational drug use, legal and illegal, is morally tainted. In Chapter 1 I dismissed arguments for LAD that attempted to show that all recreational drug use is incompatible with the attainment of human excellence. However, these arguments might have merit if they are not designed to support criminal legislation. I remain skeptical that a virtue-based objection to all recreational drug use can be defended, although no one should be confident until some philosopher attempts to do so. In any event, some instances of recreational drug use are morally objectionable, beyond those in the special circumstances in which users create an impermissible risk of harm to others. These objectionable instances might be described by the pejorative term *drug abuse.*

Labeling some acts as drug abuse does not advance the inquiry very far, unless the distinction between use and abuse can be drawn. This distinction is vague and imprecise. But the following behavioral symptoms from the Diagnostic and Statistical Manual of Mental Disorders (DSM-III) are central to any reasonable conception of drug abuse:

> The user devotes significant time to procuring, using, and withdrawing. . . . Intoxication and/or withdrawal symptoms interfere with activities of daily living. . . . [Non-related] life activities are reduced or eliminated in preference to the drug activities.[145]

If the moral right to use drugs recreationally is to be respected, the need to minimize disutility leaves society with little choice but to discourage drug abuse. The process by which this goal is reached might loosely be described as "drug education." But this process differs from drug education as it is usually conceived. Most educational programs are prevention programs. As so designed, education has generally been deemed a failure, largely because it has not been shown to achieve its objective of decreasing drug use. Yet there may be more reason for optimism if the goal of education is to decrease drug abuse.

As so construed, drug education may never have been tried. No existing educational program has attempted either to separate use from abuse or to indicate how abuse might be avoided by means other than abstinence.[146] The introduction of scientifically respectable materials in drug education programs has been politically unacceptable. As Mitchell notes: "Because some parents insist that their children learn the official lies about the drug menace, well-informed teachers are caught in another superstition–science conflict except that the drug conflict has far greater legal repercussions for all involved than the evolution–creation debate."[147] Bruce Alexander adds: "The outrageously exaggerated scare stories about drugs that fill the electronic media are often called 'education' or 'prevention.' These measure are part of the War on Drugs, not alternatives to it."[148] He proposes "domestication: learning to treat drugs with the same pragmatism that society applies to other familiar and sometimes dangerous household articles."[149] Other theorists have made similar pleas. James Bakalar and Lester Grinspoon describe this process as "integration."[150] Stephen Mugford proposes that illegal drugs should be "brought in from the cold."[151]

Since I make no attempt to solve America's drug problem as a matter of social policy, I will hazard only one final observation about the prospects for success that drug education as so conceived will minimize drug abuse. To demand that recreational drug users show restraint over the time, place, and quantity of their consumption is not to require the impossible. In fact, virtually every drug user exhibits some degree of control over her consumption.[152] The means by which users manage to avoid abuse deserve careful study and extensive publicity. Perhaps a successful educational program should seek out responsible drug users.[153] In no other context is experience perceived as a liability, unless the experience was so devastating to the educator that he now appreciates the folly of his drug use and counsels total abstinence. Still, informal cultural controls over the use of the most dangerous drugs (such as those that exist in Peru[154]) do not emerge quickly. To respect the moral right of adults to use recreational drugs may be painful, at least in the short run. But the protection of moral rights has a value to Americans that is not easily expressed in the utilitarian calculus of costs and benefits in which the decriminalization debate is usually cast.

Notes

1 DRUGS, DRUG USE, AND CRIMINALIZATION

1 "Drug War Underlines Fickleness of Public," *New York Times*, 6 September 1990, p. A22:6.

2 "War on Drugs Remains Top Priority, Bush Says," *New York Times*, 6 September 1990, p. A22:4.

3 William Bennett, *National Drug Control Strategy* (Washington: Office of the National Drug Control Policy, 1990), p. 9.

4 Thomas Mieczkowski, "The Accuracy of Self-Reported Drug Use: An Evaluation and Analysis of New Data," in *Drugs, Crime, and the Criminal Justice System*, ed. Ralph Weisheit (Cincinnati: Anderson Publishing Co., 1990), p. 275.

5 Ethan A. Nadelmann, "The Case for Legalization," *The Public Interest* 92 (1988): 3.

6 National Institute on Drug Abuse, *National Household Survey on Drug Abuse* (1990).

7 Ibid.

8 "New York Reports a Drop in Crack Traffic," *New York Times*, 27 December 1990, p. B1:2; "Drop in Youths' Cocaine Use May Reflect a Societal Shift," *New York Times*, 25 January 1991, p. A14:1; and "Crack May Be Cracking," *New York Times*, 10 August 1991, p. 18:1. For more troublesome news, see "Falling Off the Wagon for Cocaine," *Washington Post* 2–8 December 1991, National Weekly Edition, pp. 34–5.

9 Franklin Zimring and Gordon Hawkins, *The Search for Rational Drug Control* (New York: Cambridge University Press, 1992), p. 42.

10 Ronald Hamowy, "Introduction: Illicit Drugs and Govern-

ment Control," in *Dealing with Drugs*, ed. Ronald Hamowy (Lexington, MA: D.C. Heath & Co., 1987), pp. 1–2.

11 Chester Mitchell, *The Drug Solution* (Ottawa: Carleton University Press, 1990), p. 133.

12 *Harmelin v. Michigan*, 111 S. Ct. 2680 (1991).

13 "Hitting a Small Nail with a Very Large Hammer," *Washington Post*, 10–16 December 1990, National Weekly Edition, p. 25:2.

14 Uniform Crime Reports, "Crime in the United States" (1989).

15 *Chapman et al. v. United States*, 111 S. Ct. 1919 (1991).

16 Julie Bach, ed., *Drug Abuse: Opposing Viewpoints* (St. Paul: Greenhaven Press, 1988), p. 147.

17 Mitchell, *Drug Solution*, p. 138.

18 See Doug Bandow, "Once Again, a Drug War Panic," in *The Crisis in Drug Prohibition*, ed. David Boaz (Washington: Cato Institute, 1990), p. 93.

19 See Steven Jonas, "Solving the Drug Problem: A Public Health Approach to the Reduction of the Use and Abuse of Both Legal and Illegal Recreational Drugs," *Hofstra Law Review* 18 (1990): 751, 774.

20 *Newsweek*, 11 August 1986, 18.

21 House Select Committee on Narcotics Abuse and Control, *Legalization of Illicit Drugs: Impact and Feasibility*, 100th Cong., 2d sess., 1989, 1:133.

22 William Bennett, "Drug Policy and the Intellectuals" (Speech delivered at the Kennedy School of Government, Harvard University, 11 December 1989).

23 See Mitchell, *Drug Solution*, p. 27.

24 See Harold W. Lewis, *Technological Risk* (New York: W.W. Norton & Co., 1990).

25 "Our Multibillion-Dollar Bill for Getting the Lead Paint Out," *Washington Post* 1–7 July 1991, National Weekly Edition, p. 32.

26 Herbert Needleman, "Why We Should Worry about Lead Poisoning," *Contemporary Pediatrics* 34 (1988): 34.

27 Bennett, *National Drug Control Strategy*, (1990), p. 3.

28 Zimring and Hawkins, *Search for Rational Drug Control*, p. 23.

29 Gerald F. Uelmen and Victor G. Haddox, eds., *Drug Abuse and the Law Sourcebook* (New York: Clark Boardman Co., 1988), pp. 1–1.

30 Ibid., pp. 1–3.

31 See Jonas, "Solving the Drug Problem," 756.

32 A. Lee Fritschler, *Smoking and Politics,* 2d ed. (Englewood Cliffs, NJ: Prentice-Hall, 1975), pp. 34–5.
33 William Bennett, *National Drug Control Strategy.* (Washington: Office of the National Drug Control Policy, 1989), p. 4.
34 21 *U.S.C.* sec. 321 (g) (1).
35 *Food* is defined as "articles used for food or drink for man or other animals" (21 *U.S.C.* sec. 321 [f] [1]).
36 21 *U.S.C.* sec. 802 (6).
37 21 *U.S.C.* sec. 802(6).
38 Mark Moore, "Drugs: Getting a Fix on the Problem and the Solution," *Yale Law & Policy Review* 8 (1990): pp. 8, 19.
39 Bennett, *National Drug Control Strategy,* p. 8.
40 See Jonas, "Solving the Drug Problem," 757–8.
41 Uelmen and Haddox, *Drug Abuse and the Law Sourcebook,* pp. 3–4.
42 21 *U.S.C.* sec. 812.
43 *U.S. v. Fogarty,* 692 F.2d 542, 548 (1982).
44 *NORML v. Bell,* 488 F.Supp. 123 (1980).
45 21 *U.S.C.* sec. 355 (d) (6).
46 See *Grinspoon v. Drug Enforcement Agency,* 828 F.2d 881, 891 (1987).
47 Unapproved dispensing of any controlled substance for the purpose of continuing the dependence of a narcotic drug-dependent person is expressly prohibited by 21 *U.S.C.* sec. 828 (e). See also *Webb v. U.S.,* 249 U.S. 96 (1919).
48 Robert Bogomolny, Michael Sonnenreich, and Anthony Roccograndi, *A Handbook of the 1970 Federal Drug Act* (Springfield, IL: Charles C. Thomas, 1975), pp. 75–6.
49 "Survey Finds Support for Marijuana Use by Cancer Patients," *New York Times,* 1 May 1991, p. D22:1.
50 *U.S. v. Pastor,* 557 F.2d 930 (1977).
51 *Grinspoon v. Drug Enforcement Agency,* p. 895.
52 See Edward Lipinski, "Motivation in Drug Misuse: Some Comments on Agent, Environment, Host," *Journal of the American Medical Association* 219 (1972): 171.
53 *Grinspoon v. Drug Enforcement Agency,* p. 894 n. 14.
54 Jerome Beck and Marsha Rosenbaum, "The Scheduling of MDMA ('Ecstasy')," in *Handbook of Drug Control in the United States,* ed. James Inciardi (New York: Greenwood Press, 1990), pp. 303, 308.

55 21 *U.S.C.* sec. 844 (a).
56 David Musto, *The American Disease: Origins of Narcotic Control,* exp. ed. (New York: Oxford University Press, 1987), p. 260.
57 *Grinspoon v. Drug Enforcement Agency,* p. 27.
58 *Vance v. Bradley,* 440 U.S. 93, 111 (1979).
59 *U.S. v. DiLaura,* 394 F.Supp. 770, 772 (1974).
60 *McLaughlin v. Florida,* 379 U.S. 184, 196 (1964).
61 Robert E. Goodin, *No Smoking* (Chicago: University of Chicago Press, 1989), p. 65.
62 Ibid.
63 537 P.2d 494, 504 (1975).
64 Ibid., p. 498.
65 "Life, Liberty, and Maybe Marijuana," *New York Times,* 5 February 1991, p. A16:4.
66 See "Judge's Overturning of Crack Law Brings Turmoil," *New York Times,* 11 January 1991, p. B5:3; and "Minnesota Upholds Ruling That Crack Law Was Biased," *New York Times,* 14 December 1991, p. A8:2.
67 Laurence Tribe, *American Constitutional Law,* 2d ed. (Mineola, NY: Foundation Press, 1988), p. 1614.
68 Ibid., p. 1610.
69 Ibid., p. 1324.
70 Nadelmann, "Case for Legalization," 4.
71 Tribe, *American Constitutional Law,* p. 1386.
72 David Richards, *Sex, Drugs, Death, and the Law* (Totowa, NJ: Rowman & Littlefield, 1982).
73 See Frederick Schauer, "Decriminalization and the Constitution," *Criminal Justice Ethics* 3 (1984): 76.
74 See *Bowers v. Hardwick,* 478 U.S. 186 (1986). But see David Richards, *Toleration and the Constitution* (New York: Oxford University Press, 1986).
75 Thomas Jefferson, *Notes on the State of Virginia* (Boston: Thomas & Andrews, 1801), p. 236.
76 Musto, *American Disease,* p. 9.
77 Ibid., p. 247.
78 See Jonas, "Solving the Drug Problem," 751.
79 Andrew Weil, *The Natural Mind,* 2d ed. (Boston: Houghton Mifflin Co., 1986), pp. 2, 36.
80 Bruce Alexander, *Peaceful Measures: Canada's Way out of the "War on Drugs"* (Toronto: University of Toronto Press, 1990), p. 338.

81 See Norman E. Zinberg, *Drug, Set, and Setting: The Basis for Controlled Intoxicant Use* (New Haven: Yale University Press, 1984), p. 28.
82 "Federal Judge Would Make All Illicit Drugs Legal," *New York Times*, 13 December 1989, p. B10:5.
83 Weil, *Natural Mind*, p. 19.
84 Ibid.
85 Ronald K. Siegel, *Intoxication: Life in Pursuit of Artificial Paradise* (New York: E.P. Dutton & Co., 1989), p. 313.
86 See ibid., p. 308.
87 Ibid., p. 311.
88 Ibid., p. 312.
89 Norman E. Zinberg, "The Use and Misuse of Intoxicants," in Hamowy, *Dealing with Drugs*, pp. 247, 255.
90 James Bakalar and Lester Grinspoon, *Drug Control in a Free Society* (Cambridge: Cambridge University Press, 1984), p. 129.
91 Ray Brown, "The Black Community and the 'War on Drugs,' " in *The Great Issues of Drug Policy*, ed. Arnold Trebach and Kevin Zeese (Washington: Drug Policy Foundation, 1990), pp. 83, 85.
92 Nadelmann, "Case for Legalization," 4. See also Michael Letwin, "Report from the Front Line: The Bennett Plan, Street-Level Drug Enforcement in New York City and the Legalization Debate," *Hofstra Law Review* 18 (1990): 795.
93 James Inciardi and Duane McBride, "Legalization: A High-Risk Alternative to the War on Drugs," *American Behavioral Scientist* 32 (1989): 259, 278.
94 Ibid., 278.
95 See Samuel Myers, "Drugs and Market Structure: Is There Really a Drug Crisis in the Black Community?" in Trebach and Zeese, *Great Issues of Drug Policy*, p. 98.
96 Marsha Rosenbaum, *Just Say What?* (San Francisco: National Council on Crime and Delinquency, 1989), p. 9.
97 National Institute on Drug Abuse, *National Household Survey on Drug Abuse* (1990).
98 Ethan Nadelmann, "Drug Prohibition in the United States: Costs, Consequences, and Alternatives," *Science* 245 (1989): 940.
99 Inciardi and McBride, "Legalization," 239.

100 "Anti-Drug Effort Drags Outside U.S.," *New York Times*, 25 November 1990, p. A9:1.

101 Peter Reuter, "Can the Borders Be Sealed?" *The Public Interest* 92 (1989): 51.

102 National Institute on Drug Abuse, *High School Senior Survey* (1990).

103 Nadelmann, "Drug Prohibition," 941.

104 Nadelmann, "Case for Legalization," 16.

105 James Ostrowski, "The Moral and Practical Case for Drug Legalization," *Hofstra Law Review* 18 (1990): 607, 685.

106 David Carter, "An Overview of Drug-Related Misconduct of Police Officers: Drug Abuse and Narcotic Corruption," in Weisheit, *Drugs, Crime, and the Criminal Justice System*, pp. 79, 105.

107 Mark Deninger, "The Economics of Heroin: Key to Optimizing the Legal Response," *Georgia Law Review* 10 (1976): 565, 583.

108 Mark Kleiman and Aaron Saiger, "Drug Legalization: The Importance of Asking the Right Question," *Hofstra Law Review* 18 (1990): 527, 542.

109 Nadelmann, "Drug Prohibition," 941.

110 James Ostrowski, "Thinking about Drug Legalization," in Boaz, *Crisis in Drug Prohibition*, pp. 45, 61.

111 Richard Cowan, "How the Narcs Created Crack," *National Review*, 5 December 1986, 26.

112 Nadelmann, "Case for Legalization," 7.

113 John Kaplan, *The Hardest Drug: Heroin and Public Policy* (Chicago: University of Chicago Press, 1983), p. 128.

114 Jon Gettman, "Decriminalizing Marijuana," *American Behavioral Scientist* 32 (1989): 243, 244.

115 See Mark Kleiman, *Marijuana: Costs of Abuse, Costs of Control* (New York: Greenwood Press, 1989), pp. 164–7.

116 Nadelmann, "Drug Prohibition," 942.

117 See Alexander, *Peaceful Measures*, pp. 165–6.

118 Ostrowski, "Thinking about Drug Legalization," p. 62.

119 "New Tactics in the War on Drugs Tilt Scales of Justice Off Balance," *New York Times*, 29 December 1989, p. A1:1.

120 Ostrowski, "Thinking about Drug Legalization," p. 58.

121 James Austin and Aaron McVey, *The 1989 NCCD Prison Population Forecast: The Impact of the War on Drugs* (Washington: National Council on Crime and Delinquency, 1989), p. 1.

122 See Jonathan Schonsheck, "On Various Hypocrisies of the 'Drugs' in Sports Scandal," *The Philosophical Forum* 20 (1989): 247.

123 Weil, *Natural Mind*, p. 46.

124 *Sports Illustrated*, 24 September 1990, 27.

125 Gerry Fitzgerald, "Dispatches from the Drug War," *Common Cause* 16 (January/February 1990): 13, 19.

126 See Peter Dale Scott and Jonathan Marshall, *Cocaine Politics* (Berkeley: University of California Press, 1991).

127 See Steven Wisotsky, "The Emerging 'Drug Exception' to the Bill of Rights," *Hastings Law Journal* 38 (1987): 889.

128 David Evans, "How Many Liberties Are We Losing?" *Human Rights* 17 (1990): 14, 15.

129 "Hitting a Small Nail with a Very Large Hammer," p. 25:1.

130 Ibid.

131 See Zimring and Hawkins, *Search for Rational Drug Control*, p. 106.

132 John Stuart Mill, *On Liberty* (New York: E.P. Dutton & Co., 1951), p. 126.

133 *Legalization of Illicit Drugs*, p. 9.

134 See James Jacobs, "Imagining Drug Legalization," *The Public Interest* 101 (1990): 28.

135 John Lawn, "The Issue of Legalizing Illicit Drugs," *Hofstra Law Review* 18 (1990): 703, 715.

136 See Herbert Packer, *The Limits of the Criminal Sanction* (Stanford: Stanford University Press, 1968).

137 See Douglas Husak, *Philosophy of Criminal Law* (Totowa, NJ: Rowman & Littlefield, 1987).

138 See the polls in the *Washington Post*, 18–24 September 1989, Weekly Edition, p. 37; and *New York Times*, 15 September 1988, p. A26:5. See also Robert Peterson, "Legalization: The Myth Exposed," in *Searching For Alternatives*, eds. Melvyn B. Krauss and Edward P. Lazear (Stanford: Hoover Institution Press, 1991), p. 324.

139 National Institute on Drug Abuse, *High School Senior Survey* (1988).

140 Arnold Trebach and Kevin Zeese, eds., *Drug Prohibition and the Conscience of Nations* (Washington: Drug Policy Foundation, 1990) p. 226.

141 Joel Feinberg, *Harm to Others* (New York: Oxford University Press, 1984); idem, *Offense to Others* (New York: Oxford Uni-

versity Press, 1985); idem, *Harm to Self* (New York: Oxford University Press, 1986); and idem, *Harmless Wrongdoing* (New York: Oxford University Press, 1988). Feinberg allows for the criminalization of some offensive conduct, but this exception to the general requirement of harm is unimportant for present purposes.

142 See Douglas Husak, "Rights, Harmless Immorality, and In-choate Criminal Offenses" (forthcoming).
143 William Bennett: "The Plea to Legalize Drugs Is a Siren Call to Surrender," in *Drugs in Society*, ed. Michael Lyman and Gary Potter (Cincinnati: Anderson Publishing Co., 1991), p. 339.
144 James Inciardi and Duane McBride: "Debating the Legalization of Drugs," in Inciardi, *Handbook of Drug Control*, p. 283.
145 John Kaplan, *Marijuana: The New Prohibition* (New York: World Publishing Co., 1970), p. xi.
146 Feinberg, *Harmless Wrongdoing*.
147 Richards, *Sex, Drugs, Death, and the Law*, p. 168.
148 Weil, *Natural Mind*.
149 Richards, *Sex, Drugs, Death, and the Law*.
150 Ibid., p. 169.
151 Ibid., p. 170.
152 Alexander, *Peaceful Measures*, p. 337.
153 Bennett, *National Drug Control Strategy*, (1989), p. 9.
154 James Q. Wilson, "Against the Legalization of Drugs," *Commentary* 89 (1990): 21, 26.
155 Richards, *Sex, Drugs, Death, and the Law*, pp. 171–2.
156 Zimring and Hawkins, *Search for Rational Drug Control*, p. 9.
157 Ibid., p. 8.
158 Ibid., p. 10.

2 DRUGS AND HARM TO USERS

1 See Douglas Husak, "Recreational Drugs and Paternalism," *Law and Philosophy* 8 (1989): 353.
2 James Q. Wilson, "Drugs and Crime," in *Drugs and Crime*, ed. Michael Tonry and James Q. Wilson (Chicago: Chicago University Press, 1990), pp. 521, 523.
3 William Bennett, *National Drug Control Strategy* (Washington: Office of the National Drug Control Policy, 1989), p. 7.

4   See Joel Feinberg, *Harmless Wrongdoing* (New York: Oxford University Press, 1988).

5   Vincent Bugliosi, *Drugs in America* (New York: Knightsbridge Publishing Co., 1991), p. 183 (emphasis in original).

6   Claudia Mills, "The War on Drugs: Is It Time to Surrender?," *Philosophy & Public Policy* 9 (Spring/Summer 1989): 3.

7   California, Research Advisory Panel, *20th Annual Report of the Research Advisory Panel* (San Francisco: Research Advisory Panel, 1990), Commentary.

8   See Arnold Trebach, "Arrest (Even Lobotomize) My Child," in *Drug Prohibition and the Conscience of Nations*, ed. Arnold Trebach and Kevin Zeese (Washington: Drug Policy Foundation, 1990), p. 166.

9   "Explosive Drug Use Creating New Underworld in Prisons," *New York Times*, 30 December 1989, p. A2:2.

10 See Lynn Kozlowski et al., "Comparing Tobacco Cigarette Dependence with Other Drug Dependencies," *Journal of the American Medical Association* 26 (1989): 898.

11 Bennett, *National Drug Control Strategy*, (1989), p. 9.

12 William Bennett, "The Plea to Legalize Drugs Is a Siren Call to Surrender," in *Drugs in Society*, ed. Michael Lyman and Gary Potter (Cincinnati: Anderson Publishing Co., 1991), pp. 336, 339.

13 See Jefferson Morley, "Aftermath of a Crack Article," *The Nation*, 20 November 1989, 592.

14 C. L. Ten, *Mill on Liberty* (Oxford: Clarendon Press, 1980), p. 116.

15 See Douglas Husak, "Paternalism and Autonomy," *Philosophy and Public Affairs* 10 (1981): 27.

16 Gerald Dworkin, "The Value of Autonomy," in *The Theory and Practice of Autonomy*, by Gerald Dworkin (Cambridge: Cambridge University Press, 1988), pp. 21, 31.

17 Gerald Dworkin, "The Nature of Autonomy," in Dworkin, *Theory and Practice of Autonomy*, pp. 3, 20.

18 Gerald Dworkin, "Autonomy and Behavior Control," *Hastings Center Report* 6 (1976): 23.

19 Harry Frankfurt, "Freedom of the Will," in *The Importance of What We Care About*, by Harry Frankfurt (New York: Cambridge University Press, 1988), pp. 11, 20.

20 Joel Feinberg, *Harm to Self* (New York: Oxford University Press, 1986), p. 54.

21 John Rawls, *A Theory of Justice* (Cambridge, MA: Harvard University Press, 1971), p. 249.
22 See Mark Kleiman and Aaron Saiger, "Drug Legalization: The Importance of Asking the Right Question," *Hofstra Law Review* 18 (1990): 527, 533.
23 Ron Paul, "Improving National Drug Policy," *American Criminal Law Review* 26 (1989): 1689.
24 See Robert Paul Wolff, *In Defense of Anarchism* (New York: Harper & Row, 1970).
25 See Ronald Dworkin, *Taking Rights Seriously* (Cambridge, MA: Harvard University Press, 1977). See also David Lyons, "Utility and Rights," in *Nomos XXIV: Ethics, Economics, and the Law*, ed. J. Roland Pennock and John Chapman (New York: New York University Press, 1982), p. 107; and Judith Jarvis Thomson, *The Realm of Rights* (Cambridge, MA: Harvard University Press, 1990).
26 Feinberg, *Harm to Self*, p. 61.
27 Ibid.
28 Ibid., p. 26 (emphasis in original).
29 Kleiman and Saiger, "Drug Legalization," 543.
30 William Bennett, "Drug Policy and the Intellectuals" (Speech delivered at the Kennedy School of Government, Harvard University, 11 December 1989).
31 James Inciardi and Duane McBride, "Debating the Legalization of Drugs," in *Handbook of Drug Control in the United States*, ed. James Inciardi (New York: Greenwood Press, 1990), p. 295.
32 "Death Toll from Smoking Is Worsening," *New York Times*, 1 February 1991, p. A14:4.
33 Richard Peto, "Possible Ways of Explaining to Ordinary People the Quantitative Dangers of Smoking," *Health Education Journal* 39 (1980): 45.
34 "Cocaine Epidemic May Have Peaked," *New York Times*, 2 September 1990, p. A32:6.
35 See Bruce Alexander and Linda Wong, "Cocaine Related Deaths: Media Coverage in the War on Drugs," *Journal of Drug Issues* 21 (1991): 105.
36 See Marsha Rosenbaum, *Just Say What?* (San Francisco: National Council on Crime and Delinquency, 1989), p. 6.
37 Steven Jonas, "Is the Drug Problem Soluble?" *American Be-*

havioral Scientist 32 (1989): 295, 299. See also David Musto, *The American Disease: Origins of Narcotic Control*, exp. ed. (New York: Oxford University Press, 1987), p. 260.

38 Mark Moore, "Actually, Prohibition Was a Success," *New York Times*, 16 October 1989, p. A21:1.

39 National Safety Council, *Accident Facts* (1988), p. 60.

40 *Traveling Healthy* 3 (September/October 1990): 3.

41 Steven Jonas, "Solving the Drug Problem: A Public Health Approach to the Reduction of the Use and Abuse of Both Legal and Illegal Recreational Drugs," *Hofstra Law Review* 18 (1990): 751, 765.

42 Ibid., 767.

43 Ibid., 768.

44 Ibid., 769.

45 Ibid., 770.

46 See the discussion of physical, psychological, motivational, and behavioral effects of marijuana in Mark Kleiman, *Marijuana: Costs of Abuse, Costs of Control* (New York: Greenwood Press, 1989), pp. 5–11.

47 Jonathan Shedler and Jack Block, "Adolescent Drug Use and Psychological Health," *American Psychologist* 45 (1990): 612, 625.

48 Ibid., 628.

49 Richard Merrill and Michael Taylor, "Saccharin: A Case Study of Government Regulation of Environmental Carcinogens," *Agriculture and Human Values* 3 (1986): 33, 36.

50 Deborah Johnson, "The Ethical Dimensions of Acceptable Risk in Food Safety," *Agriculture and Human Values* 3 (1986): 171, 178.

51 However, see the evidence for the inability of experienced cocaine users to differentiate cocaine from other drugs or even from a placebo in Craig Van Dyke and Robert Byck, "Cocaine," *Scientific American* 246 (1982): 128, 139.

52 See the practical proposals suggested by Michael Aldrich, "Legalize the Lesser to Minimize the Greater: Modern Applications of Ancient Wisdom," *Journal of Drug Issues* 20 (1990): 543.

53 Robert E. Goodin, *No Smoking* (Chicago: University of Chicago Press, 1989), p. 7.

54 Ibid., p. 99. For a competing view, see Bruce Alexander,

Peaceful Measures: Canada's Way out of the "War on Drugs" (Toronto: University of Toronto Press, 1990): "Addiction is as likely to be a benefit as a curse" (p. 125).

55 James Bakalar and Lester Grinspoon, *Cocaine: A Drug and Its Social Evolution* (New York: Basic Books, 1976), p. 176.

56 Norman E. Zinberg, *Drug, Set, and Setting: The Basis for Controlled Intoxicant Use* (New Haven: Yale University Press, 1984), p. 26.

57 "America's Addiction to Addictions," *U.S. News & World Report*, 5 February 1990, 62.

58 Thomas Szasz, *Ceremonial Chemistry* (Garden City, NY: Anchor Press, 1974), p. xvii.

59 Howard Shaffer and Stephanie Jones, *Quitting Cocaine* (Lexington, MA: D.C. Heath & Co., 1989), p. 38.

60 See Stanton Peele, *Visions of Addiction* (Lexington, MA: D.C. Heath & Co., 1988).

61 Zinberg, *Drug, Set, and Setting*, pp. 35–6.

62 See S. Blume, "Gambling: Disease or 'Excuse'? High Rollers Suffer from an Illness," *U.S. Journal of Drug and Alcohol Dependence* (August 1989), 15.

63 Shaffer and Jones, *Quitting Cocaine*, p. 42.

64 Ibid., p. 43.

65 American Law Institute, *Model Penal Code* (Philadelphia: American Law Institute, 1985), sec. 2.09.

66 See Leo Katz, *Bad Acts and Guilty Minds* (Chicago: University of Chicago Press, 1987), p. 69.

67 American Law Institute, *Model Penal Code* (1985), sec. 2.09(2).

68 Kozlowski et al., "Comparing Tobacco Cigarette Dependence with Other Drug Dependencies," 900.

69 Ibid., 898.

70 Peter Mansky, "Opiates: Human Psychopharmacology," in 12 *Handbook of Psychopharmacology*, ed. Leslie Iversen, Susan Iversen, and Solomon Snyder (New York: Plenum Press, 1978), pp. 95, 158.

71 Herbert Fingarette and Anne Hasse, *Mental Disabilities and Criminal Responsibility* (Berkeley: University of California Press, 1979), p. 166.

72 486 F.2d 1139 (1973).

73 Ibid., p. 1183.

74 See "Court Backs Curb on Marijuana Use," *New York Times*, 27 July 1991, p. A8:6.
75 Morgan Cloud III, "Cocaine, Demand, and Addiction: A Study of the Possible Convergence of Rational Theory and National Policy," *Vanderbilt Law Review* 42 (1989): 725, 742.
76 Frank Gawin and Everett Ellinwood, "Cocaine and Other Stimulants: Action, Abuse, and Treatment," *New England Journal of Medicine* 318 (1988): 1173, 1176.
77 Robert Byck, "Cocaine, Marijuana, and the Meaning of Addiction," in *Dealing with Drugs*, ed. Ronald Hamowy (Lexington, MA: D.C. Heath & Co., 1987), pp. 221, 233.
78 See Ronald Akers, "Addiction: The Troublesome Concept," *Journal of Drug Issues* 21 (1991): 777–93.
79 Van Dyke and Byck, "Cocaine," 140.
80 John Stuart Mill, *On Liberty* (New York: E.P. Dutton & Co., 1951), p. 213.
81 Goodin, *No Smoking*, p. 28.
82 Feinberg, *Harm to Self*, p. 77.
83 Goodin, *No Smoking*, p. 29 (emphasis in original).
84 John Kaplan, *The Hardest Drug: Heroin and Public Policy* (Chicago: University of Chicago Press, 1983), p. 37.
85 See Charles Winick, "Maturing out of Narcotic Addiction," *Bulletin on Narcotics* 14 (1962): 1. See also Chester Mitchell, *The Drug Solution* (Ottawa: Carleton University Press, 1990), p. 20.
86 See Stanton Peele and Archie Brodsky, *The Truth about Addiction and Recovery* (New York: Simon & Schuster, 1991), pp. 80–4. See also the motivations for quitting described in Dan Waldorf, Craig Reinarnan, and Sheigla Murphy, *Cocaine Changes* (Philadelphia: Temple University Press, 1991), p. 196.
87 See Vernon Johnson, *Intervention: How to Help Someone Who Doesn't Want Help* (Minneapolis: Johnson Institute Books, 1986).
88 See Patrick Biernacki, *Pathways from Heroin Addiction: Recovery without Treatment* (Philadelphia: Temple University Press, 1986); and Shaffer and Jones, *Quitting Cocaine*, pp. 96–7.
89 Lee Robins et al., "Vietnam Veterans Three Years after Vietnam," in 2 *Yearbook of Substance Use and Abuse*, ed. Leon Brill and Charles Winick (New York: Human Sciences Press, 1980), p. 213.

90 Jane Porter and Hershel Jick, "Addiction Rare in Patients Treated with Narcotics," *New England Journal of Medicine* 302 (1980): 123.
91 See Zinberg, *Drug, Set, and Setting;* and Patricia Erickson et al., *The Steel Drug: Cocaine in Perspective* (Lexington, MA: D.C. Heath & Co., 1987).
92 National Institute on Drug Abuse, *National Household Survey on Drug Abuse* (1990).
93 One reviewer recommended censorship of Zinberg's book, which defends the possibility of moderate, controlled use of opiates. See Mitchell, *Drug Solution,* p. 132.
94 Erickson et al., *Steel Drug,* p. 83.
95 National Institute on Drug Abuse, *National Household Survey on Drug Abuse* (1990).
96 "Treatment for Crack Addicts: Drug Experts Report Finding Clues to a Cure," *New York Times,* 24 August 1989, p. B7:1. See also Henry Brownstein, "Demilitarization of the War on Drugs: Toward an Alternative Drug Strategy," in *The Great Issues of Drug Policy,* ed. Arnold Trebach and Kevin Zeese (Washington: Drug Policy Foundation, 1990), p. 114.
97 Yuet Cheung, Patricia Erickson, and Tammy Landau, "Experiences of Crack Use: Findings from a Community-Based Sample in Toronto," *Journal of Drug Issues* 2 (1991): 121, 134.
98 Ralph Weisheit, "Declaring a 'Civil' War on Drugs," in *Drugs, Crime, and the Criminal Justice System,* ed. Ralph Weisheit (Cincinnati: Anderson Publishing Co., 1990), pp. 1, 5.
99 "Treatment for Crack Addicts," *New York Times,* 24 August 1989, p. B7:1.
100 Kleiman and Saiger, "Drug Legalization," 564.
101 Kaplan, *Hardest Drug,* p. 34.
102 Ibid.
103 Steven Wisotsky, "Images of Death and Destruction in Drug Law Cases," in Trebach and Zeese, *Great Issues of Drug Policy,* p. 47.
104 *Robinson v. California,* 370 U.S. 660, 672 (Douglas, J., concurring).
105 Hamowy, *Dealing with Drugs,* p. 190.
106 Mark Cooper, "Up in Smoke," *American Film,* March 1987, 53, 54.
107 "Rogers of Saints Said to Admit Use of Cocaine," *New York Times,* 25 June 1982, p. A21:5.

108 U.S. Department of Labor, *What Works: Workplaces without Drugs* (Washington: U.S. Government Printing Office, 1991), p. 5.
109 "New York Told to Hire Advisers on Drug Abuse," *New York Times* 27 September 1990, p. B3:1.
110 Andrew Weil and Winifred Rosen, *Chocolate to Morphine: Understanding Mind-Active Drugs* (Boston: Houghton Mifflin Co., 1983), p. 115.
111 Feinberg, *Harm to Self*, p. 12 (emphasis in original).
112 Ibid., p. 116.
113 Joel Feinberg, *Harm to Others* (New York: Oxford University Press, 1984), p. 116.
114 Feinberg, *Harm to Self*, p. 117.
115 Ibid., p. 133.
116 Ibid.
117 Ibid., p. 188.
118 Goodin, *No Smoking*, p. 21.
119 Gilbert Botvin, "Substance Abuse Prevention: Theory, Practice, and Effectiveness," in Tonry and Wilson, *Drugs and Crime*, pp. 461, 487.
120 "Bennett Doubts Value of Drug Education," *New York Times*, 3 February 1990, p.A1:7.
121 Goodin, *No Smoking*, p. 18.
122 See Terry Bulych and Garry L. Beyerstein, "Authoritarianism and Misinformation as Sources of Support for the War on Drugs," *New Frontiers in Drug Policy*, eds., Arnold Trebach and Kevin Zeese (Washington: Drug Policy Foundation, 1991), p. 151.
123 See James Bakalar and Lester Grinspoon, *Drug Control in a Free Society* (Cambridge: Cambridge University Press, 1984), p. 17.
124 Goodin, *No Smoking*, p. 23.
125 For an example of such a warning, see James Jacobs, "Imagining Drug Legalization," *The Public Interest* 101 (1990): 28, 33, n. 4.
126 Tal Scriven, "Utility, Autonomy, and Drug Regulation," *International Journal of Applied Philosophy* 2 (1984): 27, 31.
127 John Kleinig, *Paternalism* (Totowa, NJ: Rowman & Allanheld, 1983).
128 Ibid., p. 67.
129 Ibid., p. 68.

3 DRUGS AND HARM TO OTHERS

1 William Bennett, *National Drug Control Strategy* (Washington: Office of the National Drug Control Policy, 1989), p. 7.
2 James Q. Wilson, "Drugs and Crime," in *Drugs and Crime,* ed. Michael Tonry and James Q. Wilson (Chicago: University of Chicago Press, 1990), pp. 521, 524.
3 John Lawn, "The Issue of Legalizing Illicit Drugs," *Hofstra Law Review* 18 (1990): 703.
4 John Kaplan, "Taking Drugs Seriously," *The Public Interest* 92 (1988): 32, 37.
5 See Lee Nisbet, ed., *The Gun Control Debate* (Buffalo: Prometheus Books, 1990).
6 Kaplan, "Taking Drugs Seriously," 42.
7 A. M. Rosenthal, "How Much Is a Baby's Life Worth?," *New York Times,* 15 December 1989, p. A43:6.
8 Mark Kleiman, *Marijuana: Costs of Abuse, Costs of Control* (New York: Greenwood Press, 1989), p. 173.
9 See Arnold Trebach, "A Bundle of Peaceful Compromises," *Journal of Drug Issues* 4 (1990): 515, 521.
10 Steven Wisotsky, *Breaking the Impasse in the War on Drugs* (New York: Greenwood Press, 1986), p. 215.
11 See Arnold Trebach and Kevin Zeese, eds., *Drug Prohibition and the Conscience of Nations* (Washington: Drug Policy Foundation, 1990), p. 227.
12 See Patricia Erickson et al., *The Steel Drug: Cocaine in Perspective* (Lexington, MA: D.C. Heath & Co., 1987), p. 119.
13 Steven Wisotsky, "Exposing the War on Cocaine: The Futility and Destructiveness of Prohibition," *Wisconsin Law Review* (1983), 1305, 1381.
14 Vincent Bugliosi, *Drugs in America* (New York: Knightsbridge Publishing Co., 1991), p. 186. See also Joseph D. McNamara, "Comment," in *Searching for Alternatives,* eds. Melvyn B. Krauss and Edward P. Lazear (Stanford: Hoover Institution Press, 1991), p. 292, 293.
15 See Dan Waldorf, Craig Reinarman, and Sheigla Murphy, *Cocaine Changes* (Philadelphia: Temple University Press, 1991), p. 196. See also Patricia Erickson and Glenn Murray, "The Undeterred Cocaine User: Intention to Quit and Its Relationship to Perceived Legal and Health Threats," 16 *Contemporary Drug Problems* (1989): 141.

16 See Arnold Trebach, "In the Age of Cocaine – What Is America's Drug Problem?" *Harper's,* December 1985, 44.
17 See Gilbert Botvin, "Substance Abuse Prevention: Theory, Practice, and Effectiveness," in Tonry and Wilson, *Drugs and Crime,* p. 461.
18 Edward M. Brecher and the Editors of *Consumer Reports, Licit and Illicit Drugs* (Boston: Little, Brown & Co., 1972), p. 3.
19 David Musto, "The History of Legislative Control over Opium, Cocaine, and Their Derivatives," in *Dealing with Drugs,* ed. Ronald Hamowy (Lexington, MA: D.C. Heath & Co., 1987), pp. 37, 40.
20 David Musto, "Opium, Cocaine, and Marijuana in American History," *Scientific American* 265 (1991): 40, 44.
21 James Ostrowski, "Thinking about Drug Legalization," in *The Crisis in Drug Prohibition,* ed. David Boaz (Washington: Cato Institute, 1990), pp. 45, 66.
22 Brecher et al., *Licit and Illicit Drugs,* p. 7.
23 James Ostrowski, "The Moral and Practical Case for Drug Legalization," *Hofstra Law Review* 18 (1990): 607, 613.
24 James Bakalar and Lester Grinspoon, *Drug Control in a Free Society* (New York: Cambridge University Press, 1984), p. 33.
25 Hodding Carter III, "We're Losing the Drug War Because Prohibition Never Works," in Boaz, *Crisis in Drug Prohibition,* p. 102.
26 Mark Moore, "Actually, Prohibition Was a Success," *New York Times,* 16 October 1989, p. A21:1.
27 "The Unspeakable Is Debated: Should Drugs Be Legalized?," *New York Times,* 15 May 1988, p. A1:1.
28 William Bennett, "Drug Policy and the Intellectuals" (Speech delivered at the Kennedy School of Government, Harvard University, 11 December 1989).
29 Bennett, *National Drug Control Strategy,* (1989), p. 3.
30 See special issues of *Contemporary Drug Problems* 16 (1989): 527–700 and 17 (1990): 1–156. See also Bruce Johnson, Elsayed Elmoghazy, and Eloise Dunlap, *Crack Abusers and Noncrack Abusers: A Comparison of Drug Use, Drug Sales, and Nondrug Criminality* (New York: Narcotic and Drug Research, 1990).
31 Jeffrey Fagan, "Myths and Realities about Crack," *Contemporary Drug Problems* 16 (1989): 527, 528.
32 Ostrowski, "Thinking about Drug Legalization," p. 46.
33 Bernard Segal, "Drug-Taking Behavior among School-Aged

Youth: The Alaska Experience and Comparisons with Lower-48 States," *Drugs & Society* 4 (1989): 1.

34 Kleiman, *Marijuana*, p. 176.

35 See Erickson et al., *Steel Drug*.

36 "None of an Employer's Business," *New York Times*, 7 July 1991, sec. 4, p. 10:1

37 Ostrowski, "Moral and Practical Case for Drug Legalization," 619.

38 For an argument that increased consumption should be construed as an economic benefit, see Jeffrey A. Miron, "Drug Legalization and the Consumption of Drugs: An Economist's Perspective," in *Searching for Alternatives*, p. 68.

39 "Death Toll from Smoking Is Worsening," *New York Times*, 1 February 1991, p. A14:4.

40 Robert Goodin, *No Smoking* (Chicago: University of Chicago Press, 1989), p. 41.

41 John Kaplan, *The Hardest Drug: Heroin and Public Policy* (Chicago: University of Chicago Press, 1983), p. 103.

42 Ibid.

43 Ibid.

44 Mark Moore, "Drugs: Getting a Fix on the Problem and the Solution," *Yale Law & Policy Review* 8 (1990): 8, 15.

45 Ibid., 15.

46 George Fletcher, *Rethinking Criminal Law* (Boston: Little, Brown & Co., 1978), p. 404 (emphasis in original).

47 See Joel Feinberg, *Harm to Others* (New York: Oxford University Press, 1984).

48 Ibid., p. 31.

49 Ibid., pp. 34, 36.

50 Ibid., p. 34.

51 Bennett, *National Drug Control Strategy*, (1989), p. 7. See also the list of evils presented in Mitchell S. Rosenthal, "The Logic of Legalization: A Matter of Perspective," in Krauss and Lazear, *Searching For Alternatives*, p. 226, 228.

52 See Amartya Sen and Bernard Williams, eds., *Utilitarianism and Beyond* (New York: Cambridge University Press, 1982).

53 See Ronald Dworkin, *Taking Rights Seriously* (Cambridge, MA: Harvard University Press, 1977), pp. 184, 194. See also the "monstrous" theory of "social rights" attacked by John Stuart Mill, *On Liberty* (London: E.P. Dutton & Company, 1951), p. 210.

54 Some libertarians have argued that restitution to victims can and should replace criminal punishment altogether. See Randy Barnett, "Restitution: A New Paradigm of Criminal Justice," in *Assessing the Criminal*, ed. Randy Barnett and John Hagel III (Cambridge, MA: Ballinger Publishing Co., 1977), p. 349.

55 Joel Feinberg, "Harm to Others – A Rejoinder," *Criminal Justice Ethics* 5 (1986): 16, 17.

56 Ibid., p. 23.

57 Chester Mitchell, *The Drug Solution* (Ottawa: Carleton University Press, 1990), p. 224. Mitchell argues that still other alternatives are preferable to either criminal or civil liability.

58 Ibid., p. 222.

59 Ibid., pp. 191–2.

60 Ibid., p. 224.

61 Lester Grinspoon and James Bakalar, "Arguments for a Harmfulness Tax," *Journal of Drug Issues* 20 (1990): 599–604.

62 Some commentators respond that the tax on substances such as cocaine would be so exorbitant that the black market would reappear. See Joel W. Hay, "The Harm They Do To Others: A Primer on the External Costs of Drug Abuse," in Krauss and Lazear, *Searching For Alternatives*, p. 200, 218.

63 Lawrence Becker, "Criminal Attempt and the Theory of the Law of Crimes," *Philosophy and Public Affairs* 3 (1974): 262, 275.

64 Ibid., 273.

65 Robert Nozick, *Anarchy, State, and Utopia* (New York: Basic Books, 1974), p. 67.

66 John Kleinig, "Criminally Harming Others," *Criminal Justice Ethics* 5 (1986): 3, 8.

67 James Inciardi and Duane McBride, "Legalization: A High-Risk Alternative to the War on Drugs," *American Behavioral Scientist* 32 (1989): 259, 265.

68 Ibid., 268.

69 Barbara Baum Levenbook, "Criminal Harm," *Criminal Justice Ethics* 1 (1982): 48, 52.

70 See Guido Calabresi and Douglas Melamed, "Property Rules, Liability Rules, and Inalienability: One View of the Cathedral," *Harvard Law Review* 85 (1972): 1089.

71 For an account of what persons should not be permitted to do, even if they compensate their victims, see Robert Goodin,

"Theories of Compensation, in *Liability and Responsibility*, eds. R. G. Frey and Christopher Morris (New York: Cambridge University Press, 1991), p. 257.

72 Kaplan, *Heroin*, p. 112.

73 Bennett, *National Drug Control Strategy*, (1989), p. 7.

74 See Stephen Chapman, "Nancy Reagan and the Real Villains in the Drug War," in Boaz, *Crisis in Drug Prohibition*, p. 105.

75 See Joshua Dressler, *Understanding Criminal Law* (New York: Matthew Bender, 1987), pp. 422–3.

76 See Wayne LaFave and Austin Scott, 2 *Substantive Criminal Law* (St. Paul: West Publishing Co., 1986), pp. 20–1.

77 See Fletcher, *Rethinking Criminal Law*, p. 133.

78 Ibid., p. 402.

79 See Jerri Husch, "Of Work and Drugs: Notes on Prevention," *Drug Policy 1989–1990: A Reformer's Catalogue*, ed. Arnold Trebach and Kevin Zeese (Washington: Drug Policy Foundation, 1989), p. 228.

80 Kaplan, *Heroin*, p. 132.

81 See Paul Robinson, "Legality and Discretion in the Distribution of Criminal Sanctions," *Harvard Journal on Legislation* 25 (1988): 393, 431–4.

82 See *People v. Feldman*, 342 N.Y.S. 2d 956 (1973).

83 See John Kleinig, "Crime and the Concept of Harm," *American Philosophical Quarterly* 15 (1978) 27.

84 Lawn, "Issue of Legalizing Illicit Drugs," 713–4. See also the estimates in Joel W. Hay, "The Harm They Do To Others," in Krauss and Lazear, *Searching For Alternatives*, p. 200.

85 See Lonn Lanza-Kaduce and Donna Bishop, "Legal Fictions and Criminology: The Jurisprudence of Drunk Driving," *Journal of Criminal Law & Criminology* 77 (1986): 358, 363.

86 Ethan A. Nadelmann, "The Case for Legalization," *The Public Interest* 92 (1988): 3.

87 Mitchell, *Drug Solution*, p. 203.

88 Ibid.

89 *Bottom Line* 7 (1986): 17.

90 See Mitchell, *Drug Solution*, p. 284.

91 See Andrew von Hirsch and Nils Jareborg, "Gauging Criminal Harm: A Living-Standard Analysis," *Oxford Journal of Legal Studies* 11 (1991): 1.

92 My emphasis on agency creates the possibility that the remoteness principle can be subsumed under the empirical

principle, since some theorists have argued that conduct not sufficiently proximate to a consummate harm does not cause that harm. See H. L. A. Hart and Tony Honore, *Causation in the Law* (Oxford: Clarendon Press, 1959).

93 See American Law Institute, *Model Penal Code* (Philadelphia: American Law Institute, 1985), sec. 5.01(4).

94 Ibid., sec. 5.01(1) (c).

95 See Feinberg, *Harm to Others*, pp. 199–202.

96 See Norman Zinberg, *Drug, Set, and Setting: The Basis for Controlled Intoxicant Use* (New Haven: Yale University Press, 1984); and Erickson et al., *Steel Drug.*

97 Bennett, *National Drug Control Strategy*, (1989), p. 11.

98 Ibid. (emphasis in original).

99 See Feinberg, *Harm to Others*, p. 216.

100 See von Hirsch and Jareborg, "Gauging Criminal Harm."

101 Craig Zwerling, James Ryan, and Endel Orav, "The Efficacy of Preemployment Drug Screening for Marijuana and Cocaine in Predicting Employment Outcome," *Journal of the American Medical Association* 264 (1990): 2639, 2642.

102 Drug Use Forecasting Annual Report, *Drugs and Crime* (Washington: Department of Justice, 1990), p. 4.

103 Ibid., p. 7.

104 Jan Chaiken and Marcia Chaiken, "Drugs and Predatory Crime," in Tonry and Wilson, *Drugs and Crime*, pp. 203, 214.

105 Bennett, *National Drug Control Strategy*, (1989), p. 7.

106 Wilson, "Drugs and Crime," p. 522.

107 Michael Tonry, "Research on Drugs and Crime," in Tonry and Wilson, *Drugs and Crime*, pp. 1, 3.

108 See Steven Jonas, "Solving the Drug Problem: A Public Health Approach to the Reduction of the Use and Abuse of Both Legal and Illegal Recreational Drugs," *Hofstra Law Review* 18 (1990): 751, 767.

109 Chaiken and Chaiken, "Drugs and Predatory Crime," p. 219.

110 National Institute on Drug Abuse, *National Household Survey on Drug Abuse* (1990).

111 Paul Goldstein, "The Drugs/Violence Nexus: A Tripartite Conceptual Framework," *Journal of Drug Issues* 15 (1985): 493.

112 Ko-Lin Chin and Jeffrey Fagan, "Violence as Regulation and Social Control in the Distribution of Crack," in Research Monograph 103, *Drugs and Violence: Causes, Correlates, and Consequences*, edited by Mario De LaRosa, Elizabeth W. Lan-

bert, and Bernard Gropper, (Washington: National Institute of Drug Administration, 1990), p. 8.

113 Ostrowski, "Moral and Practical Case for Drug Legalization," 685.

114 Paul Goldstein et al., "Most Drug-Related Murders Result from Crack Sales, Not Use," in Trebach and Zeese, *Drug Prohibition and the Conscience of Nations*, p. 75.

115 Ostrowski, "Moral and Practical Case for Drug Legalization," 651.

116 Bennett, *National Drug Control Strategy*, (1989), p. 7.

117 Chaiken and Chaiken, "Drugs and Predatory Crime," p. 205.

118 Ibid., p. 216.

119 Cheryl Carpenter et al., *Kids, Drugs, and Crime* (Lexington, MA: D.C. Heath & Co., 1988), p. 85.

120 Chaiken and Chaiken, "Drugs and Predatory Crime," p. 217.

121 Ibid., p. 234.

122 Ibid., p. 212 (emphasis in original).

123 See Bruce Johnson et al., "Concentrations of Delinquent Offending: Serious Drug Involvement and High Delinquency Rates," *Journal of Drug Issues* 21 (1991): 205.

124 See Jonathan Caulkins, "Punishment Policies' Effect on Illicit Drug Users' Purchasing Habits" (Cambridge, MA: Operations Research Center, Massachusetts Institute of Technology, 1989, Microform).

125 See Zinberg, *Drug, Set, and Setting;* and Erickson et al., *Steel Drug*. See also Waldorf et al., *Cocaine Changes*.

126 William Bennett, "The Plea to Legalize Drugs Is a Siren Call to Surrender," in *Drugs in Society*, ed. Michael Lyman and Gary Potter (Cincinnati: Anderson Publishing Co., 1991), p. 338.

127 Helene White, "The Drug-Use Delinquency Connection in Adolescence," in *Drugs, Crime, and the Criminal Justice System*, ed. Ralph Weisheit (Cincinnati: Anderson Publishing Co., 1990), pp. 215, 221.

128 Carpenter et al., *Kids, Drugs, and Crime*, p. 35.

129 Ibid., p. 36.

130 Ibid.

131 Jeffrey Fagan, "Intoxication and Aggression," in Tonry and Wilson, *Drugs and Crime*, p. 241.

132 Ibid., p. 298.

133 Ibid., p. 243.

134 Ibid., p. 299.
135 Ibid., p. 243.
136 James Swartz, "Cocaine and Opiates: Prevalence Estimates of Their Use by Arrestees and a Theoretical and Empirical Investigation of Their Relationship to the Commission of Violent Crimes" (Ph.D. diss., Northwestern University, 1990).
137 Fagan, "Intoxication and Aggression," p. 243.
138 Erickson et al., *Steel Drug*, p. 94.
139 See Richard Clayton and Barry Tuchfeld, "The Drug–Crime Debate: Obstacles to Understanding the Relationship," *Journal of Drug Issues* 12 (1982): 153.
140 See James Collins, Robert Hubbard, and J. Valley Rachal, "Expensive Drug Use and Illegal Income: A Test of Explanatory Hypotheses," *Criminology* 23 (1985): 743.
141 See Zwerling, Ryan, and Orav, "Preemployment Drug Screening."
142 See Edward Kaufman, "The Relationship of Alcoholism and Alcohol Abuse to the Abuse of Other Drugs," *American Journal of Drug and Alcohol Abuse* 9 (1982): 1.
143 Andrew Weil, *The Natural Mind* (Boston: Houghton Mifflin Co., 1972), p. 8.
144 Chaiken and Chaiken, "Drugs and Predatory Crime," p. 216.
145 Fagan, "Intoxication and Aggression," p. 244.
146 Denise Kandel, Ronald Kessler, and Rebecca Margulies, "Antecedents of Adolescent Initiation into Stages of Drug Use: A Developmental Analysis," in *Longitudinal Research on Drug Use: Empirical Findings and Methodological Issues*, ed. Denise Kandel (New York: John Wiley, 1978), p. 73.
147 White, "Drug-Use Delinquency Connection in Adolescence," p. 236.
148 Ibid., p. 224.
149 Ibid., p. 228.
150 Franklin Zimring and Gordon Hawkins, *The Search for Rational Drug Control* (New York: Cambridge University Press, 1992), p. 140.
151 David Musto, *The American Disease: Origins of Narcotic Control*, exp. ed. (New York: Oxford University Press, 1987), p. 246.
152 Richard Condon, *The Manchurian Candidate* (New York: McGraw-Hill, 1958).

4 RESTRICTIONS ON DRUG USE

1   See Mark Kleiman and Aaron Saiger, "Drug Legalization: The Importance of Asking the Right Question," *Hofstra Law Review* 18 (1990): 527, 540.
2   See Franklin Zimring and Gordon Hawkins, *The Search for Rational Drug Control* (New York: Cambridge University Press, 1992), p. 107.
3   One reformer seems prepared to legalize all drugs but crack. See David Elkins, "Drug Legalization: Cost Effective and Morally Permissible," *Boston College Law Review* 32 (1991): 575.
4   Barbara Baum Levenbook, "Criminal Harm," *Criminal Justice Ethics* 1 (1982): 48.
5   Dan Beauchamp, "The Ethical Debate," in *Alcohol: The Prevention Debate*, ed. Marcus Grant and Bruce Ritson (New York: St. Martin's Press, 1983), pp. 166, 167.
6   See Will Kymlicka, *Contemporary Political Philosophy* (Oxford: Clarendon Press, 1990), pp. 199–237.
7   See Michael Sandel, *Liberalism and the Limits of Justice* (Cambridge: Cambridge University Press, 1982).
8   Joel Feinberg, *Harm to Self* (New York: Oxford University Press, 1986), p. 133.
9   See Daniel Benjamin and Roger Miller, *Undoing Drugs* (New York: Basic Books, 1991).
10 See Arnold Trebach, "A Bundle of Peaceful Compromises," *Journal of Drug Issues* 20 (1990): 515, 517.
11 David Musto, *The American Disease: Origins of Narcotic Control*, exp. ed. (New Haven: Yale University Press, 1987), pp. 91–120.
12 Govert F. van de Wijngaart, "The Dutch Approach: Normalization of Drug Problems," *Journal of Drug Issues* 20 (1990): 667, 671.
13 See Musto, *American Disease*, p. 244.
14 David Richards, *Sex, Drugs, Death, and the Law* (Totowa, NJ: Rowman & Littlefield, 1982), pp. 179–80.
15 Ibid., p. 179.
16 See Feinberg, *Harm to Self*.
17 See the polls in the *Washington Post*, 18–24 September 1989, Weekly Edition, p. 37; and *New York Times*, 15 September 1988, p. A26:5.

18 See Ronald Dworkin, *Taking Rights Seriously* (Cambridge, MA: Harvard University Press, 1977), pp. 184, 194.
19 See Ronald Dworkin, "Liberal Community," *California Law Review* 77 (1989): 479, 481.
20 According to one commentator who objects to pornography, "What is at stake is civilization and humanity, nothing less." See Irving Kristol, "Pornography, Obscenity, and the Case for Censorship," in *Philosophy of Law*, 5th ed., ed. Joel Feinberg and Hyman Gross (Belmont, CA: Wadsworth Publishing Co., 1991), pp. 332, 335.
21 See Steven Jonas, "Solving the Drug Problem: A Public Health Approach to the Reduction of the Use and Abuse of Both Legal and Illegal Recreational Drugs," *Hofstra Law Review* 18 (1990): 751, 760.
22 Jeremy Waldron, "Particular Values and Critical Morality," *California Law Review* 77 (1989): 561, 583.
23 National Institute on Drug Abuse, *National Household Survey on Drug Abuse* (1991).
24 Musto, *American Disease*, pp. 1–8.
25 See John Haaga and Peter Reuter, "The Limits of the Czar's Ukase: Drug Policy at the Local Level," *Yale Law & Policy Review* 8 (1990): 36.
26 National Institute on Drug Abuse, *National Household Survey on Drug Abuse* (1991).
27 National Institute on Drug Abuse, *National Household Survey on Drug Abuse* (1990).
28 U.S. Department of Health and Human Services, "HHS News," 13 February 1990, Table 19.
29 Ibid., Table 20.
30 See Arnold Trebach and Kevin Zeese, eds., *Drug Prohibition and the Conscience of Nations* (Washington: Drug Policy Foundation, 1990), p. 226.
31 Waldron, "Particular Values and Critical Morality," 581.
32 Ibid., 585.
33 Joel Feinberg, *Harmless Wrongdoing* (New York: Oxford University Press, 1988), p. 108.
34 See Richard Stephens, "The Hard Drug Scene," in *Drugs and the Youth Culture*, ed. Frank Scarpitti and Susan Datesman (Beverly Hills: Sage Publications, 1980), pp. 59, 67.
35 National Institute on Drug Abuse, *National Household Survey on Drug Abuse* (1990).

36 See James Bakalar and Lester Grinspoon, *Drug Control in a Free Society* (New York: Cambridge University Press, 1984), p. 144.

37 See Norman Zinberg, *Drug, Set, and Setting: The Basis for Controlled Intoxicant Use* (New Haven: Yale University Press, 1984); and Patricia Erickson et al., *The Steel Drug: Cocaine in Perspective* (Lexington, MA: D.C. Heath & Co., 1987).

38 Aldous Huxley, *Brave New World* (Garden City, NY: Doubleday, 1932).

39 Ironically, Iran has perhaps the highest rate of heroin addiction in the world, with approximately one million addicts in a nation of forty million people. See Michael Lyman and Gary Potter, eds., *Drugs in Society* (Cincinnati: Anderson Publishing Co., 1991), p. 110.

40 James Inciardi and Duane McBride, "Legalization: A High-Risk Alternative to the War on Drugs," *American Behavioral Scientist* 32 (1989): 259, 266.

41 Daniel Koshland, "Thinking Tough," *Science* 241 (1988): 1273.

42 See the proposals in Joseph Galiber, "A Bill to Repeal Criminal Drug Laws: Replacing Prohibition with Regulation," *Hofstra Law Review* 18 (1990): 831–80; Nancy Lord, "A Practical Model for Drug Regulation," in *Drug Policy 1989–1990: A Reformer's Catalogue*, ed. Arnold Trebach and Kevin Zeese (Washington: Drug Policy Foundation, 1989), p. 371; and Richard Karel, "A Model Legalization Proposal," in *The Drug Legalization Debate*, ed. James Inciardi (London: Sage Publications, 1991), p. 80.

43 See Milton Friedman, "The War We Are Losing," in *Searching For Alternatives*, eds. Melvyn B. Krauss and Edward P. Lazear (Stanford: Hoover Institution Press, 1991), p. 53.

44 James Ostrowski, "Answering the Critics of Drug Legalization," *Notre Dame Journal of Law, Ethics, & Public Policy* 5 (1991): 823, 845 (emphasis in original).

45 See Mark Moore, "Regulating Heroin: Kaplan and Trebach on the Dilemmas of Public Policy," *American Bar Foundation Research Journal* (1984), 723, 724–8.

46 Chester Mitchell, *The Drug Solution* (Ottawa: Carleton University Press, 1990), p. 173.

47 Richard Evans, "The Many Forms of Legalization: Beyond 'Whether' to 'How,' " in *The Great Issues of Drug Policy*, ed.

Arnold Trebach and Kevin Zeese (Washington: Drug Policy Foundation, 1990), pp. 6, 8.

48 Mitchell, *Drug Solution*, p. 245.

49 J. J. Boddewyn, "Tobacco Advertising in a Free Society," in *Smoking and Society*, ed. Robert Tollison (Lexington, MA: D.C. Heath & Co., 1986), pp. 309, 320.

50 Robert E. Goodin, *No Smoking* (Chicago: University of Chicago Press, 1989), p. 104.

51 Evans, "Many Forms of Legalization," p. 10.

52 See Joseph Galiber, "Treat It Like Alcohol," in *The Crisis in Drug Prohibition*, ed. David Boaz (Washington: Cato Institute, 1990), p. 116.

53 See Distilled Spirits Council of the United States, *Summary of State Laws and Regulations Relating to Distilled Spirits*, 26th ed. (Washington, 1989).

54 See Richards, *Sex, Drugs, Death, and the Law*, p. 189.

55 Ibid., p. 190.

56 Jerome Rabow and Ronald Watts, "Alcohol Availability, Alcohol Beverage Sales, and Alcohol-Related Problems," *Journal of Studies on Alcohol* 43 (1982): 767.

57 See Brenda Walsh, "The Economics of Alcohol Taxation," in *Economics and Alcohol*, ed. Marcus Grant, Martin Plant, and Alan Williams (New York: Gardner Press, 1983), pp. 173, 180.

58 P. Cook, "Alcohol Taxes as a Public Health Measure," in Grant, Plant, and Williams, *Economics and Alcohol*, pp. 190–5.

59 Mitchell, *Drug Solution*, pp. 297–8.

60 John Stuart Mill, *On Liberty* (New York: E.P. Dutton & Co., 1951), p. 210.

61 Michael Aldrich, "Legalize the Lesser to Minimize the Greater: Modern Applications of Ancient Wisdom," *Journal of Drug Issues* 20 (1990): 543, 548.

62 See John Kaplan, *Marijuana: The New Prohibition* (New York: World Publishing Co., 1970).

63 Licensing models for marijuana use are described in Norman Zinberg and John Robertson, *Drugs and the Public* (New York: Simon & Schuster, 1972), pp. 254–6, 259–62; and Frank Logan, ed., *Cannabis: Options for Control* (Sunbury, U.K.: Quartermaine House, 1979), pp. 39–46.

64 Mitchell, *Drug Solution*, p. 268.

65 See Joel Feinberg, *Harm to Others* (New York: Oxford University Press, 1984), p. 194.

66 Mitchell, *Drug Solution*, p. 257.
67 See James Jacobs, *Drunk Driving* (Chicago: University of Chicago Press, 1989), p. 62.
68 Ibid., p. 59.
69 Goodin, *No Smoking*, p. 61.
70 Ibid., p. 62.
71 "Secondhand Smoke Assailed in Report," *New York Times*, 30 May 1991, p. A22:1.
72 Dorothy Roberts, "Punishing Drug Addicts Who Have Babies: Women of Color, Equality, and the Right of Privacy," *Harvard Law Review* 104 (1991): 1419, 1421, n. 5.
73 Ibid., 1421.
74 See Dale Gieringer, "How Many Crack Babies?," in Trebach and Zeese, *Drug Prohibition and the Conscience of Nations*, p. 71.
75 Jan Bays, "Substance Abuse and Child Abuse: The Impact of Addiction on the Child," *Pediatric Clinics of North America* 37 (1990): 881.
76 Kathleen Nolan, "Protecting Fetuses from Prenatal Hazards: Whose Crimes? What Punishment?" *Criminal Justice Ethics* 9 (1990): 13, 14.
77 Roberts, "Punishing Drug Addicts Who Have Babies," 1429.
78 *Johnson v. State*, No. 89–1765 (Fla. Dist. Ct. App., 5th Dist., 1989).
79 *People v. Hardy* (Mich. Ct. App., No. 128458, 1991).
80 Dawn Korver, "The Constitutionality of Punishing Pregnant Substance Abusers under Drug Trafficking Laws: The Criminalization of a Bodily Function," *Boston College Law Review* 32 (1991): 629, 655.
81 See *People v. Bolar*, 440 N.E.2d 639 (1982).
82 Nolan, "Protecting Fetuses from Prenatal Hazards," 20.
83 Ibid., 14.
84 See I. Cushner, "Maternal Behavior and Perinatal Risks: Alcohol, Smoking, and Drugs," *Annual Review of Public Health* 2 (1981): 201.
85 R. Bower, "Drinking While Pregnant Risks Child's IQ," *Science News* 135 (1989): 68.
86 See Roberts, "Punishing Drug Addicts Who Have Babies," 1434–5, n. 80.
87 John Myers, "A Limited Role for the Legal System in Responding to Maternal Substance Abuse during Pregnancy,"

Notre Dame Journal of Law, Ethics, & Public Policy 5 (1991): 747, 755.
88 Roberts, "Punishing Drug Addicts Who Have Babies," 1434.
89 Ibid., 1435.
90 Lynn Paltrow, "When Becoming Pregnant Is a Crime," *Criminal Justice Ethics* 9 (1990): 41, 43.
91 Nolan, "Protecting Fetuses from Prenatal Hazards," 19.
92 See Paltrow, "When Becoming Pregnant Is a Crime," 43.
93 Ibid., 45.
94 But see Paul Logli, "Drugs in the Womb: The Newest Battlefield in the War on Drugs," *Criminal Justice Ethics* 9 (1990), 23, 27.
95 Wendy Mariner, Leonard Glantz, and George Annas, "Pregnancy, Drugs, and the Perils of Prosecution," *Criminal Justice Ethics* 9 (1990): 30, 35.
96 Ibid., 30.
97 See Philip Johnson, "The ACLU Philosophy and the Right to Abuse the Unborn," *Criminal Justice Ethics* 9 (1990): 48.
98 See Note, "Maternal Rights and Fetal Wrongs: The Case Against the Criminalization of 'Fetal Abuse,' " *Harvard Law Review*, 101: 994, 1007.
99 Roberts, "Punishing Drug Addicts Who Have Babies," 1445 (emphasis in original).
100 *Eisenstadt v. Baird*, 405 U.S. 438, 453 (1972).
101 Roberts, "Punishing Drug Addicts Who Have Babies," 1462–3.
102 486 F.2d 1139 (1973).
103 Paltrow, "When Becoming Pregnant Is a Crime," 42.
104 Ibid.
105 Ibid.
106 See Dan Waldorf and Patrick Biernacki, "The Natural Recovery from Opiate Addiction: Some Preliminary Findings," *Journal of Drug Issues* 11 (1981): 61, 66; and E. Waterson, C. Evans, and I. Murray-Lyon, "Is Pregnancy a Time of Changing Drinking and Smoking Patterns for Fathers as Well as Mothers?," *British Journal of Addiction* (1990): 389.
107 Waldorf and Biernacki, "Natural Recovery from Opiate Addiction," 66.
108 Kurt Schmoke, "An Argument in Favor of Decriminalization," *Hofstra Law Review* 18 (1990): 501, 513.

109 Mitchell, *Drug Solution*, pp. 305–6.
110 Mariner, Glantz, and Annas, "Pregnancy, Drugs, and the Perils of Prosecution," 36.
111 See Deborah Frank et al., "Cocaine Use during Pregnancy: Prevalence and Correlates," *Pediatrics* 82 (1988): 888–95.
112 Nolan, "Protecting Fetuses from Prenatal Hazards," 14.
113 Gieringer, "How Many Crack Babies?," p. 72.
114 Mariner, Glantz, and Annas, "Pregnancy, Drugs, and the Perils of Prosecution," 33.
115 Gieringer, "How Many Crack Babies?" p. 73.
116 Nolan, "Protecting Fetuses from Prenatal Hazards," 33.
117 Some theorists suggest that there has been a bias against the dissemination of scientific studies failing to observe reproductive hazards of cocaine use. See G. Koren; K. Graham; H. Shear; and T. Einarson, "Bias Against the Null Hypothesis: The Reproductive Hazards of Cocaine," *The Lancet* (December 16, 1989): 1440.
118 E. Davis and I. Fennoy, "Growth and Development in Children of Cocaine Abusing Mothers," *American Journal of Diseases of Children* 144 (1990): 426.
119 "Are Cocaine Babies Doomed to a Lifetime of Failure?" *Pediatric News* (November 1990), 2:3.
120 Myers, "Role for the Legal System in Responding to Maternal Substance Abuse," 754.
121 Zimring and Hawkins, *Search for Rational Drug Control*, p. 117.
122 See "Choice for Youths: Tobacco or a Fine," *New York Times*, 1 July 1991, p. A8:4.
123 See S. Kenneth Schonberg and Sidney Schnoll, "Drugs and Their Effects on Adolescent Users," in *Teen Drug Use*, ed. George Beschner and Alfred Friedman (Lexington, MA: D.C. Heath & Co., 1985), p. 43.
124 See Alexander Wagenaar, *Alcohol, Young Drivers, and Traffic Accidents* (Lexington, MA: Lexington Books, 1983).
125 See Morris Paulson, Robert Coombs, and Mark Richardson, "School Performance, Academic Aspirations, and Drug Use among Children and Adolescents," *Journal of Drug Education* 20 (1990): 289.
126 See Michael Newcomb and P. M. Bentler, "Drug Use, Educational Aspirations, and Work Force Involvement: The Transition from Adolescence to Young Adulthood," *American Journal of Community Psychology* 14 (1986): 303.

127 U.S. Department of Education, *Schools without Drugs* (Rockville, MD: National Clearinghouse for Alcohol and Drug Information, 1989), p. v.

128 J. Michael Polich et al., *Strategies for Controlling Adolescent Drug Use* (Santa Monica, CA: Rand Publication Series, 1984), p. 155.

129 Feinberg, *Harm to Self*, p. 104.

130 For a criticism of some of these bases for justifying paternalism over adolescents, see Laurence Houlgate, "Children, Paternalism, and Rights to Liberty," in *Having Children*, ed. Onora O'Neill and William Ruddick (New York: Oxford University Press, 1979), p. 266.

131 See Zimring and Hawkins, *Search for Rational Drug Control*, p. 121.

132 John Kaplan, *The Hardest Drug: Heroin and Public Policy* (Chicago: University of Chicago Press, 1983), p. 105.

133 "Just Say Alcohol," *Washington Post*, 17–23 June 1991, National Weekly Edition, p. A37:1.

134 Musto, *American Disease*, pp. 270–1.

135 National Institute on Drug Abuse, *National Household Survey on Drug Abuse* (1990).

136 Goodin, *No Smoking*, p. 128.

137 Vincent Blasi and Henry Monaghan, "The First Amendment and Cigarette Advertising," *Journal of the American Medical Association* 256 (1986): 502, 503.

138 Howard Leventhal, Kathleen Glynn, and Raymond Fleming, "Is the Smoking Decision an 'Informed Choice'?" *Journal of the American Medical Association* 257 (1987): 3373.

139 Waldorf and Biernacki, "Natural Recovery from Opiate Addiction," 64.

140 Jonathan Shedler and Jack Block, "Adolescent Drug Use and Psychological Health," *American Psychologist* 45 (1990): 612–30.

141 Ibid.

142 John Lawn, "The Issue of Legalizing Illicit Drugs," *Hofstra Law Review* 18 (1990): 703, 710.

143 Ed Leuw, "Drugs and Drug Policy in the Netherlands," in 14 *Crime and Justice*, ed. Michael Tonry (Chicago: University of Chicago Press, 1991), pp. 229, 231.

144 Mark Kleiman, *Marijuana: Costs of Abuse, Costs of Control* (New York: Greenwood Press, 1989), pp. xvii–xviii.

145 See Howard Shaffer and Stephanie Jones, *Quitting Cocaine* (Lexington, MA: Lexington Books, 1989), p. 44.

146 Ibid., p. xvi.

147 Mitchell, *Drug Solution*, p. 307.

148 Bruce Alexander, *Peaceful Measures: Canada's Way out of the "War on Drugs"* (Toronto: University of Toronto Press, 1990), p. xi.

149 Ibid.

150 Bakalar and Grinspoon, *Drug Control in a Free Society*, p. 99.

151 Stephen Mugford, "Drug Legalization and the 'Goldilocks' Problem: Thinking About Costs and Control of Drugs," in Krauss and Lazear, *Searching For Alternatives*, p. 33, 48.

152 See Zinberg, *Drug, Set, and Setting*, p. 7; and Walter Weiss, "User Careers: Implications for Preventing Drug Misuse," in *Alcohol and Drugs: Research and Policy*, ed. Martin Plant et al. (Edinburgh: Edinburgh University Press, 1990), p. 142.

153 See Andrew Weil, *The Natural Mind*, 2d ed. (Boston: Houghton Mifflin Co., 1986), pp. 197–8.

154 See Anthony Henman, "Coca and Cocaine: Their Role in 'Traditional' Cultures in South America," 20 *Journal of Drug Issues* (1990), p. 577.

Works cited

Akers, Ronald. "Addiction: The Troublesome Concept." *Journal of Drug Issues* 21 (1991): 777–93.

Aldrich, Michael. "Legalize the Lesser to Minimize the Greater: Modern Applications of Ancient Wisdom." *Journal of Drug Issues* 20 (1990): 543–53.

Alexander, Bruce. *Peaceful Measures: Canada's Way out of the "War on Drugs."* Toronto: University of Toronto Press, 1990.

Alexander, Bruce, and Wong, Linda. "Cocaine Related Deaths: Media Coverage in the War on Drugs." *Journal of Drug Issues* 21 (1991): 105–19.

American Law Institute. *Model Penal Code.* Philadelphia: American Law Institute, 1985.

Austin, James, and McVey, Aaron. *The 1989 NCCD Prison Population Forecast: The Impact of the War on Drugs.* Washington: National Council on Crime and Delinquency, 1989.

Bach, Julie, ed. *Drug Abuse: Opposing Viewpoints.* St. Paul: Greenhaven Press, 1988.

Bakalar, James, and Grinspoon, Lester. *Cocaine: A Drug and Its Social Evolution.* New York: Basic Books, 1976.

Drug Control in a Free Society. Cambridge: Cambridge University Press, 1984.

Bandow, Doug. "Once Again, a Drug War Panic." In *The Crisis in Drug Prohibition*, edited by David Boaz. Washington: Cato Institute, 1990.

Barnett, Randy. "Restitution: A New Paradigm of Criminal Justice." In *Assessing the Criminal*, edited by Randy Barnett and John Hagel III. Cambridge, MA: Ballinger Publishing Co., 1977.

Bays, Jan. "Substance Abuse and Child Abuse: The Impact of Ad-

diction on the Child." *Pediatric Clinics of North America* 37 (1990):
881.

Beauchamp, Dan. "The Ethical Debate." In *Alcohol: The Prevention Debate*, edited by Marcus Grant and Bruce Ritson. New York: St. Martin's Press, 1983.

Beck, Jerome, and Rosenbaum, Marsha. "The Scheduling of MDMA ('Ecstasy')." In *Handbook of Drug Control in the United States*, edited by James Inciardi. New York: Greenwood Press, 1990.

Becker, Lawrence. "Criminal Attempt and the Theory of the Law of Crimes." *Philosophy and Public Affairs* 3 (1974): 262–94.

Benjamin, Daniel, and Miller, Roger. *Undoing Drugs*. New York: Basic Books, 1991.

Bennett, William. "Drug Policy and the Intellectuals." Speech delivered at the Kennedy School of Government, Harvard University, 11 December 1989.

National Drug Control Strategy. Washington: Office of the National Drug Control Policy, 1989.

National Drug Control Strategy. Washington: Office of the National Drug Control Policy, 1990.

"The Plea to Legalize Drugs Is a Siren Call to Surrender." In *Drugs in Society*, edited by Michael Lyman and Gary Potter. Cincinnati: Anderson Publishing Co., 1991.

Bernheim, David. *Defense of Narcotics Cases*. New York: Matthew Bender, 1989.

Beschner, George, and Friedman, Alfred. *Teen Drug Use*. Lexington, MA: D.C. Heath & Co., 1986.

Biernacki, Patrick. *Pathways from Heroin Addiction: Recovery without Treatment*. Philadelphia: Temple University Press, 1986.

Blasi, Vincent, and Monaghan, Henry. "The First Amendment and Cigarette Advertising." *Journal of the American Medical Association* 256 (1986): 502–9.

Blume, S. "Gambling: Disease or 'Excuse'? High Rollers Suffer from an Illness." *U.S. Journal of Drug and Alcohol Dependence* (August 1989).

Boaz, David, ed. *The Crisis in Drug Prohibition*. Washington: Cato Institute, 1990.

Boddewyn, J. J. "Tobacco Advertising in a Free Society." In *Smoking and Society*, edited by Robert Tollison. Lexington, MA: D.C. Heath & Co., 1986.

Works cited

Bogomolny, Robert; Sonnenreich, Michael; and Roccograndi, Anthony. *A Handbook of the 1970 Federal Drug Act*. Springfield, IL: Charles C. Thomas, 1975.

Bonnie, Richard. *Marijuana Use and Criminal Sanctions*. Charlottesville: Michie Co., 1980.

Botvin, Gilbert. "Substance Abuse Prevention: Theory, Practice, and Effectiveness." In *Drugs and Crime*, edited by Michael Tonry and James Q. Wilson. Chicago: University of Chicago Press, 1990.

Bower, R. "Drinking While Pregnant Risks Child's IQ." *Science News* 135 (4 February 1989): 68.

Brecher, Edward M., and the Editors of *Consumer Reports*. *Licit and Illicit Drugs*. Boston: Little, Brown & Co., 1972.

Brown, Ray. "The Black Community and the 'War on Drugs.' " In *The Great Issues of Drug Policy*, edited by Arnold Trebach and Kevin Zeese. Washington: Drug Policy Foundation, 1990.

Brownstein, Henry. "Demilitarization of the War on Drugs: Toward an Alternative Drug Strategy." In *The Great Issues of Drug Policy*, edited by Arnold Trebach and Kevin Zeese. Washington: Drug Policy Foundation, 1990.

Bugliosi, Vincent. *Drugs in America*. New York: Knightsbridge Publishing Co., 1991.

Bulych, Terry, and Beyerstein, Barry L. "Authoritarianism and Misinformation as Sources of Support for the War on Drugs." In *New Frontiers in Drug Policy*, edited by Arnold Trebach and Kevin Zeese. Washington: Drug Policy Foundation, 1991.

Byck, Robert. "Cocaine, Marijuana, and the Meaning of Addiction." In *Dealing with Drugs*, edited by Ronald Hamowy. Lexington, MA: D.C. Heath & Co., 1987.

Calabresi, Guido, and Melamed, Douglas. "Property Rules, Liability Rules, and Inalienability: One View of the Cathedral." *Harvard Law Review* 85 (1972): 1089–1128.

Carpenter, Cheryl; Glassner, Barry; Johnson, Bruce; and Loughlin, Julia. *Kids, Drugs, and Crime*. Lexington, MA: D.C. Heath & Co., 1988.

Carter, David. "An Overview of Drug-Related Misconduct of Police Officers: Drug Abuse and Narcotic Corruption." In *Drugs, Crime, and the Criminal Justice System*, edited by Ralph Weisheit. Cincinnati: Anderson Publishing Co., 1990.

Carter, Hodding, III. "We're Losing the Drug War Because Prohibition Never Works." In *The Crisis in Drug Prohibition*, edited by David Boaz. Washington: Cato Institute, 1990.

Caulkins, Jonathan. "Punishment Policies' Effect on Illicit Drug Users' Purchasing Habits." Cambridge, MA: Operations Research Center, Massachusetts Institute of Technology, 1989. Microform.

Chaiken, Jan, and Chaiken, Marcia. "Drugs and Predatory Crime." In *Drugs and Crime*, edited by Michael Tonry and James Q. Wilson. Chicago: University of Chicago Press, 1990.

Chapman, Stephen. "Nancy Reagan and the Real Villains in the Drug War." In *The Crisis in Drug Prohibition*, edited by David Boaz. Washington: Cato Institute, 1990.

Cheung, Yuet; Erickson, Patricia; and Landau, Tammy. "Experiences of Crack Use: Findings from a Community-Based Sample in Toronto." *Journal of Drug Issues* 21 (1991): 121–40.

Chin, Ko-lin, and Fagan, Jeffrey. "Initiation into Crack and Cocaine: A Tale of Two Epidemics." *Contemporary Drug Problems* (1989): 579–617.

"Violence as Regulation and Social Control in the Distribution of Crack." In Research Monograph 103, *Drugs and Violence: Causes, Correlates, and Consequences*, edited by Mario De La Rosa, Elizabeth W. Lambert, and Bernard Gropper. Washington: National Institute of Drug Administration, 1990.

Clayton, Richard, and Tuchfeld, Barry. "The Drug–Crime Debate: Obstacles to Understanding the Relationship." *Journal of Drug Issues* 12 (1982): 153–66.

Cloud, Morgan, III. "Cocaine, Demand, and Addiction: A Study of the Possible Convergence of Rational Theory and National Policy." *Vanderbilt Law Review* 42 (1989): 725–818.

Collins, James; Hubbard, Robert; and Rachal, J. Valley. "Expensive Drug Use and Illegal Income: A Test of Explanatory Hypotheses." *Criminology* 23 (1985): 743–64.

Condon, Richard. *The Manchurian Candidate*. New York: McGraw-Hill, 1958.

Cook, P. "Alcohol Taxes as a Public Health Measure." In *Economics and Alcohol*, edited by Marcus Grant, Martin Plant, and Alan Williams. New York: Gardener Press, 1983.

Cooper, Mark. "Up in Smoke." *American Film* (March 1987), 53–7.

Cowan, Richard. "How the Narcs Created Crack." *National Review* (5 December 1986), 26.

Works cited

Cushner, I. "Maternal Behavior and Perinatal Risks: Alcohol, Smoking, and Drugs." *Annual Review of Public Health* 2 (1981): 201–18.

Davis, E., and Fennoy, I. "Growth and Development in Children of Cocaine Abusing Mothers." *American Journal of Diseases of Children* 144 (1990): 426.

Deninger, Mark. "The Economics of Heroin: Key to Optimizing the Legal Response." *Georgia Law Review* 10 (1976): 565–618.

Distilled Spirits Council of the United States. *Summary of State Laws and Regulations Relating to Distilled Spirits.* 26th ed. Washington D.C., 1989.

Donovan, Dennis M., and Marlatt, G. Alan, eds. *Assessment of Addictive Behaviors.* New York: Guilford Press, 1988.

Dressler, Joshua. *Understanding Criminal Law* New York: Matthew Bender, 1987.

Duster, Troy. *The Legislation of Morality: Law, Drugs, and Moral Judgment.* New York: Free Press, 1970.

Dworkin, Gerald. "Autonomy and Behavior Control." *Hastings Center Report* 6 (1976): 23–28.

"The Nature of Autonomy." In *The Theory and Practice of Autonomy,* by Gerald Dworkin. Cambridge: Cambridge University Press, 1988.

"The Value of Autonomy." In *The Theory and Practice of Autonomy,* by Gerald Dworkin. Cambridge: Cambridge University Press, 1988.

Dworkin, Ronald. "Liberal Community." *California Law Review* 77 (1989): 479–504.

Taking Rights Seriously. Cambridge, MA: Harvard University Press, 1977.

Elkins, David. "Drug Legalization: Cost Effective and Morally Permissible." *Boston College Law Review* 32 (1991): 575–627.

Erickson, Patricia; Adlaf, Edward; Murray, Glenn; and Smart, Reginald. *The Steel Drug: Cocaine in Perspective.* Lexington, MA: D.C. Heath & Co., 1987.

Erickson, Patricia, and Murray, Glenn. "The Undeterred Cocaine User: Intention to Quit and Its Relationship to Perceived Legal and Health Threats." *Contemporary Drug Problems* 16 (1989): 141–56.

Evans, David. "How Many Liberties Are We Losing?" *Human Rights* 17 (1990): 14–17.

Evans, Richard. "The Many Forms of Legalization: Beyond 'Whether' to 'How.' " In *The Great Issues of Drug Policy,* edited by Arnold Trebach and Kevin Zeese. Washington: Drug Policy Foundation, 1990.

Fagan, Jeffrey. "Intoxication and Aggression." In *Drugs and Crime*, edited by Michael Tonry and James Q. Wilson. Chicago: University of Chicago Press, 1990.

"Myths and Realities about Crack." *Contemporary Drug Problems* 16 (1989): 527–33.

Feinberg, Joel. *Harmless Wrongdoing.* New York: Oxford University Press, 1988.

Harm to Others. New York: Oxford University Press, 1984.

"Harm to Others – A Rejoinder." *Criminal Justice Ethics* (1986), 5:16–29.

Harm to Self. New York: Oxford University Press, 1986.

Offense to Others. New York: Oxford University Press, 1985.

Fingarette, Herbert. *Heavy Drinking.* Berkeley: University of California Press, 1988.

Fingarette, Herbert, and Hasse, Anne. *Mental Disabilities and Criminal Responsibility.* Berkeley: University of California Press, 1979.

Fishbein, Diana. "Medicalizing the Drug War." *Behavioral Sciences and the Law* 9 (1991): 323–44.

Fitzgerald, Gerry. "Dispatches from the Drug War." *Common Cause* (January/February 1990): 13–19.

Fletcher, George. *Rethinking Criminal Law.* Boston: Little, Brown & Co., 1978.

Frank, Deborah, et al. "Cocaine Use During Pregnancy: Prevalence and Correlates." *Pediatrics* 82 (1988): 888–95.

Frankfurt, Harry. "Freedom of the Will." In *The Importance of What We Care About*, by Harry Frankfurt. New York: Cambridge University Press, 1988.

Friedman, Milton. "The War We Are Losing." In *Searching for Alternatives*, edited by Melvyn B. Krauss and Edward P. Lazear. Stanford: Hoover Institution Press, 1991.

Fritschler, A. Lee. *Smoking and Politics.* 2d ed. Englewood Cliffs, NJ: Prentice-Hall, 1975.

Galiber, Joseph. "A Bill to Repeal Criminal Drug Laws: Replacing Prohibition with Regulation." *Hofstra Law Review* 18 (1990): 831–80.

"Treat It Like Alcohol." In *The Crisis in Drug Prohibition*, edited by David Boaz. Washington: Cato Institute, 1990.

Gawin, Frank, and Ellinwood, Everett. "Cocaine and Other Stimulants: Action, Abuse, and Treatment." *New England Journal of Medicine* 318 (1988): 1173–82.

Gettman, Jon. "Decriminalizing Marijuana." *American Behavioral Scientist* 32 (1989): 243–8.

Gieringer, Dale. "How Many Crack Babies?" In *Drug Prohibition and the Conscience of Nations*, edited by Arnold Trebach and Kevin Zeese. Washington: Drug Policy Foundation, 1990.

Goldstein, Paul. "The Drugs/Violence Nexus: A Tripartite Conceptual Framework." *Journal of Drug Issues* 15 (1985): 493.

Goldstein, Paul, et al. "Most Drug-Related Murders Result from Crack Sales, Not Use." In *Drug Prohibition and the Conscience of Nations*, edited by Arnold Trebach and Kevin Zeese. Washington: Drug Policy Foundation, 1990.

Goodin, Robert E. *No Smoking.* Chicago: University of Chicago Press, 1989.

"Theories of Compensation." In *Liability and Responsibility*, edited by R. G. Frey and Christopher Morris. New York: Cambridge University Press, 1991.

Grant, Marcus, and Ritson, Bruce. *Alcohol: The Prevention Debate.* New York: St. Martin's Press, 1983.

Grinspoon, Lester, and Bakalar, James. "Arguments for a Harmfulness Tax." *Journal of Drug Issues* 20 (1990): 599–604.

Haaga, John, and Reuter, Peter. "The Limits of the Czar's Ukase: Drug Policy at the Local Level." *Yale Law & Policy Review* 8 (1990): 36–74.

Hamowy, Ronald, ed. *Dealing with Drugs.* Lexington, MA: D.C. Heath & Co., 1987.

Hart, H. L. A., and Honore, Tony. *Causation in the Law.* Oxford: Clarendon Press, 1959.

Hay, Joel W. "The Harm They Do To Others: A Primer on the External Costs of Drug Abuse." In *Searching for Alternatives*, edited by Melvyn B. Krauss and Edward P. Lazear. Stanford: Hoover Institution Press, 1991.

Hellman, Arthur. *Laws against Marijuana: The Price We Pay.* Urbana, IL: University of Illinois Press, 1975.

Henman, Anthony. "Coca and Cocaine: Their Role in 'Traditional' Cultures in South America." *Journal of Drug Issues* 20 (1990): 577–88.

Himmelstein, Jerome. *The Strange Career of Marijuana.* Westport, CT: Greenwood Press, 1983.

Works cited

Husak, Douglas. "Paternalism and Autonomy." *Philosophy and Public Affairs* 10 (1981): 27–46.

Philosophy of Criminal Law. Totowa, NJ: Rowman & Littlefield, 1987.

"Recreational Drugs and Paternalism." *Law and Philosophy* 8 (1989): 353–81.

"Rights, Harmless Immorality, and Inchoate Criminal Offenses." Forthcoming.

Husch, Jerri. "Of Work and Drugs: Notes on Prevention." In *Drug Policy 1989–1990: A Reformer's Catalogue,* edited by Arnold Trebach and Kevin Zeese. Washington: Drug Policy Foundation, 1989.

Huxley, Aldous. *Brave New World.* Garden City, NY: Doubleday, 1932.

Inciardi, James. "Debating the Legalization of Drugs." *American Behavioral Scientist* 32 (1989): 233–42.

The War on Drugs: Heroin, Cocaine, Crime, and Public Policy. Palo Alto, CA: Mayfield Publishing Co., 1986.

ed. *Handbook of Drug Control in the United States.* New York: Greenwood Press, 1990.

ed. *The Drug Legalization Debate.* London: Sage Publications, 1991.

Inciardi, James, and McBride, Duane. "Debating the Legalization of Drugs." In *Handbook of Drug Control in the United States,* edited by James Inciardi. New York: Greenwood Press, 1990.

"Legalization: A High-Risk Alternative to the War on Drugs." *American Behavioral Scientist* 32 (1989): 259–89.

Jacobs, James. *Drunk Driving.* Chicago: University of Chicago Press, 1989.

"Imagining Drug Legalization." *The Public Interest* 101 (1990): 28–42.

Jefferson, Thomas. *Notes on the State of Virginia.* Boston: Thomas & Andrews, 1801.

Johnson, Bruce; Wish, Eric; Schmeidler, James; and Huizinga, David. "Concentrations of Delinquent Offending: Serious Drug Involvement and High Delinquency Rates." *Journal of Drug Issues* 21 (1991): 205–29.

Johnson, Deborah. "The Ethical Dimensions of Acceptable Risk in Food Safety." *Agriculture and Human Values* 3 (1986): 171–9.

Johnson, Vernon. *Intervention: How to Help Someone Who Doesn't Want Help.* Minneapolis: Johnson Institute Books, 1986.

Works cited

Jonas, Steven. "Is the Drug Problem Soluble?" *American Behavioral Scientist* 32 (1989): 295–315.

"Solving the Drug Problem: A Public Health Approach to the Reduction of the Use and Abuse of Both Legal and Illegal Recreational Drugs." *Hofstra Law Review* 18 (1990): 751–93.

Kandel, Denise; Kessler, Ronald; and Margulies, Rebecca. "Antecedents of Adolescent Initiation into Stages of Drug Use: A Developmental Analysis." In *Longitudinal Research on Drug Use: Empirical Findings and Methodological Issues*, edited by Denise Kandel. New York: John Wiley, 1978.

Kaplan, Howard. "Social Sanctions, Self-Referent Responses, and the Continuation of Substance Abuse: A Person–Environment Interaction Perspective." *Drugs & Society* 2 (1987): 31–55.

Kaplan, John. *The Hardest Drug: Heroin and Public Policy.* Chicago: University of Chicago Press, 1983.

Marijuana: The New Prohibition. New York: World Publishing Co., 1970.

"Taking Drugs Seriously." *The Public Interest* 92 (1988): 32–50.

Karel, Richard. "A Model Legalization Proposal." In *The Drug Legalization Debate*, edited by James Inciardi. London: Sage Publications, 1991.

Katz, Leo. *Bad Acts and Guilty Minds.* Chicago: University of Chicago Press, 1987.

Kaufman, Edward. "The Relationship of Alcoholism and Alcohol Abuse to the Abuse of Other Drugs." *American Journal of Drug and Alcohol Abuse* 9 (1982): 1–17.

Kirsch, M. M. *Designer Drugs.* Minneapolis: CompCare Publications, 1986.

Kleiman, Mark. *Marijuana: Costs of Abuse, Costs of Control.* New York: Greenwood Press, 1989.

Kleiman, Mark, and Saiger, Aaron. "Drug Legalization: The Importance of Asking the Right Question." *Hofstra Law Review* 18 (1990): 527–65.

Kleinig, John. "Crime and the Concept of Harm." *American Philosophical Quarterly* 15 (1978): 27–36.

"Criminally Harming Others." *Criminal Justice Ethics* 5 (1986): 3–10.

Paternalism. Totowa, NJ: Rowman & Allanheld, 1983.

Koren, G.; Graham, K.; Shear, H.; and Einarson, T. "Bias Against the Null Hypothesis: The Reproductive Hazards of Cocaine." *The Lancet* (December 16, 1989): 1440–42.

Works cited

Korver, Dawn. "The Constitutionality of Punishing Pregnant Substance Abusers under Drug Trafficking Laws: The Criminalization of a Bodily Function." *Boston College Law Review* 32 (1991): 629–62.

Koshland, Daniel. "Thinking Tough." *Science* 241 (1988): 1273.

Kozlowski, Lynn; Wilkinson, Adrian; Skinner, Wayne; Kent, Karl; Franklin, Tom; and Pope, Marilyn. "Comparing Tobacco Cigarette Dependence with Other Drug Dependencies." *Journal of the American Medical Association* 261 (1989): 898–901.

Kristol, Irving. "Pornography, Obscenity, and the Case for Censorship." In *Philosophy of Law*, 5th ed., edited by Joel Feinberg and Hyman Gross. Belmont, CA: Wadsworth Publishing Co., 1991.

Kymlicka, Will. *Contemporary Political Philosophy*. Oxford: Clarendon Press, 1990.

LaFave, Wayne, and Scott, Austin. *Substantive Criminal Law*. 2 vols. St. Paul: West Publishing Co., 1986.

Lanza-Kaduce, Lonn, and Bishop, Donna. "Legal Fictions and Criminology: The Jurisprudence of Drunk Driving." *Journal of Criminal Law & Criminology* 77 (1986): 358–78.

Lawn, John. "The Issue of Legalizing Illicit Drugs." *Hofstra Law Review* 18 (1990): 703–15.

Letwin, Michael. "Report from the Front Line: The Bennett Plan, Street-Level Drug Enforcement in New York City and the Legalization Debate." *Hofstra Law Review* 18 (1990): 795–830.

Leuw, Ed. "Drugs and Drug Policy in the Netherlands." In *Crime and Justice*, vol. 14, edited by Michael Tonry. Chicago: University of Chicago Press, 1991.

Levenbook, Barbara Baum. "Criminal Harm." *Criminal Justice Ethics* 1 (1982): 48–53.

Leventhal, Howard; Glynn, Kathleen; and Fleming, Raymond. "Is the Smoking Decision an 'Informed Choice'?" *Journal of the American Medical Association* 257 (1987): 3373–6.

Lewis, Harold. *Technological Risk*. New York: W.W. Norton & Co., 1990.

Lipinski, Edward. "Motivation in Drug Misuse: Some Comments on Agent, Environment, Host." *Journal of the American Medical Association* 219 (1972): 171–5.

Logan, Frank, ed. *Cannabis: Options for Control*. Sunbury, U.K.: Quartermaine House, 1979.

Works cited

Logli, Paul. "Drugs in the Womb: The Newest Battlefield in the War on Drugs." *Criminal Justice Ethics* 9 (1990): 23–29.

Lord, Nancy. "A Practical Model for Drug Regulation." In *Drug Policy 1989–1990: A Reformer's Catalogue,* edited by Arnold Trebach and Kevin Zeese. Washington: Drug Policy Foundation, 1989.

Lyman, Michael, and Potter, Gary, eds. *Drugs in Society.* Cincinnati: Anderson Publishing Co., 1991.

Lyons, David. "Utility and Rights." In *Ethics, Economics, and the Law,* edited by J. Roland Pennock and John Chapman. New York: New York University Press, 1982.

Mansky, Peter. "Opiates: Human Psychopharmacology." In *Handbook of Psychopharmacology,* vol. 12, edited by Leslie Iversen, Susan Iversen, and Solomon Snyder. New York: Plenum Press, 1978.

Mariner, Wendy; Glantz, Leonard; and Annas, George. "Pregnancy, Drugs, and the Perils of Prosecution." *Criminal Justice Ethics* 9 (1990): 30–41.

McNamara, Joseph D. "Comment." In *Searching For Alternatives,* edited by Melvyn B. Krauss and Edward P. Lazear. Stanford: Hoover Institution Press, 1991.

Merrill, Richard, and Taylor, Michael. "Saccharin: A Case Study of Government Regulation of Environmental Carcinogens." *Agriculture and Human Values* 3 (1986): 33–72.

Mieczkowski, Thomas. "The Accuracy of Self-Reported Drug Use: An Evaluation and Analysis of New Data." In *Drugs, Crime, and the Criminal Justice System,* edited by Ralph Weisheit. Cincinnati: Anderson Publishing Co., 1990.

Mill, John Stuart. *On Liberty.* New York: E.P. Dutton & Co., 1951.

Miller, Richard Lawrence. *The Case for Legalizing Drugs.* New York: Praeger Publishing Co., 1991.

Mills, Claudia. "The War on Drugs: Is It Time to Surrender?" *Philosophy & Public Policy* 9 (1989): 3–5.

Miron, Jeffrey A. "Drug Legalization and the Consumation of Drugs: An Economist's Perspective. In *Searching For Alternatives,* edited by Melvyn B. Krauss and Edward P. Lazear. Stanford: Hoover Institution Press, 1991.

Mitchell, Chester. *The Drug Solution.* Ottawa: Carleton University Press, 1990.

Works cited

Moore, Mark. "Drugs: Getting a Fix on the Problem and the Solution." *Yale Law & Policy Review* 8 (1990): 8–35.

"Regulating Heroin: Kaplan and Trebach on the Dilemmas of Public Policy." *American Bar Foundation Research Journal* (1984): 723–31.

Morley, Jefferson. "Aftermath of a Crack Article." *The Nation* (20 November 1989), 592.

Mugford, Stephen. "Drug Legalization and the 'Goldilocks' Problem: Thinking About Costs and Control of Drugs." In *Searching For Alternatives*, edited by Melvyn B. Krauss and Edward P. Lazear. Stanford: Hoover Institution Press, 1991.

Musto, David. *The American Disease: Origins of Narcotic Control.* Exp. ed. New York: Oxford University Press, 1987.

"The History of Legislative Control over Opium, Cocaine, and Their Derivatives." In *Dealing with Drugs*, edited by Ronald Hamowy. Lexington, MA: D. C. Heath & Co., 1987.

"Opium, Cocaine, and Marijuana in American History." *Scientific American* 265 (1991): 40–7.

Myers, John. "A Limited Role for the Legal System in Responding to Maternal Substance Abuse during Pregnancy." *Notre Dame Journal of Law, Ethics, & Public Policy* 5 (1991): 747–81.

Myers, Samuel. "Drugs and Market Structure: Is There Really a Drug Crisis in the Black Community?" In *The Great Issues of Drug Policy*, edited by Arnold Trebach and Kevin Zeese. Washington: Drug Policy Foundation, 1990.

Nadelmann, Ethan A. "The Case for Legalization." *The Public Interest* 92(1988): 3–31.

"Drug Prohibition in the United States: Costs, Consequences, and Alternatives." 245 *Science* (1989): 939–47.

National Institute on Drug Abuse. *National Household Survey on Drug Abuse.* Rockville, MD, 1990.

Needleman, Herbert. "Why We Should Worry about Lead Poisoning." *Contemporary Pediatrics* 34 (1988): 34.

Newcomb, Michael, and Bentler, P. M. "Drug Use, Educational Aspirations, and Work Force Involvement: The Transition from Adolescence to Young Adulthood." *American Journal of Community Psychology* 14 (1986): 303–21.

Nisbet, Lee, ed. *The Gun Control Debate.* Buffalo: Premetheus Books, 1990.

Nolan, Kathleen. "Protecting Fetuses from Prenatal Hazards:

Works cited

Whose Crimes? What Punishment?" *Criminal Justice Ethics* 9 (1990): 13–23.

Note. "Maternal Rights and Fetal Wrongs: The Case against the Criminalization of 'Fetal Abuse.' " *Harvard Law Review* 101 (1988): 994–1012.

Nozick, Robert. *Anarchy, State, and Utopia*. New York: Basic Books, 1974.

Nurco, David; Hanlon, Thomas; and Kinlock, Timothy. "Recent Research on the Relationship between Illicit Drug Use and Crime." *Behavioral Sciences and the Law* 9 (1991): 221–42.

O'Neill, Onora, and Ruddick, William, eds. *Having Children*. New York: Oxford University Press, 1979.

Ostrowski, James. "Answering the Critics of Drug Legalization." *Notre Dame Journal of Law, Ethics, & Public Policy* 5 (1991): 823–51.

"The Moral and Practical Case for Drug Legalization." *Hofstra Law Review* 18 (1990): 607–702.

"Thinking about Drug Legalization." In *The Crisis in Drug Prohibition*, edited by David Boaz. Washington: Cato Institute, 1990.

Packer, Herbert. *The Limits of the Criminal Sanction*. Stanford: Stanford University Press, 1967.

Paltrow, Lynn. "When Becoming Pregnant Is a Crime." *Criminal Justice Ethics* 9 (1990): 41–7.

Paul, Ron. "Improving National Drug Policy." *American Criminal Law Review* 26 (1989): 1689–92.

Paulson, Morris; Coombs, Robert; and Richardson, Mark. "School Performance, Academic Aspirations, and Drug Use among Children and Adolescents." *Journal of Drug Education* 20 (1990): 289–303.

Peele, Stanton. *Diseasing of America: Addiction Treatment Out of Control*. Lexington, MA: D. C. Heath & Co., 1989.

Visions of Addiction. Lexington, MA: D C. Heath & Co., 1988.

Peele, Stanton, and Brodsky, Archie. *The Truth about Addiction and Recovery*. New York: Simon & Schuster, 1991.

Peterson, Robert." Legalization: The Myth Exposed." In *Searching for Alternatives*, edited by Melvyn B. Krauss and Edward P. Lazear. Stanford: Hoover Institution Press, 1991.

Peto, Richard. "Possible Ways of Explaining to Ordinary People the Quantitative Dangers of Smoking." *Health Education Journal* 39 (1980): 45–6.

Works cited

Polich, J. Michael; Ellickson, Phyllis; Reuter, Peter; and Kahan, James. *Strategies for Controlling Adolescent Drug Use.* Santa Monica, CA: Rand Publication Series, 1984.

Porter, Jane, and Jick, Hershel. "Addiction Rare in Patients Treated with Narcotics." *New England Journal of Medicine* 302 (1980): 123.

Rabow, Jerome, and Watts, Ronald. "Alcohol Availability, Alcohol Beverage Sales, and Alcohol-Related Problems." *Journal of Studies on Alcohol* 43 (1982): 767–801.

Raschke, Carl. *Painted Black: From Drug Killings to Heavy Metal – The Alarming True Story of How Satanism Is Terrorizing Our Communities.* New York: Harper & Row, 1990.

Rawls, John. *A Theory of Justice.* Cambridge, MA: Harvard University Press, 1971.

Reuter, Peter. "Can the Borders Be Sealed?" *The Public Interest* 92 (1989): 51–65.

Richards, David. *Sex, Drugs, Death, and the Law.* Totowa NJ: Rowman & Littlefield, 1982.

   Toleration and the Constitution. New York: Oxford University Press, 1986.

Roberts, Dorothy. "Punishing Drug Addicts Who Have Babies: Women of Color, Equality, and the Right of Privacy." *Harvard Law Review* 104 (1991): 1419–82.

Robins, Lee; Helzer, J.; Hesselbrock, M.; and Wish, C. "Vietnam Veterans Three Years after Vietnam." In *Yearbook of Substance Use and Abuse*, vol. 2, edited by Leon Brill and Charles Winick. New York: Human Sciences Press, 1980.

Robinson, Paul. "Legality and Discretion in the Distribution of Criminal Sanctions." *Harvard Journal on Legislation* 25 (1988): 393–460.

Rosenbaum, Marsha. *Just Say What?* San Francisco: National Council on Crime and Delinquency, 1989.

Rosenthal, Mitchell S. "The Logic of Legalization: A Matter of Perspective." In *Searching For Alternatives*, edited by Melvyn B. Krauss and Edward P. Lazear. Stanford: Hoover Institution Press, 1991.

Sagoff, Mark. "Paternalism and the Regulation of Drugs." *International Journal of Applied Philosophy* 2 (1984): 43–57.

Sandel, Michael. *Liberalism and the Limits of Justice.* Cambridge: Cambridge University Press, 1982.

Works cited

Schauer, Frederick. "Decriminalization and the Constitution." *Criminal Justice Ethics* 3 (1984): 76–84.

Schmoke, Kurt. "An Argument in Favor of Decriminalization." *Hofstra Law Review* 18 (1990): 501–25.

Schonberg, S. Kenneth, and Schnoll, Sidney. "Drugs and Their Effects on Adolescent Users." In *Teen Drug Use*, edited by George Beschner and Alfred Friedman. Lexington, MA: D. C. Heath & Co., 1985.

Schonsheck, Jonathan. "On Various Hypocrisies of the 'Drugs' in Sports Scandal." *The Philosophical Forum* 20 (1989): 247–85.

Scott, Peter Dale, and Marshall, Jonathan. *Cocaine Politics*. Berkeley: University of California Press, 1991.

Scriven, Tal. "Utility, Autonomy, and Drug Regulation." *International Journal of Applied Philosophy* 2 (1984):27–42.

Segal, Bernard. "Drug-Taking Behavior among School-Aged Youth: The Alaska Experience and Comparisons with Lower–48 States." *Drugs & Society* 4 (1989):1–174.

Sen, Amartya, and Williams, Bernard, eds. *Utilitarianism and Beyond*. Cambridge: Cambridge University Press, 1982.

Shaffer, Howard, and Jones, Stephanie. *Quitting Cocaine*. Lexington, MA: Lexington Books, 1989.

Shedler, Jonathan, and Block, Jack. "Adolescent Drug Use and Psychological Health." *American Psychologist* 45 (1990): 612–30.

Shulgin, Alexander. *The Controlled Substances Act: A Resource Manual of the Current Status of the Federal Drug Laws*. Berkeley: Ronin Publishing, 1988.

Siegel, Ronald K. *Intoxication: Life in Pursuit of Artificial Paradise*. New York: E.P. Dutton & Co., 1989.

Spitz, Henry, and Rosecan, Jeffrey, eds. *Cocaine Abuse: New Directions in Treatment and Research*. New York: Brunner/Mazel, 1987.

Stephens, Richard. "The Hard Drug Scene." In *Drugs and the Youth Culture*, edited by Frank Scarpitti and Susan Datesman. Beverley Hills: Sage Publications, 1980.

Mind Altering Drugs. New York: Sage Publishing Co., 1987.

Swartz, James. "Cocaine and Opiates: Prevalence Estimates of Their Use by Arrestees and a Theoretical and Empirical Investigation of Their Relationship to the Commission of Violent Crimes." Ph.D. diss., Northwestern University, 1990.

Works cited

Szasz, Thomas. *Ceremonial Chemistry*. Garden City, NY: Anchor Press, 1974.

Ten, C. L. *Mill on Liberty*. Oxford: Clarendon Press, 1980.

Thomson, Judith Jarvis. *The Realm of Rights*. Cambridge, MA: Harvard University Press, 1990.

Tollison, Robert, ed. *Smoking and Society*. Lexington, MA: D.C. Heath & Co., 1986.

Tonry, Michael, ed. *Crime and Justice*, vol. 14. Chicago: University of Chicago Press, 1991.

Tonry, Michael, and Wilson, James Q., eds. *Drugs and Crime*. Chicago: Chicago University Press, 1990.

Trebach, Arnold. "A Bundle of Peaceful Compromises." *Journal of Drug Issues* 20 (1990): 515–31.

The Great Drug War: Radical Proposals that Could Make America Safe Again. New York: Macmillan, 1987.

"In the Age of Cocaine – What Is America's Drug Problem?" *Harper's* (December 1985), 39–51.

Trebach, Arnold, and Zeese, Kevin, eds. *Drug Policy 1989–1990: A Reformer's Catalogue*. Washington: Drug Policy Foundation, 1989.

Drug Prohibition and the Conscience of Nations. Washington: Drug Policy Foundation, 1990.

The Great Issues of Drug Policy. Washington: Drug Policy Foundation, 1990.

Tribe, Laurence. *American Constitutional Law*. 2d ed. Mineola, NY: Foundation Press, 1988.

Uelmen, Gerald F., and Haddox, Victor G. *Drug Abuse and the Law Sourcebook*. New York: Clark Boardman Co., 1988.

United States Congress, House Select Committee on Narcotics Abuse and Control. *Legalization of Illicit Drugs: Impact and Feasibility: Hearings before the Select Committee on Narcotics Abuse and Control*. 2 vols. 100th Cong., 2d sess., 1989.

United States Department of Education. *Schools without Drugs*. Rockville, MD: National Clearinghouse for Alcohol and Drug Information, 1989.

United States Department of Labor. *What Works: Workplaces without Drugs*. Washington: U.S. Government Printing Office, 1991.

VanDeVeer, Donald. *Paternalistic Intervention*. Princeton: Princeton University Press, 1986.

van de Wijngaart, Govert F. "The Dutch Approach: Normalization of Drug Problems." *Journal of Drug Issues* 20 (1990): 667–78.

Works cited

Van Dyke, Craig, and Byck, Robert. "Cocaine." *Scientific American* 246 (1982): 128–41.

von Hirsch, Andrew, and Jareborg, Nils. "Gauging Criminal Harm: A Living-Standard Analysis." *Oxford Journal of Legal Studies* 11 (1991): 1–38.

Wagenaar, Alexander. *Alcohol, Young Drivers, and Traffic Accidents.* Lexington, MA: Lexington Books, 1983.

Waldorf, Dan, and Biernacki, Patrick. "The Natural Recovery from Opiate Addiction: Some Preliminary Findings." *Journal of Drug Issues* 11 (1981): 61–74.

Waldorf, Dan; Reinarman, Craig; and Murphy, Sheigla. *Cocaine Changes.* Philadelphia: Temple University Press, 1991.

Waldron, Jeremy. "Particular Values and Critical Morality." *California Law Review* 77 (1989): 561–89.

Walsh, Brenda. "The Economics of Alcohol Taxation." In *Economics and Alcohol*, edited by Marcus Grant, Martin Plant, and Alan Williams. New York: Gardner Press, 1983.

Warner, Roger. *Invisible Hand: The Marijuana Business.* New York: Beech Tree Books, 1986.

Waterson, E.; Evans, C.; and Murray-Lyon, I. "Is Pregnancy a Time of Changing Drinking and Smoking Patterns for Fathers as Well as Mothers?" *British Journal of Addiction* 85 (1990): 389–97.

Weil, Andrew. *The Natural Mind.* 2d ed. Boston: Houghton Mifflin Co., 1986.

Weil, Andrew, and Rosen, Winifred. *Chocolate to Morphine: Understanding Mind-Active Drugs.* Boston: Houghton Mifflin Co., 1983.

Weisheit, Ralph, ed. *Drugs, Crime, and the Criminal Justice System.* Cincinnati: Anderson Publishing Co., 1990.

Weiss, Walter. "User Careers: Implications for Preventing Drug Misuse." In *Alcohol and Drugs: Research and Policy*, edited by Martin Plant et. al. Edinburgh: Edinburgh University Press, 1990.

White, Helene. "The Drug-Use Delinquency Connection in Adolescence." In *Drugs, Crime, and the Criminal Justice System*, edited by Ralph Weisheit. Cincinnati: Anderson Publishing Co., 1990.

Whitlock, F. *Drugs, Morality, and the Law.* St. Lucia, Australia: University of Queensland Press, 1975.

Wilson, James Q. "Against the Legalization of Drugs." *Commentary* 89 (February 1990): 21–8.

"Drugs and Crime." In *Drugs and Crime,* edited by Michael Tonry and James Q. Wilson. Chicago: Chicago University Press, 1990.

Winick, Charles. "Maturing out of Narcotic Addiction." *Bulletin on Narcotics* 14 (1962): 1–17.

Wisotsky, Steven. *Beyond the War on Drugs.* Buffalo: Prometheus Books, 1990.

Breaking the Impasse in the War on Drugs. New York: Greenwood Press, 1986.

"Crackdown: The Emerging 'Drug Exception' to the Bill of Rights." *Hastings Law Journal* 38 (1987): 889–926.

"Exposing the War on Cocaine: The Futility and Destructiveness of Prohibition." *Wisconsin Law Review* (1983): 1305–1426.

"Images of Death and Destruction in Drug Law Cases." In *The Great Issues of Drug Policy,* edited by Arnold Trebach and Kevin Zeese. Washington: Drug Policy Foundation, 1990.

Wolff, Robert Paul. *In Defense of Anarchism.* New York: Harper & Row, 1970.

Zimring, Franklin, and Hawkins, Gordon. *The Search for Rational Drug Control.* New York: Cambridge University Press, 1992.

Zinberg, Norman E. *Drug, Set, and Setting: The Basis for Controlled Intoxicant Use.* New Haven: Yale University Press, 1984.

"The Use and Misuse of Intoxicants." In *Dealing with Drugs,* edited by Ronald Hamowy. Lexington, MA: D. C. Heath & Co., 1987.

Zinberg, Norman, and Robertson, John. *Drugs and the Public.* New York: Simon & Schuster, 1972.

Zwerling, Craig; Ryan, James; and Orav, Endel. "The Efficacy of Preemployment Drug Screening for Marijuana and Cocaine in Predicting Employment Outcome." *Journal of the American Medical Association* 264 (1990): 2639.

Index

Index

Index

Index

Index